SECURITIZATION
OF CREDIT

SECURITIZATION OF CREDIT

Inside the
New Technology of Finance

James A. Rosenthal

Juan M. Ocampo

McKinsey & Company, Inc.

WILEY

John Wiley & Sons, Inc.

New York • Chichester • Brisbane • Toronto • Singapore

Publisher: Stephen Kippur
Editor: Karl Weber
Managing Editor: Ruth Greif
Editing, Design, and Production:
   Publications Development Company of Crockett, Texas

Library of Congress Cataloging in Publication Data:

Rosenthal, James A.
    Securitization of credit : inside the new technology of finance/
James A. Rosenthal, Juan M. Ocampo
      p. cm.
    Includes index.

ISBN: 0-471-61368-1

Printed in the United States of America

88 89 10 9 8 7 6 5 4 3 2

9-29-89

Special thanks to
Kate Ballen
and
Anne Ocampo
our wives, who offered
enthusiasm and support
throughout the writing of this book

Acknowledgments

This book is a product of the McKinsey & Company Securitization Project, a research project on credit (i.e., loan or asset-backed) securitization sponsored by McKinsey & Company during 1987–1988. It reflects the thinking of many McKinsey colleagues, most particularly that of the authors, James Rosenthal and Juan Ocampo. As in any cooperative venture, component parts of the work are not easily attributable to any single person; nonetheless, for those who would seek to unweave the intellectual threads, Chapters 1 and 9 are primarily the work of Ocampo, with 2–8 primarily that of Rosenthal.

The Securitization Project itself was directed by Lowell Bryan whose thought and leadership have been central to the analytical framework and conclusions contained herein. Significant McKinsey contributions were also made by Guy Moszkowski, Engagement Manager of the Project; Brook Manville, who coordinated and added to the writing of this book; and Jack Fuchs, Philippe Giry-Deloison, Arnab Gupta, Tim Koller, Kewsong Lee, and Sameer Shah.

The book also benefited from the insights and suggestions of several people not part of McKinsey & Company, but to whom special thanks are due: Neil Baron, of Booth and Baron, who helped develop the legal framework and whose detailed knowledge of structured finance was extraordinarily helpful; James Peaslee of Cleary, Gottlieb, Steen & Hamilton, for his invaluable assistance with the taxation concepts related to securitization; Ron Wippern, (formerly professor of finance at Harvard Business School and the Yale School of Management) who now heads his own financial consulting firm, for his insights concerning financial analysis; Morris Simkin, of Siller, Welk, Mencher, and Simkin, for his assistance with the securities law concepts related to securitization.

Grateful acknowledgment is also made for the assistance and cooperation of the many participants in those transactions on which the analysis has been based. McKinsey & Company would like to express its appreciation to: William Haley and David Tibbals of Salomon Brothers; Terry Watson of Bank of America; Howard Altarescu and J. Christopher Kersey of Goldman Sachs; Glenn McClelland and William Stengel of Citicorp North America; James Welch of Morgan Guaranty Trust Company of New York; Marge Wolf of Citibank, N.A.; Raleigh Hortenstine III of First Republic Bank; Donald L. McWorter of Banc One; and Dennis M. Cantwell of Chrysler Financial Corporation. Notwithstanding all this valuable assistance, the authors alone are solely responsible for the contents herein.

Finally, thanks to Susan Benthall who helped edit the manuscript; to Margaret Blake, Karen Drummond, Kathleen Mullins, Cynthia Rhule-Harris, and the McKinsey Report Production Department for their thoughtful and essential help in the manuscript preparation; and to Karl Weber of John Wiley & Sons, the sponsoring editor of this book.

Contents

Part 1

Securitized Credit: The New Lending Technology

1

An Introduction to Credit Securitization

Superconductors, gene-splicing, artificial intelligence, robotic-driven manufacturing—daily we hear of new technologies that are making old standards obsolete and delivering products and services once thought impossible. Recently, the world of finance has had its share of new technologies that are changing the course and manner of business around the world. Although little celebrated outside the financial community, these new technologies are increasing the efficiencies of financing and capital formation. This book is about one of the newest and most important of them, the process we call "credit securitization." It is a technology that is fundamentally altering traditional forms of fund raising.

Credit securitization is the carefully structured process whereby loans and other receivables are packaged, underwritten, and sold in the form of securities (instruments commonly known as asset-backed securities). As such, it is a subset of a broader trend seen throughout the capital markets for many years, "securitization," that is, the general phenomenon whereby more and more fund raising is occurring through the agency of securities. In what follows, however, we focus particularly on credit securitization,

3

examining in some detail the nature and value of this technological innovation.

From its first beginnings with the development of the residential mortgage-backed securities business in the 1960s, credit securitization now includes products backed by a range of loans and receivables, including commercial mortgages, auto loans, credit card receivables, trade receivables and an expanding list of other assets. In this book, we use the term "credit securitization" to emphasize that these instruments have *credit risk* which must be structured. From our perspective, "credit securitization" is the most accurate name for the variety of asset-backed financings, such as are described in the following pages of this book.

This book provides the reader with an understanding of how credit securitization works—both in general and in particular—through a number of case studies. As an overview of the new technology, the book gives a basic understanding of its nature and process, the values that can be derived from it, and case studies to illustrate its economic benefits. We have found this material to be of broad interest. Financial institutions and corporations need to understand the competitive opportunities and challenges created by the new technology. Bankers, investment bankers, attorneys, accountants, investment managers, corporate treasurers, strategic planners, and many others can professionally benefit from an understanding of how the technology works.

This book is organized into four sections. Part 1, Chapter 1 provides a theoretical overview of credit securitization and a platform upon which to build an understanding of why this technology is so significant. Part 1, Chapter 2 represents a "tool kit"—the working knowledge one needs to understand the structure of an asset-backed transaction. Part 2 presents case examples of transactions that have already taken place as an illustration of the mechanics and sources of added value from the technology in practice. In Part 3, we offer some final thoughts about the possible future direction and growth of the technology.

As an introduction to our subject, we now turn to two questions about the technology. First, is credit securitization really a technological advance? The answer to this question leads to the fundamental and second question, who benefits from credit securitization? And what do they stand to gain from it?

IS CREDIT SECURITIZATION A TECHNOLOGICAL ADVANCE?

We adopt the economists' definition of a technological advance as encompassing a new process that yields either a comparable service from less resources than before, or a better service from the same resources as before. In our view, credit securitization represents such a technological advance—and, we will argue, a very sizable advance. The perspective herein developed is important because many observers have insisted that the recent trend of credit securitization is no more than "a game of regulatory mirrors"—no real new technology, but only a temporary exploitation of certain regulatory loopholes.

On the surface, asset-backed securities transactions look more like complex manipulations of regulatory guidelines and accounting conventions than the product of a technological process. This appearance stems from the multitude of regulatory, tax, and accounting issues behind every transaction. These issues are discussed in detail in Chapter 2. But there is much more beneath the surface of any securitized transaction. *Although credit securitization is sensitive to regulatory guidelines and other arbitrary limits, it draws its lifeblood not from regulatory arbitrage but from the way it handles risk. In this respect, it is fundamentally more efficient than conventional lending.*

Risk in lending comes from two sources. First, the borrower may not repay on time or may not repay at all (credit risk). Second, interest on the debt assumed to fund the loans may not match the terms and pricing of the loans—"mismatching"—which exposes the lender to interest rate or prepayment risks. Credit securitization transactions manage these risks more explicitly—and therefore more efficiently—than conventional lending does. It makes these risks more transparent and it also allocates them far more precisely to the players who are best able to absorb them. To illustrate the point, this section compares the old technology of lending with the new technology of credit securitization.

Traditional Lending: Costly Because It Bundles Risk

Under traditional lending, the commercial bank, thrift, or finance company that originates loans endeavors to minimize credit risk through two phases: initially, through a review process before granting the credit, and thereafter through a continuous monitoring and servicing process. Whatever risk the credit contains, the lending institution absorbs by holding the loan in its own portfolio. In other words, it insulates the depositors or other creditors that fund the loan by backing its obligations with its full faith and credit.

This "backing" requires equity capital: the lending institution must provide a buffer layer of funding that is subordinated to the claims of depositors and other providers of low cost funds. Such capital is expensive. In early 1988, it is currently estimated to run 25 percent pre-tax per annum, while the cost of marginal short-term debt funds is only 6.5 percent per annum. The capital markets effectively impose equity capital requirements upon lending institutions who turn to them in order to borrow at least a portion of the monies needed to fund their loans. In order to borrow at reasonably attractive rates, lending institutions must back up their capital market borrowings with an amount of equity capital proportionate to the risk of default, *as viewed by the fund suppliers in the capital markets.*

For unregulated lenders, such as large finance companies, the capital markets today appear to frequently require a minimum of 9 percent or more equity capital to total assets. In other words, 9 or more cents of every dollar lent by many finance companies is funded by equity. The added cost of this expensive equity currently translates into about an incremental 160 basis points of cost over what 100 percent debt funding would have permitted given today's (early 1988) market conditions.

Regulated financial institutions (e.g., commercial banks and thrifts) appear to need less capital than the finance companies. The support which commercial banks, for example, receive from FDIC, as a guarantor of deposits, and the Federal Reserve, as a lender of last resort, permits most commercial banks to tap the capital and money markets with less equity capital than independent finance companies can. Large commercial banks and bank holding companies are currently operating at a capitalization rate of about 7–8 percent capital to assets. Not all of this capital, moreover, is equity capital.

This high degree of leverage for commercial banks does not appear to be sustainable. The capital and money markets are increasingly signaling their discontent with the financial soundness of many large banking institutions by requiring a significant credit yield premium on the longer-term debt obligations issued by these institutions. The regulators, moreover, are increasing the level of equity capital which they will require commercial banks to put up in return for the deposit guarantees and other supports and privileges which a banking charter brings. Thus the regulators and the capital and money markets are moving together to *increase* the cost of capital consumed in commercial bank lending. This is very significant since the *existing* base of equity capital dedicated to the commercial banking industry costs in excess of $25 billion per year when measured in terms of the stock market required rate of return on equity. Viewed from a different perspective, the existing bank capital employed, given today's market conditions in traditional lending, translates into about an incremental 120–140 basis points or so of cost above and beyond the cost of debt funding. Whether it is measured in the aggregate or on a loan-by-loan basis, the cost of the equity buffer in lending is very large. Since credit securitization is extremely effective at reducing the amount of equity consumed in lending—and the savings are so large—it presents a fundamentally more efficient technology for lending.

At first glance, the level of equity that the capital markets are requiring may appear excessive. Net credit charge-offs for the U.S. commercial banking system have remained between 0.37 percent and 0.99 percent of total loans over the past 8 years. In this light, a bank capitalization rate running around 7 percent or 8 percent of assets seems like overkill. Similarly, the historical annual credit charge-offs for a large automobile finance company car loan portfolio approximate less than 0.4 percent. Yet the capital markets apparently want that company to maintain an equity buffer of about 7 percent of assets.

Why are the capital markets insisting on this excess layer of protection? The reason probably lies in the combination of risks that depositors, noteholders, and other senior creditors of the lending institutions absorb. Beyond the expected credit risk are at least three others:

1. Each lending institution tends to concentrate the credit risk in its portfolio—either by region, industry, demographic strata, or some other dimension. Such concentrations, which come about naturally, render the simple consideration of "expected" loss rates inadequate. Expected loss rates are a reasonable measure of total risk for diversified portfolios, but the undiversified character of the balance sheet of most banks, thrifts, and finance companies makes the unlikely but devastating risk of catastrophic loss quite relevant.

2. The lender can use the funds it obtains from the money and capital markets not only to finance its existing loan portfolio, but also to extend future loans whose risk may be greater. The *discretion* that the bank, thrift, or finance company has over the use of its funds further heightens creditors' level of uncertainty.

3. Lending institutions typically face a number of noncredit risks in the normal course of doing business. Prominent among them are interest rate and prepayment risks, which can outweigh credit risks for many lending institutions and are extremely difficult to eliminate from their balance sheets.

In return for the risk and uncertainty that these three factors add, the capital markets ask for greater protection in the form of more lender equity capitalization, higher yield on their funds, or both.

Securitized Credit: More Efficient Because It Manages Risk Better

Credit securitization greatly reduces the risks and uncertainties that arise from portfolio concentration, the lender's discretion, and its exposure to noncredit losses. At the same time, it increases the transparency of the expected credit risk. Taken together, these benefits lower the cost of lending by removing part of the "excess" equity cushions and funding yield premiums that traditional lending entails.

Credit securitization begins with the same loan-by-loan credit review and monitoring processes that traditional lending does. In fact, the same originating institution—bank, thrift, or finance company—normally performs these steps. The similarity ends here.

Credit securitization isolates the loans from the originator's balance sheet. The institution originating loans does not absorb all of the resulting risk. Instead the loans are pooled, generally into homogeneous portfolios, and sold to trusts or other special purpose vehicles. This pooling and sale of assets make the loans more transparent, and reduce uncertainties for capital markets investors. Since the pool is prespecified, investors know the risk they are absorbing: they are funding only a clearly delineated, existing pool of loans. They are not funding future discretionary lending or risk taking that the original lender may engage in. Nor are they absorbing interest rate or other risks, which may be borne by the originator but are not incorporated in the loan pool itself. Their risk exposure is strictly limited to that represented by the loan portfolio.

This aspect of credit securitization offers two other benefits. First, the grouping of loans into large, homogeneous pools facilitates the actuarial analysis of their risks. Second, it makes it easier for third parties—in particular, the rating agencies and credit enhancers—to review and reinforce the credit underwriting decisions taken by the originating lender.

Credit securitization typically splits the credit risk into three or more "vertical" tranches and places it with institutions that are in the best position to absorb it. The first loss tranche is usually capped at levels reasonably related to the "expected" or "normal" rate of portfolio credit loss. All credit losses up to this cap are borne entirely by the originator. Since the originator has direct contact with the borrower and maintains that contact through loan servicing and monitoring, it is in the best position to manage and absorb the portfolio's normal level of credit loss.

The originator is, however, often ill-suited to absorb the "catastrophe" risk that the portfolio contains. This risk arises because a good originator tends to operate best in specific lending sectors or regions. But in focusing its efforts on areas where its ability to manage and absorb the expected loss is greatest, it winds up with an undiversified portfolio. By confining the originator's exposure to a capped first loss, credit securitization reduces the problem arising from lack of diversification—a problem that is pronounced in the United States owing to our legal heritage of local and regionally focused banking and thrift institutions.

The second tranche typically covers losses that exceed the originator's cap. The risk band it delineates is itself typically capped at a level equivalent to 7 or 8 times the pool's expected losses. This tranche is borne by a high-grade, well-capitalized credit enhancer that can diversify the risk of individual loan pools by creating a portfolio of partially guaranteed loan pools. The guaranty fees earned on the entire portfolio are available to cover the possibility of loss in any given pool.

The risk absorption role of the credit enhancer is directly analogous to that of a reinsurer in the property and casualty insurance business. And the role of the loan originator corresponds to that of the primary policy underwriter. The fact that credit securitization is adopting the risk-sharing techniques long used by insurers is not surprising. For the risks are similar in each of these businesses.

The third tranche of credit risk above and beyond the second tranche is absorbed by the investors that buy the asset-backed securities themselves. Credit loss from this final tranche is exceedingly unlikely.

Credit securitization also segments interest rate risk so that it can be tailored and placed among the most appropriate investors. More often than not, the originator absorbs no interest rate risk, having sold the loans in their entirety. (Also, since most loan originators are highly leveraged institutions, they are in a poor position to incur interest rate risk.) Rather this risk is passed on to the note investors that buy the asset-backed securities and to counterparties. Structurers of asset-backed securities can fine tune the risk by creating multiple fast-pay and slow-pay tranches, backed by a common pool of primary loans. The counterparties may absorb mismatch risk through interest rate swaps, or prepayment risk through guaranteed investment contracts. The view these players take of interest rate risk depends on the eye of the beholder; one institution's exposure may well be another's hedge. The unbundling of interest rate risk that occurs in credit securitization exploits this fact. It allows the interest rate risks inherent in lending to be placed with "natural" absorbers.

The net result of asset-backed securitization's greater credit transparency, isolated risk ownership, and segmented risk absorption is lower total costs than traditional lending. Table 1.1 shows the estimated capital required to support lending under traditional and credit securitized alternatives for a number of illustrative loan portfolios.

In preparing Table 1.1, we have made a conservative assumption concerning the amount of capital required to support the originator's contingent obligation for first loss. Our calculations assume that the originator had to fully support this contingent obligation with capital, even if the level of the contingent obligation exceeded the expected loss.[1] Although the level of capital

TABLE 1.1. REQUIRED ORIGINATOR CAPITAL TRADITIONAL LENDING VERSUS ASSET-BACKED SECURITIZATION

Loan Portfolio	Expected Loss over Average Life of Loan	Traditional Lending— Originator Capital Required	Asset-Backed Securitization— Originator Capital Required
Auto loans	1.0%	7%	3.0%
Credit card loans	4.0	7	4.0
Trade receivables	0.4 (annual)	7	1.2

Source: McKinsey analysis.

[1] See Appendix A for a more detailed discussion of this point.

coverage for securitized credit still exceeds the expected rate of credit loss, the "excess" is noticeably less than for conventional lending. Moreover, this decreased level of capital gives noteholders more protection than was available from conventional lending and funding, as the next section explains. The greater level of protection translates, for many asset-backed transactions, to a lower cost of debt funding (i.e., lower yield on the asset-backed notes) which supplements the savings attained through capital efficiency.

WHO BENEFITS?

Technological advances bring benefits, and credit securitization is no exception. Borrowers, originators (here, as before, meaning the bank, thrift, finance company, or other intermediary making loans to ultimate borrowers), and investors all may reap advantages from this technology. Credit securitization can lead to a more efficient financial services industry and one that can better satisfy the regulatory objectives of safety and soundness.

Borrowers

Asset-backed securitization can provide borrowers with cheaper sources of funds. This benefit is already evident in residential mortgages. Home buyers are now paying approximately 100 basis points less in interest (versus U.S. Treasury yields) on fixed-rate mortgages than they were a decade ago when mortgage securitization was much less pervasive. In more recently securitized loans, such as automobile and credit card receivables, securitization's greater efficiency has not yet been passed on to borrowing customers in the form of lower rates, but we suspect that it will not be long in coming.

For commercial borrowers, credit securitization offers the opportunity to significantly expand their corporate finance flexibility. Through credit securitization, a corporation can tap debt markets at a cost of borrowing frequently much lower than the cost of its senior debt. It can also avoid risk from interest rate, currency exchange, and commodity price exposures. In other words, the securitizing corporation can more finely hone its claims structure and thus reserve for its equity holders only the risks and returns that are most attractive to them.

A second benefit of structured securitization for the corporate borrower is more managerial freedom. Under traditional lending, restrictive covenants limit the freedom of action of the corporation and its management. Asset sales do not involve these general covenants though they do force management to yield essentially all discretionary power over the assets that have been sold. Typically, the flexibility gained from covenant release means far more for the corporation's strategic and operating health than control over accounts receivables or other securitizable assets.

Investors

Credit securitization offers multiple new investment instruments for mutual funds, insurers, pension funds, and other investors. This increase in choice and availability is in itself attractive, but investors have other reasons to be pleased with asset-backed securities:

1. These securities typically offer a greater level of protection from rating downgrades than traditional debt securities.[2] Investors in asset-backed securities are structurally protected from the event risk that the originator's credit quality may deteriorate. Unlike a normal corporation, a special-purpose vehicle cannot be restructured by management through increased leverage or other means.

2. As a developmental asset class asset-backed securities typically provide premium yields compared to those of comparable conventional instruments.

The Financial Services Industry

Asset-backed securitization will lead to a more efficient financial services industry. Firms that capitalize on their distinctive skills will benefit from the evolving changes; firms that lack skills or fail to adapt to the forthcoming new industry structure will be hurt.

---

[2] Note that the asset-backed market is currently quite sensitive to downgrades of the financial institutions providing credit support on specific issues. We expect this vulnerability to diminish in the future as monoline (single purpose) credit insurers grow in number and importance.

Credit securitization should affect the structure of the financial services industry in three ways, each of which will improve the industry's cost effectiveness and increasingly divide financial service firms into winners and losers. First, credit securitization breaks the once vertically integrated process of lending and funding by financial intermediaries into a discrete series of steps (Figure 1.1). Each step requires skills that differ from skills in the other steps, and each displays distinctive economies of scale and scope. This breakup permits firms to focus on a limited number of roles in the process—even perhaps only one—and to build a competitive advantage through specialization and a business configuration that is tailored to that role's microeconomics.

Second, credit securitization enables a strong loan originator or servicer to expand its volume of business without expanding its capital base in the same proportion. Conventional balance sheet lenders lack this freedom. Their growth rate is limited by their ability to expand their capital base through retained earnings or new issues. Securitizing lenders that possess or develop a competitive advantage through more efficient marketing, tighter credit management, lower cost servicing, or other sources can turn the advantage against their rivals in a more potent way than was possible before. Since credit securitization permits stronger firms to increase their flow of business at many multiples of the rate that their capital base would otherwise have dictated, it should lead to massive shifts in market share within the overall lending market.

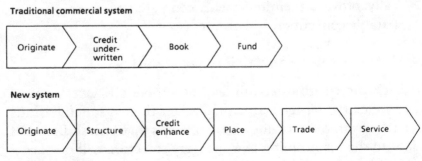

Source: McKinsey & Company.

Figure 1.1. Credit securitization is changing the traditional commercial banking business system.

Such shifts have, in fact, been under way for years in the largely securitized residential mortgage market.

Third, not only does credit securitization allow financial service firms to exploit any competitive advantage more decisively through rapid expansion of their market shares, it also magnifies the economic impact of the competitive advantages themselves. To illustrate this point, let us look at credit management, one of many potential sources of competitive advantage in securitized lending.

Figure 1.2 compares the lending costs for two hypothetical banks that are lending to the same borrower market under traditional balance sheet lending. The banks have identical capital structures and funding costs; they differ only in their credit management skills.

Bank B's loan portfolio generates 100 basis points in annual credit charge-offs; Bank A's portfolio generates 200 basis points. Not surprisingly, Bank B enjoys a 100-basis-point cost advantage over its competitor.

Figure 1.3 shows the costs for the two banks when they use credit securitization in lieu of balance sheet lending. As the figure shows, credit securitization drops the cost of lending considerably for both banks, but Bank B, the superior credit manager, has

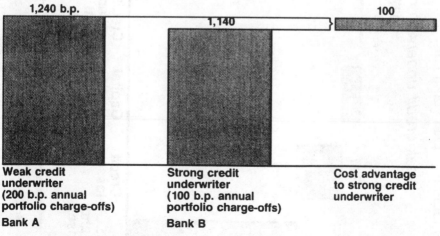

Source: McKinsey analysis.

Figure 1.2. Comparison of pretax lending costs for two hypothetical banks employing traditional lending (basis points).

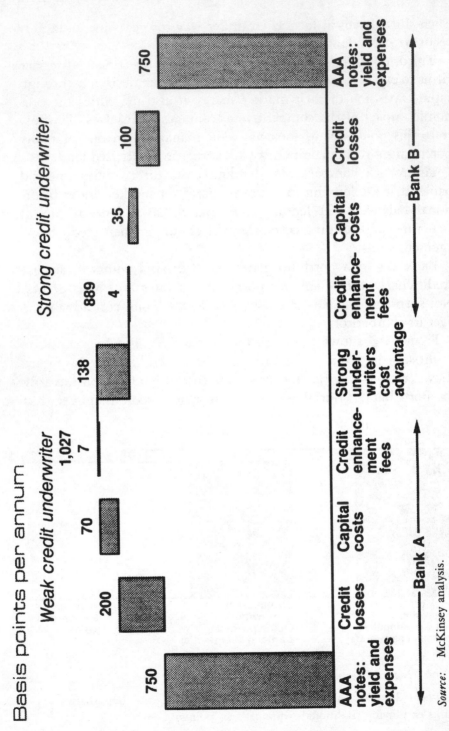

Source: McKinsey analysis.

Figure 1.3. Pretax lending cost comparison for the same hypothetical banks employing credit securitization.

benefited far more from the technology than its less skilled rival. Its cost advantage has increased from 100 basis points to about 140. As exemplified in Chapter 4's discussion of the California Credit Card Trust transaction, the main driver of Bank B's cost advantage is its significantly lower ceiling on its first-loss credit exposure, which translates into reduced capital costs.[3] This illustration underscores a major feature of securitized lending: Its great transparency. Cost and capability differences among competitors are no longer muted; rather they are highlighted and magnified.

Each of the three changes that credit securitization is bringing to financial intermediaries will increase the rivalry among firms in the business. The disaggregation of the vertically integrated roles historically played by lenders should sharpen competition for business within each function; entry barriers previously limiting more specialized new entrants will be lowered. Secondly, the removal of large equity capital requirements as a constraint on business volume will both facilitate the entry of new competitors and increase the competition for business volume among current competitors. Third, the magnification of competitive advantage in areas like credit management will further fuel rivalry among financial intermediaries. Overall, we see credit securitization as a major contributing factor to a new era of broadly increased competition in financial services, just as it has already heightened competition in the one business now dominated by the new technology—residential mortgages.

Regulators

Most of the regulators that oversee this country's financial institutions regard the trend toward securitization with caution. Two concerns arise: first, since loan originators sell the assets they generate, they will lose their incentive to maintain credit discipline; second, asset sales will undermine the impact of capital adequacy guidelines and other regulatory tools. These concerns are justified. Poorly done, securitization can magnify the risks of our financial system. History shows that some of our biggest credit debacles

---

[3] See also the economic analysis contained in Appendix A, for further explanation of how the credit loss rate can drive the economics of an asset-backed security transaction.

have come from markets where asset sales or syndications were the norm: Penn Central's default in the commercial paper market in 1975, Penn Square's fiasco in the loan sale market in 1982, the large and widely syndicated Latin American credits of the late 1970s and early 1980s, and the failure of Equity Programs Investment Co.'s (EPIC) mortgaged-backed securities in 1985. Today, segments of the commercial loan participation markets may be overheating.

It would be a grave mistake, however, to conclude from these and other examples that credit securitization is a hazardous trend that should be contained. Except for EPIC, a real estate syndication company whose affiliate sold mortgage-backed securities and mortgages, most of the failures noted previously were direct loan sales. As such, they lacked the careful structuring and risk-sharing arrangements that are the hallmarks of securitized credit. Although EPIC took the precautions of structuring and credit enhancement, it did not live up to our definition of sound securitized credit—it was marked by an inadequate initial credit review and the over-exposure of at least one credit-enhancer to such assets.

Much as we might disallow EPIC, it would be foolhardy to assume that securitized credit is fail-safe. We do, however, expect its rate of failure to be low relative to traditional credit because of the multiple levels of scrutiny that securitized credit portfolios undergo from their originators, rating agencies, and credit enhancers. Moreover, if regulators fostered the disciplined development of credit securitization, the rate of failure could conceivably be far below that of banks and thrifts.

The argument for regulators' support is straightforward. Properly managed, credit securitization would permit regulators to deploy the industry's capital in a way that covers risk more effectively; it would reduce low-skilled, excess lending capacity in an orderly fashion; and, as a consequence, it would lead to a less costly, more stable financial system. In brief, credit securitization promises to be a boon to regulators rather than a destabilizing force.

With credit securitization, regulators can deploy capital in a way that covers risk more effectively. A major issue facing regulators of depository institutions (primarily banks and thrifts) is that the industry's capital tends to build up where it is not needed. Weak lenders can run through their equity capital quickly. When measured by net credit charge-offs, the weakest 10 percent of commercial banks saw 9 percent of their loan assets written off in 1986. Given the industry's average capitalization rate, a continuation of the trend will dissipate these banks' equity in only 1 year. Once their capital is eroded, the FDIC must cover the failing institution's losses to protect its insured depositors—and in some instances also its uninsured. As things now stand, in 1988, the magnitude of this problem is difficult to overstate. Net charge-offs, nonperforming loan ratios, and bank failures have soared during the last several years of sustained economic expansion. What will a recession bring?

The problems facing commercial bank regulators pale beside those facing the thrifts. Some experts estimate that it will eventually cost $50 billion or more to restructure the nation's insolvent thrifts and keep their insured depositors whole. If this extraordinary estimate proves to be anywhere near accurate, the relevant guarantors will be the American taxpayers, since the FSLIC is far from having adequate reserves to cover a restructuring that extensive.

The regulators' natural response to this crisis is to raise the banking industry's capital adequacy targets. In an environment where the bulk of bank lending is done in a conventional, balance sheet manner, an increase in capital guidelines might cause as much harm as good. But linked with pervasive, industry-wide credit securitization, higher capital requirements can build up the level of reserves standing between industry losses and the deposit insurer's funds. Let us examine this argument.

Increased capital requirements raise the cost of traditional lending for the banks and thrifts that can afford to comply with them. Each loan originated and carried on the institution's books consumes more equity. If borrowers have no alternative to bank loans, banks can raise their loan pricing to cover their capital costs. If borrowers do have alternatives, which is the case today for a large portion of the borrowing market, banks cannot increase their pricing. They will tend to lose market share to commercial paper, junk bonds, and other funding alternatives. Strong banks, at the margin, get squeezed out of lending. Weak banks, the prime source of regulators' problems, often cannot afford to comply with the request for greater capital coverage—and, at least in the short run will not do so.

Under this scenario, the regulators wind up in a dilemma. They have hurt their stronger constituents' business by increasing their lending costs and deprived them of valuable lending volumes as a result. Meanwhile, they have not succeeded in getting their weaker constituents, those with a high chance of failing, to put up a bigger equity buffer. Although the regulators can raise the total level of capital dedicated to the banking industry, they cannot channel it to the right place. In a business dominated by traditional lending, capital tends to accumulate naturally among the strong institutions, where it serves more to increase costs than safety and where it is unavailable to the deposit insurance corporations that are buttressing the assets of failing institutions.

Credit securitization can greatly enhance the benefits, and reduce or eliminate the drawbacks, of regulators' plans to increase capital guidelines. Under credit securitization, the guidelines do not hinder strong banks because they no longer carry loans on their books. The capital that these banks do have tied up in loans is there to satisfy their maximum first-loss credit exposure (originator's cap), not regulatory capital guidelines. Capital guidelines thus become irrelevant in determining a bank's capital cost for securitizable loans, and regulators can increase capital requirements without driving strong banks out of competitive lending markets. For loans that do not lend themselves to the credit securitization technology, banks should be able to pass along their increased capital costs because borrowers are unlikely to have any alternatives for such loans.

It is worth noting that the credit securitization process just described, in which bank equity is earmarked for coverage of explicit loan pool loss expectation, is in effect risk-adjusted capital allocation. Bank regulators have recently adopted this form of allocation as an overarching policy goal. By allowing the capital markets to arbitrate the amount of capital that is adequate to cover specific loan pools, credit securitization can bring about a more finely tuned and unbiased risk-adjusted capital scheme than administered guidelines ever will.

Credit securitization permits the orderly reduction of low-skilled, excess lending capacity. As securitized credit becomes prevalent and capital requirements increase, weak banks with poor credit management records should see their loan origination volumes curtailed. As this happens, they will have two choices: Either to securitize their loan production, using expensive structures that require them to retain high first-loss exposures; or to keep that loan production on their books, thus incurring a large capital cost, which is rising along with capital adequacy guidelines. Either choice puts them at a cost disadvantage vis-à-vis banks that have strong credit management capabilities. Because this cost differential is significant, it should cause strong credit underwriters to displace poor risk managers over time—a stabilizing trend that regulators will welcome.

In summary, credit securitization could lead to a far more stable and less costly financial system. By working in a coordinated way to foster well-structured credit securitization, while also phasing in increasing capital guidelines for depositary institutions, regulators can help forge such a system. The phased increases would prompt lenders to adopt the new technology and capture its cost advantage over balance sheet funding. Any acceleration in the adoption of the technology would be beneficial from the regulators' standpoint: not only does credit securitization offer a means of regulating the industry's capital coverage without today's harmful side effects, but it also deploys industry capital more efficiently (that is, requiring less total capital) and more effectively to cover the true risk exposure of depositors.

Table 1.2 shows the total coverage that securitized credit provides depositors or high-grade note purchasers—the risk averse investors whose interests the regulators must protect with particular diligence.

In constructing Table 1.2, we used approximate guidelines for AAA asset-backed securities to calculate the level of "final investor coverage" for the hypothetical loan portfolios listed in Table 1.1. In each instance, the noteholder or depositor (these are essentially equivalent here) receives a far greater degree of coverage than under traditional lending. Since this coverage is generated from

TABLE 1.2. CREDIT PROTECTION PROVIDED BY SECURITIZED CREDIT

Loan Portfolio	Expected Loss over Average Life of Loan	Traditional Lending—Originator Capital Required	Asset-Backed Securitization—Originator Capital Required	Asset-Backed Securitization—Credit Enhancer Capital Required	Asset-Backed Securitization—Credit Enhancer Loss Protection	Asset-Backed Securitization—Final Investor Coverage
Auto loans	1.0%	7%	3.0%	0.2%	8%	8.0%
Credit card loans	4.0	7	4.0	0.4	12	16.0
Trade receivables	0.4 (annual)	7	1.2	0.1	4	5.2

Source: McKinsey analysis.

private capital, it affords much greater protection for the FDIC and FSLIC, and should dramatically reduce their costs from charge-offs.

The greater coverage, which is counterintuitively provided with *less* industry capital, comes about for two reasons. First, the credit enhancer's capital is fully available to absorb catastrophe risks in all of these portfolios. In contrast, most of the industry's capital today redundantly supports the portfolios of strong banks and is unavailable to support the local "catastrophes" that blow through the capital coverage of weaker banks and deplete the deposit insurers' reserves. Second, the credit insurers' capital is preserved, and good loan origination practices are reinforced through the use of "custom tailored" first-loss exposures, which the originating lenders bear.

SUMMARY

Credit securitization promises to create a stronger and more efficient financial system. It is a lower cost financing vehicle that also neutralizes a number of the risks that bedevil balance sheet lending. This technology benefits everyone—borrowers, investors, financial institutions, and regulators.

USING THIS BOOK

Credit securitization is not a simple technology, as the complexity of some of the following chapters quickly suggests. But few technologies are simple in the beginning; they both reflect and cause great change, and thus take "getting used to."

What follows is intended to help you do just that, by providing a working blueprint, both in theory and in practice, of this new technology. Our discussion has been designed to equip you with the vocabulary and the technical background to play any of a variety of roles in the growing business that credit securitization represents.

Many of the details of credit securitization are transaction-specific, but an examination of the details cannot be avoided if one is to truly understand the technology. Our focus on the particulars of actual transactions has necessarily involved a trade-off: By examining the intricate elements of real securitized financings, we have been forced to shorten the "shelf life" of much of what has been written. Credit securitization is very much a moving target, and nothing within this book should be understood as the last word on a process that is evolving literally daily.

In fact, we have made an effort in the particular transaction descriptions to give the reader a sense of this diverse evolutionary process. Thus, we describe both transactions that are highly structured to fully separate the credit of the asset-backed issue from that of the originator and transactions in which structures were selected with less credit separation. We describe both public issues of asset-backed securities and also structured private market loan sales. Not withstanding the diversity and constant evolution of credit securitization, the obvious beginning for any work in the area is a firm grasp of what has come before, and how and why credit securitization has actually been employed by the pioneering practitioners. In that spirit, it is hoped that readers will find this a useful tool.

2

Overview of Securitized Credit Product Structures

As discussed in Chapter 1, we broadly define securitization to be the trend toward financial assets being securities rather than loans. In our definition, a security is a financing in which the originator is not the investor, and a loan is a financing in which the originator is the investor. These are functional definitions, rather than legal ones. Securitization has affected many asset classes and taken many forms—from traditional debt securities and loan sales to a variety of newer forms in which outstanding loans are converted into asset-backed securities. Credit securitization is the process of creating these newer forms by converting loans into securities. In other words, credit securitization separates the originator from the ultimate investors. Credit securitization typically involves the use of structures which separate the credit of the assets backing an issue from the general credit of the originator.

In this chapter, we will examine a range of securitizing structures to see their legal and economic advantages and limitations. We will look at two types of structures:

- *Traditional, direct structures,* which include traditional securities (commercial paper, notes, bonds) and loan sales and participations

- *Emerging credit securitization structures,* which create asset-backed securities whose credit is independent of that of the originator.

The advantages, disadvantages, and flexibility of these structures can only be appreciated in the context of the legal, regulatory, and accounting infrastructure that lies beneath them. Accordingly, we will look at the relevant securities laws, tax laws, bankruptcy and insolvency laws, and accounting treatment of these various structuring options. This framework will provide the analytical background for understanding the specific securitized credit transactions described in Part 2.

TRADITIONAL, DIRECT STRUCTURES

We will now briefly discuss the structure of traditional debt securities, and the laws and accounting rules that affect these securities. Many of these laws and rules are equally applicable to the newer credit securitization structures discussed later. We will also examine the structure of the other traditional direct form of securitization—loan sales—before proceeding to an in-depth examination of the newer structures.

DEBT SECURITIES

Traditional corporate debt securities typically are bonds, notes, and commercial paper.[1] With these, a corporation contracts to pay investors principal and interest at fixed intervals over a certain time period. These debt securities are usually backed by the general credit of the corporation.

The structure of a typical corporate debt securities issue is illustrated in Figure 2.1. In that example, Corporation X sells $100 million in 20-year bonds to Underwriter Y, who then immediately

---

[1] The term "bond" generally refers to a long-term (typically 10 years or more) debt instrument. The very shortest debt instrument, "commercial paper," generally matures in no more than 9 months. The term "note" refers to a debt instrument whose maturity is greater than that of commercial paper and less than that of a bond.

Figure 2.1. Typical structure of corporate bond issue ($100 million Corporation X 12% bonds).

sells the bonds to investors.[2] The bonds essentially are contracts by which Corporation X promises to pay investors 12 percent annual interest on their investment. Typically, such corporate bonds will pay interest semiannually and the principal will be repaid upon the maturity of the bond.

While the bond structure in Figure 2.1 appears simple, the issuance of a corporate bond cannot be that simple, since it is accompanied by large quantities of paperwork and sizeable legal fees. We will briefly summarize the relevant legal and accounting aspects of the bond issue by Corporation X.

Credit Risk

As previously noted, the 20-year bonds issued by Corporation X represent a contract to pay the bondholders interest semiannually and principal at maturity. While this contract assures bondholders of relative priority in payment to equity holders, the bondholders are exposed to the credit risk that adverse business conditions could cause Corporation X to default on its obligation to pay timely interest and principal. Independent rating agencies, like Standard & Poor's and Moody's, assess this risk of default on a scale that ranges from least likely to default (AAA/Aaa or equivalent) to already in default (D or equivalent). While a default on a bond obligation may precede a corporate bankruptcy, companies that are in the most serious financial trouble sometimes end up in

---

[2] Figure 2.1 shows a traditional "firm-commitment" underwriting in which the underwriter purchases the securities and resells them to investors and/or dealers. Most debt securities are issued on this firm-commitment basis. Alternatively, a securities issue may be placed through "best efforts" underwriting in which the underwriter simply acts as a sales agent of the securities on a commission basis. The underwriter neither purchases securities itself, nor guarantees that investors will completely purchase the issue.

bankruptcy.[3] A company enters bankruptcy when a bankruptcy petition is filed in the bankruptcy court, either by the company itself or by its creditors. Upon such a filing, the company's operations become controlled by the United States Bankruptcy Code (Bankruptcy Code). During this period, the bankrupt company is aided by provisions in the Bankruptcy Code that provide special flexibility by, among other things, stopping collection actions by creditors.

The Bankruptcy Code also sets a schedule of priorities among the claims of creditors. Investors in the corporate bonds of a bankrupt company frequently lose more of their investment than secured creditors. Bondholders typically are general unsecured creditors, whose claims the Bankruptcy Code subordinates to the claims of the secured and other priority creditors. Therefore, investors in traditional corporate bonds are typically exposed to the corporation's general business risk, and the rating agencies will rate the credit quality of that corporation's bonds by analyzing the overall ability of the business to pay bondholders' principal and interest in a timely manner.

It is important to note that a corporate bankruptcy exposes investors to two sorts of undesirable credit risk. First, investors are exposed to the risk that they will not ultimately be paid the principal and interest to which they are entitled. Second, even when investors are ultimately paid in full, they are exposed to the risk of delayed payment and, therefore, the loss of the time value of money. In fact, the structure of the Bankruptcy Code almost guarantees substantial delays in a bankrupt corporation's payments to lenders. The automatic stay provision of the Bankruptcy Code stops the collection of all prebankruptcy filing debts from the entity that has filed for bankruptcy. Creditors are not permitted to take any action to collect such prefiling debts without court permission. Generally, debt payments are not resumed until the adoption of a plan of reorganization or a liquidation, either of which may not occur until years after the initial bankruptcy filing.

---

[3] However, the Bankruptcy Code does not apply to certain types of institutions, including commercial banks and thrifts. The impact of insolvency upon these institutions will be discussed later in this chapter.

At that time, all, some, or none of the creditors' claims will be satisfied in accordance with their respective priorities and the company's debt-paying capacity.

You might think that an investor in corporate debt could be protected from such risks if he could obtain a security interest in a valuable corporate asset. A security interest is simply a priority legal claim on the asset or collateral for the investor's loan to the corporation. Unfortunately, though, even a properly established security interest in valuable collateral would serve only to protect the investor against the credit risk that he will not ultimately be repaid principal and interest. While the law requires that the secured creditor ultimately not be deprived of the value of the collateral up to the amount of the debt, the operation of the Bankruptcy Code ordinarily delays payment even for secured debts. Therefore, the credit rating agencies will not rate the secured debt of a corporation subject to the Bankruptcy Code much more highly than the corporation's general unsecured debt, since the investor in the secured debt remains exposed to the same risk of untimely payment.

In contrast, one of the major advantages of the new credit securitization structures discussed later in this chapter is that they are structured in a manner that provide uninterrupted access to the underlying assets even after a bankruptcy of the originating corporation—thus permitting credit quality to be substantially higher than that of the originator.

Tax/Accounting Aspects of Traditional Corporate Debt

Traditionally, corporations have been financed with debt and equity. Debt instruments can offer a significant tax advantage to corporations. The interest costs of debt are deductible from the taxable federal income of the corporation, while distributions to equity investors are not tax-deductible. Since the federal tax rate on corporate income is sizeable (presently 34 percent), the "tax shield" advantage of debt financing is quite valuable. In addition to the federal income tax, many businesses are also subject to state income taxes. While these state taxes vary, it is generally true that interest costs of corporate debt are also tax-deductible under these state statutes, while distributions to equity holders are not deductible.

The accounting treatment of traditional corporate debt securities is straightforward. They are carried on the business's balance sheet as liabilities.

Federal Securities Laws

Several federal securities laws apply to all domestic issues of debt securities. While a detailed understanding of these laws is not necessary for our purposes, it is important to have a general understanding of the constraints imposed by these statutes. These constraints affect all traditional debt securities, and they play an important role in the structuring of the new asset-backed securities.

Securities Act of 1933.   The Securities Act of 1933 (1933 Act) generally requires issuers of securities to publicly disclose in a registration statement, including a prospectus, a great deal of financial and other information about the issuer and the proposed issue. The federal Securities and Exchange Commission (SEC) must declare the registration statement to be effective before the securities may be sold. Issues of securities so registered with the SEC are termed "public offerings" and may be sold to the general public as well as institutional investors. The cost and time required for a registered public offering may be quite substantial. Costs include relatively large legal, accounting, and printing fees, together with a 2bp SEC registration fee. The time required for the SEC registration process may be 3 or 4 months or more. However, a "shelf registration" process is available to substantially shorten this period for some issues.

In summary, the major advantages of a registered public securities offering are that the securities may be publicly advertised, sold to the general public, and thereafter resold in the secondary market to the public at large. The disadvantages are the costs and delays of the registration process.

For issuers who desire to avoid the registration process, there are several statutory exemptions from the 1933 Act's registration requirement. Three of these exemptions are of general significance to asset securitization. The first exemption is the "commercial paper" exemption for high-quality debt instruments whose maturity is no more than 9 months. The second exemption is for private offerings of securities. While the legal definition of a private offering is quite complicated, SEC Regulation D generally provides a "safe harbor" as a private offering for issues sold to "accredited investors" (which include institutional investors, wealthy individuals, and purchasers of $150,000 or more). Securities sold through private offerings cannot be publicly sold through general solicitation or advertising, and are somewhat limited in transferability. The third relevant exemption is for participation interests in mortgages originated by regulated financial institutions for which the minimum sale price is not less than $250,000.[4]

Securities Exchange Act of 1934.   While the purpose of the 1933 Act is to assure potential investors of adequate and accurate information prior to a securities issue coming to market, the purpose of the Securities Exchange Act of 1934 (1934 Act) is to assure investors of a continuing stream of accurate information about the issuer after the initial issuance of the securities. The 1934 Act requires every issuer of securities registered under the 1933 Act, with certain exceptions, to file regular reports with the SEC about its operations and financial condition. These reports allow investors to monitor the condition of the issuer. The 1934 Act is also noteworthy for its Rule 10b-5, which prohibits the use of fraud or any manipulative or deceptive practice in connection with any sale of securities.

Trust Indenture Act of 1939.   While the 1933 and 1934 Acts provide investors with information about publicly issued securities, the Trust Indenture Act of 1939 (1939 Act) creates certain structural protections for investors in most publicly issued debt securi-

---

[4] The 1933 Act contains other exemptions including one for securities issued by banks and thrifts. However, while this exemption applies to general credit bank debt issues, it does not apply to issues of debt securities backed by discrete bank asset pools. Hence, for our purposes, this exemption is not important in the context of credit securitization.

ties. The 1939 Act generally provides that the issuer of debt must enter into a bond indenture agreement with an independent qualified trustee. The trustee is then legally responsible for monitoring the issuer's compliance with its obligations to the bondholders. If the issuer defaults on any of these obligations, the trustee must notify the bondholders and take necessary prudent actions to protect their interests.

As with the 1933 Act, the 1939 Act contains a number of exemptions. These exemptions include private placements, commercial paper, and certain mortgage securities.

Public Offerings versus Private Placements under the 1933, 1934, and 1939 Acts.

The combined effect of the 1933, 1934, and 1939 Acts is to impose substantial costs, delays, and financial disclosure obligations upon public offerings of securities. Legal, accounting, and printing costs must be paid for the initial registration of the securities. Further legal and accounting costs result from the issuer's continuing obligation to file regular reports of its financial condition during the life of the issue. Also, the issuer must pay a fee to retain an independent trustee during the life of the issue. Private placements of securities to institutional or wealthy individual investors may avoid some of the costs, delays, and disclosures of this registration, reporting, and monitoring process.

On the other hand, public issues may have a major advantage over private placements. Since public issues may be widely advertised, distributed, and sold, a public issue is likely to be very liquid. Because many investors prefer to have the option of selling their interests prior to maturity with minimal transaction costs, they will accept a slightly lower yield for such liquidity. Private offerings tend to be less liquid, and investors typically demand a higher yield for this reduced liquidity.[5]

---

[5] In addition to the 1933, 1934, and 1939 Acts that we have already discussed, there is another federal securities-related law that has a significant impact on certain issues of debt securities. That law, the Investment Company Act of 1940, primarily affects the new forms of asset-backed securities rather than traditional debt securities. As a result, it is discussed later in connection with the asset-backed securities structures.

LOAN SALES

Securities, whether publicly issued or privately placed, are not the only form of traditional, unstructured securitization. Loan sales are another form of such traditional securitization. A loan is a contract between an originating lending institution and a borrower which calls for the borrower to receive a certain amount of funds for a specified time at a contractual interest rate. Loans are similar to traditional securities in that the originating institution depends primarily on the general credit of the borrower to assure timely repayment of the loan. However, some "secured" loans are further protected by security interests in property of the borrower. Such a security interest typically does not guarantee the lender timely payment of interest and principal in the event of a default of the borrower. Rather, it simply gives the lender a prior claim to the collateral in the event of a default. A bankruptcy of the borrower would be likely to impair the ability of the lender to exercise such secured claims in a timely manner, though the lender would ultimately be entitled to collect the value of his collateral to the extent of his secured claim.

The term "loan sale" includes both sales of whole loans from an originator to a single investor and sales of portions of loans (participations) from an originator to investors. The structure of a typical loan sale is diagrammed in Figure 2.2. In that example, originating Bank A lends $90 million to investment-grade Corporation X. Bank A then sells a $30 million participation in the loan to Japanese Bank B, $30 million of the loan to Regional Bank C, and another $20 million to a third bank. Bank A thereby participates out $80 million of the $90 million loan. In this manner, the purchasing banks effectively become direct lenders to Corporation X by each purchasing the right to stand in the place of Bank A with respect to their portion of the loan. The purchasing banks decide to participate in such transactions either because they have a true funding cost advantage, which allows them comparatively greater profit from the loan (this is true for many foreign banks), because they are overcapitalized and lack a more attractive use of funds, or because they want to diversify their loan portfolio.

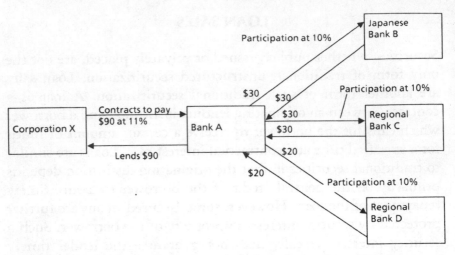

Figure 2.2. Typical structure of loan participation ($90 million loan to Corporation X) ($ millions).

Usually, Bank A then services the loan on behalf of all four banks by collecting the loan payments, monitoring the loan covenants, and remitting payments to the other banks. For this, Bank A typically collects a servicing fee before remitting the loan payments to the other banks, and through this fee captures a spread between the interest rate paid by Corporation X and a lower interest rate on the loan participations. Or, Bank A may charge an origination fee or premium price to the participating banks.

For the purposes of this book, we are distinguishing loan sales from loan syndications. In a loan syndication, two or more banks each initially make discrete portions of a total package of loans to a borrower. In our terminology, syndications are not forms of securitization since the credit originator and the ultimate investor are the same entity. By contrast, in a loan sale, the credit originator initially makes the loan and then resells all or part of it to other investors.

From a structural perspective, there are usually four major considerations in a loan sale: (1) that the loan sale not violate the Glass-Steagall Act; (2) that the loan sale not create a security requiring registration under the previously discussed securities laws; (3) that the loan sale be a "true sale" for insolvency purposes; and (4) that the loan sale qualify as a sale for accounting purposes. Let us look at each of these in more detail.

1. Banks and bank affiliates are prohibited by the Glass-Steagall Act from underwriting most securities. Many loan sales involve loans that have been originated by commercial banks. The structure of a typical bank loan sale is not unlike that of a debt security underwritten by an investment bank. In both cases, the financial institution raises money for the borrower by booking a general debt of the borrower and then selling that obligation to investors. This apparent resemblance between the selling of loans and the underwriting of debt securities is of legal concern since one of the federal banking laws, the Glass-Steagall Act, prohibits banks from underwriting most securities. Essentially, the Glass-Steagall Act prohibits national banks and state Federal Reserve system member banks from underwriting and dealing in domestic, nongovernment debt securities. The Act also bars any such bank from being affiliated with an organization "engaged principally" in the underwriting of such securities. The Federal Reserve Board also applies this affiliation limitation to bank holding companies and their subsidiaries pursuant to its supervisory powers under the Bank Holding Company Act.

Banks have sold loan participations for many years, and the relevant case law suggests that the courts will be reluctant to label such traditional banking activity as securities underwriting prohibited by Glass-Steagall. Nevertheless, the status of some of the newer loan participation programs under Glass-Steagall is not certain. Depending upon how it is structured, such a program may raise Glass-Steagall concerns. If a participated loan has a large number of purchasers, small dollar amount participations, a large proportion of nonbank purchasers, and an active secondary market, then it could begin to look somewhat like a Glass-Steagall security. If a participated loan has a relatively small number of bank purchasers, each of whom purchases and holds large dollar amount participations, then the loan sale bears little resemblance to a Glass-Steagall security. As a result, bank loan participations often are sold to a relatively limited number of purchasers under conditions that may limit to whom such participations may be resold.[6]

2. Loan participation programs also raise issues under the securities laws.

While the question of whether placement of particular loan participations constitutes securities underwriting prohibited by Glass-Steagall is of particular concern to banks, all issuers of loan participations must be concerned about the federal securities laws. As noted earlier, these laws require that all securities, with certain exceptions, undergo a somewhat costly and time-consuming registration process, that issuers regularly disclose financial information, and that debt securities comply with various structural standards. Since it is possible for a loan participation to be viewed as a "security" covered by the securities laws, originators of loan participations must take measures to guard against unintentionally violating the securities laws. As a result, loan participations are typically structured to fall under one of two previously discussed securities registration exemptions. Either the participations are of relatively short maturity loans,[7] or they are only privately placed with "accredited" investors.[8] Accordingly, the participations would be exempt from the registration requirements of the 1933 Act and the trustee requirement of the 1939 Act.[9] However, there is growing legal and regulatory authority for the proposition that a sale of interests in a commercial loan to institutions regularly engaged in making such loans may not involve "securities."

---

[6] The rights of banks to structure and place loan participations and "securities" are in a state of turmoil. The federal banking regulators, Congress, and the courts are constantly developing their positions concerning the rights of banks in this area. Accordingly, it is advisable to consult with a well-informed attorney before drawing any final conclusions concerning Glass-Steagall and Bank Holding Company Act "underwriting" limitations on banks and their affiliates.

[7] Term of 9 months or less in order to fall within the "commercial paper" registration exemption.

[8] "Accredited" investors include institutional investors and relatively wealthy individual purchasers.

[9] The originator of the participations might or might not also be exempt from the reporting requirements of the 1934 Act depending upon the type of originator and whether its other securities activities already required it to file 1934 Act reports.

3. Loan sales must be properly structured and documented to protect against insolvency risk. Purchasers of loans and loan participations originated by banks believe that they are stepping into the shoes of the originating bank, and that the only credit risk they are incurring is that of the borrower. Until the failure of the Penn Square Bank in 1982, such loan sales were relatively informal arrangements. However, the Penn Square failure eliminated the informality of loan sale structures. Penn Square had sold several billion dollars of loans to other financial institutions, which had not thought themselves exposed to credit losses from a failure of Penn Square. While a bank like Penn Square was technically exempt from the federal Bankruptcy Code, banks can become "insolvent" and thereby fail. If an FDIC-insured bank fails, the FDIC usually either liquidates as receiver or merges the failed bank in order to minimize losses to its insurance fund.

In the Penn Square case, the FDIC, as receiver of Penn Square, took the position that the "purchasers" of Penn Square loans were merely lenders to and unsecured creditors of Penn Square. Thus the FDIC treated the loan "sales" as borrowings by Penn Square, rather than true sales of the loans. The FDIC took this position in order to continue to count the loans "sold" by Penn Square as assets of Penn Square, and thereby minimize the losses to its insurance fund. The FDIC supported its claim before various courts with evidence that the purchasing institutions had not acquired a legally sufficient quantum of rights and responsibilities for the loans to demonstrate ownership. As a result of the FDIC's position on the Penn Square insolvency, some banks sustained losses related to loans they believed they had truly "purchased" from Penn Square.

Since that time, loan sales have been much more formally structured so that the sale of the loan effectively conveys an ownership interest which includes both the control and the risks of the loan. Thus written loan participation agreements generally specify that the loan has been sold and that the originating bank may not, without the concurrence of the participant: (1) amend the terms or conditions of the loan; (2) change the security agreement for the loan; (3) release any claims against the borrower; or (4) commence any collection action without prior consultation with the participant.

In addition, the purchaser of a participation generally has the right to revoke the originating bank's servicing authority if that bank becomes insolvent, fails to comply with its servicing obligations, or is party to an irresolvable dispute concerning the loan. Finally, a notification to the borrower that the loan has been sold is a useful, though not essential, indication of a true sale. The above structuring and documentation procedures have been adopted in order to prevent a recurrence of the Penn Square "true sale" versus "lending" problem. Of course, the ultimate determination of whether a loan sale qualifies as a true sale will be made by the courts in the event of any dispute.[10] It is critically important to note that while the above structuring may eliminate the risk of an insolvency of an originating bank, it does not eliminate the risk that the ultimate borrower may go bankrupt. In other words, Bank A may lend funds to Corporation X; Bank A then may participate the loan by a "true sale" to Banks B and C. In that event, Banks B and C are exposed to the risk that Corporation X may go bankrupt, which would cause an automatic interruption in loan payments even if the loan were secured with valuable collateral.

4. Loan sales must also be structured as sales for accounting purposes.   A bank originating a loan participation must not only structure that participation as a "true sale" for insolvency purposes, but also as a sale under Regulatory Accounting Principles (RAP) if the loans are to be removed from its balance sheet for capital adequacy purposes. The federal banking regulators permit the originating bank to remove the sold loan from its books only if the loan sale qualifies as a sale under RAP. The Federal Financial Institutions Examination Council (FFIEC) has adopted a general rule that a bank may take loans off its books only if the loan sale is

---

[10] This discussion of "true sale" requirements for loan participations has been focused upon banks since they originate most loan participations. As previously noted, banks are exempt from the Bankruptcy Code. (Thrifts, too, are exempt from the Bankruptcy Code.) However, some loans are sold by originators like finance companies who are subject to the Bankruptcy Code. Purchasers of these loans are concerned that the loan sale qualify as a "true sale" for bankruptcy purposes so that the sold loan does not remain part of the seller's estate. The bankruptcy "true sale" standard is similar to the insolvency "true sale" standard. (See the discussion later in this chapter of "true sale" under the Bankruptcy Code.)

without recourse to the originating bank.[11] Of course, finance companies and other nonbank entities are not subject to federal banking regulations. These companies may account for properly structured loan sales with recourse as sales under Generally Accepted Accounting Principles (GAAP), in accordance with Financial Accounting Standards Board (FAS) Standard No. 77. (See the last part of this chapter for a discussion of accounting for asset sales.) This is important because financings that are accounted for as debt—as opposed to sales—result in more debt on the balance sheet. Although these companies are not subject to capital adequacy regulation, capital requirements are imposed upon them by the securities markets, rating agencies, and lending banks.

SUMMARY

We have discussed the traditional securitization structures, including debt securities like notes and bonds in the public market and loan sales and participations in the private market. These traditional financing technologies typically share the characteristic that the originator of the credit (usually an investment bank or a commercial bank) is not the ultimate investor in the financial asset.

However, both traditional debt securities and loan participations have certain common disadvantages. From the perspective of the investors, both forms of finance leave the investor exposed to the risks of delayed payment and ultimate credit loss that could result from the failure of the borrower. From the perspective of the borrower, both forms of financings create debt obligations on their balance sheets that must be supported with expensive equity capital.

On the other hand, the new credit securitization structures described next represent a technology that can overcome these disadvantages of the traditional structures.

---

[11] However, the FFIEC has adopted an exception to this no-recourse policy for sales of residential mortgage loans. The federal banking regulators permit "true sales" of 1- to 4-family residential mortgages with less than "significant" recourse back to the originating bank because it is a federal policy to assist liquidity in the mortgage markets to make home ownership less expensive and, therefore, possible for more people.

EMERGING CREDIT SECURITIZATION STRUCTURES

In the last few years, structured credit securitization has become more and more sophisticated. Underlying this new technology are several generic structuring approaches which make it possible for many borrowers to access the securities markets in a broader and more efficient manner than the previously described traditional debt financing. We use the term "structured financing" with respect to asset-backed financings to mean a transaction that has been legally structured so that: (1) the cash flow from the underlying assets is packaged to attract targeted investors; (2) the tax and accounting needs of the borrower and investors are satisfied; (3) the credit criteria applied to the asset pool will generate an efficient cost of funds; and (4) a bankruptcy or insolvency of the originator will not interfere with the use of proceeds from the assets to make timely payments to investors.

Structured finance allows originators to access the securities market at debt ratings higher than their overall corporate rating, which generally enables them to secure funds at a lower cost. Structured finance also allows originators to finance assets in a manner that removes the assets and their supporting debt from the originators' balance sheets. As a result, originators of structured financings may be able to save some equity costs of on-balance sheet financing, and eliminate potential asset-liability mismatch.

Structured credit securitization began in the residential mortgage market as a result of federal government encouragement through the Federal National Mortgage Association (FNMA), the Government National Mortgage Association (GNMA), and the Federal Home Loan Mortgage Corporation (FHLMC) programs. For example, FNMA might buy eligible ("conforming") residential mortgage loans, pool a number together, guarantee payments of principal and interest, and then sell mortgage-backed securities to investors. This government-assisted securitization dominates the conforming residential mortgage market.

In 1985, the securitization technology that had been developed in the mortgage market was applied for the first time to non-mortgage assets. Creative structurers found ways to substitute private credit enhancement for the government-related credit enhancement that had assisted the securitization of conforming residential mortgages.

One example of such a structured financing is that illustrated in Figure 2.3. Corporation A, whose general credit has been rated BB by Standard & Poor's and Ba Moody's,[12] wants to raise $100 million. Corporation A establishes a special purpose vehicle, and then sells $100 million of assets to it. The special purpose vehicle funds the purchase of these assets by issuing $100 million in asset-backed securities to investors. Corporation A remains the servicer for the assets, and retains the spread between the yield on the assets and the interest paid to the investors (Figure 2.4). The investors rely upon the particular assets in the special purpose vehicle for the return on their investment. If the transaction is properly structured, a bankruptcy of Originator A will not interfere with timely payments to the investors. After all, the investors have purchased securities issued by the special purpose vehicle based on the credit strength of the asset pool, as opposed to that of

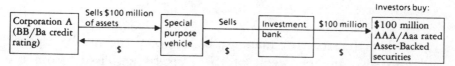

Figure 2.3. Typical structure asset-backed security ($100 million).

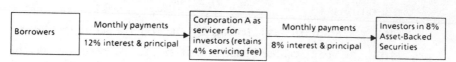

Figure 2.4. Payment stream ($100 million Corporation A asset-backed securities).

[12] Standard & Poor's and Moody's are the two most prominent national rating services. Standard & Poor's rates the ability of companies to pay their corporate debt on a scale of D (debt that is already in default) to AAA (companies whose capacity to make timely payments is extremely strong). Moody's uses a similar scale with different symbols to rate debt-paying capacity (e.g., Aaa). The better a company's credit rating, the less the risk of loss to debt security holders and the lower the yield demanded by those investors.

Corporation A. As a result of this structured separation of credit, the asset-backed securities are frequently given a higher credit rating than that of the originator. This higher credit rating may be achieved by some form of partial credit enhancement such as a letter of credit to cover first losses on the asset pool.

Another result of this structured transaction is that the assets and their supporting debt liabilities have been removed from Corporation A's balance sheet. As a result, Corporation A may realize significant savings in the amount of expensive equity that it holds on its balance sheet. Moreover, with less debt on its balance sheet, Corporation A may have more borrowing flexibility under agreements with its banks and other lenders.

FRAMEWORK FOR ANALYZING STRUCTURED, ASSET-BACKED FINANCE

In order to understand the structural options available for individual securitized credit transactions and the advantages and disadvantages of each structure, it is important to understand five fundamental concerns that underlie each such transaction. These concerns are:

- How the structure manages bankruptcy and insolvency risk to separate the credit of the asset-backed issue from the credit of the originator
- Which legal form is selected for the issuer
- How the structure is influenced by federal income tax considerations
- How the structure is affected by the federal securities laws
- How the asset-backed issue will be accounted for by the originator.

We will now look at each of these concerns.

Separating the Credit of the Asset-Backed Issue from That of the Originator

A major advantage of securitized credit is its ability to separate the credit of the assets securing an asset-backed issue from the credit risk of the originator. As previously discussed, traditional corporate debt financing is based upon the general credit of the corporation. Investors in such traditional corporate debt securities are exposed to the risk that the corporation may default on its debts and look to the U.S. Bankruptcy Code to interrupt creditors' attempts to collect prebankruptcy debts. The automatic stay provision of the Bankruptcy Code usually stops timely payments of interest and principal to bondholders. Normally, it would only be at the end of the bankruptcy proceeding (which can last for years) that the bondholders would recover some portion of the monies to which they were entitled.

Moreover, even if the corporation had pledged valuable collateral to secure the bond payments, the Bankruptcy Code would automatically stay the bondholders from exercising their rights to such collateral. Therefore, while this collateral may help assure the bondholders of ultimate repayment, the bondholders are not likely to be paid in a timely manner. Since timely payments are very important to investors, the rating agencies will not rate a traditional collateralized bond much higher than the general credit rating of the issuing corporation as a bankruptcy is likely to cause a default on the timely payment of interest and principal. However, the newer securitized credit products have been structured to protect investors in the event that the originating corporation becomes bankrupt. As a result, it has become possible to structure asset-backed securities whose credit quality is higher than the general credit of the originator.

Generally, such securitized credit products are insulated from the risk of an originator's bankruptcy by structuring the transaction so that the underlying assets are not the property of the originator. Typically, the originator will sell the assets to another entity (which we call a "special purpose vehicle"), and that special purpose vehicle will then issue asset-backed securities secured by the assets. A number of measures must be taken to ensure that the investors in these asset-backed securities are properly protected from a bankruptcy of the originator.

First, the transfer of the assets from the originator to the special purpose vehicle must qualify as a "true sale" rather than a "pledge" for bankruptcy purposes. In order to so qualify, several steps usually should be taken:

- The originator should account for the transfer as a sale on its financial statements.
- Recourse to the originator should not be for an amount much greater than the reasonably anticipated losses on the assets based primarily on historic performance of similar assets.
- Outside legal counsel to the originator should provide an opinion letter indicating that a "true sale" of the assets has occurred for bankruptcy purposes.[13]

Second, a special purpose vehicle that purchases receivables must "perfect" its right to the receivables in accordance with applicable state law. Perfection means that appropriate documents must be filed and the receivables properly marked, as required by the Uniform Commercial Code, in order to legally validate the claim to the receivables. Typically, the rights to the receivables are perfected in the name of the trustee for the asset-backed security holders.

However, if the originator remains as servicer for the assets, and if it commingles receipts from the sold assets with its own funds, the rights of the special purpose vehicle to the funds commingled for more than 10 days could become unperfected. In that event, the investors would become unsecured creditors with respect to amounts in such commingled accounts on the date of the originators. For funds commingled for less than 10 days, the investors would be perfected, but would not have priority over other creditors with secured claims to such account. Moreover, any payments made within a 90-day period (1 year if the special purpose vehicle is wholly owned by the originator) prior to a bankruptcy of the originator out of funds commingled for more than 10 days might be recaptured by the originator's bankrupt estate. In order to protect against these risks, as a general matter, collections from the sold assets generally should not be commingled with the originator's own funds, if the originator continues to act as the collection agent.

Thirdly, the special purpose vehicle must also be structured so that it cannot engage in any activity that would cause it to be-

---

[13] As you will note throughout this handbook, residential mortgages are sometimes treated more liberally by both statute and regulation because of Congress's desire to facilitate secondary mortgage market activity.

come bankrupt. Typically, the special purpose vehicle's business must be restricted to the purchase of the assets and the issuance of the debt backed by the assets. The special purpose vehicle may not incur any further debt that is less likely to be paid than the asset-backed debt, since the failure to pay such further debt could result in the vehicle's bankruptcy. The special purpose vehicle may not sell or assign the assets backing the debt to any other entity, unless that entity is also protected against bankruptcy and the assets transferred remain subject to the prior claims of the asset-backed debtholders.

In many cases, the special purpose vehicle may be a corporation that is a limited purpose subsidiary of the originator. In that event, the special purpose vehicle must also be protected from being consolidated with the parent in the event of the latter's bankruptcy. To guard against such consolidation, the special purpose finance corporation should protect its separate corporate identity by:

- Maintaining separate books and records
- Maintaining separate accounts not intermingled with those of the originator
- Holding appropriate Board of Directors meetings to authorize corporate action
- Having at least one independent officer and director
- Both the originator and the special purpose finance corporation adopting resolutions specifying that a bankruptcy filing by the originator will not cause a filing by the finance corporation
- Obtaining a legal opinion from the originator's counsel that the assets of the special purpose finance corporation could not be consolidated with the originator in the event of its bankruptcy.

While most corporations are subject to the U.S. Bankruptcy Code, some institutions (most importantly, banks and thrifts) are exempted from the Code. These institutions may pledge their assets to a special purpose vehicle or directly to asset-backed security holders, and those holders do not have to worry that the

Bankruptcy Code will interfere with timely payments to security holders. Thus bankruptcy-immune originators need not actually "sell" the assets to a special purpose vehicle. However, the rating agencies do require these "bankruptcy-immune" originators to comply with most of the other structuring steps described above (including those relating to perfecting the special purpose vehicle's or debtholder's rights in the receivables).

While banks and thrifts cannot become bankrupt, they can become insolvent. In the event of an insolvency, the Federal Deposit Insurance Corporation (FDIC) acts as the receiver for an insolvent bank and arranges to sell the bank or liquidate its assets. The Federal Savings and Loans Insurance Corporation (FSLIC) plays the same role for most insolvent thrifts. FDIC and FSLIC have indicated their positions concerning asset-backed obligations originated by banks and thrifts and secured by a pledge of assets. Generally, FSLIC will retain the option to continue to perform by the assumption of the thrift's obligations to the asset-backed debtholders. Alternately, FSLIC may liquidate the assets, accelerate payments to the debtholders, and recapture any excess value from the assets. The FDIC will generally choose this acceleration option. However, neither agency will so accelerate if the asset collateral is "underwater" in that its market value would be insufficient to fully pay the debtholders. Accordingly, when a FSLIC-insured institution is the originator, asset-backed securities should provide that they may be accelerated or assumed in the event of an insolvency of the originating institution that has pledged the assets. When a FDIC-insured institution is the originator, asset-backed securities should provide for acceleration upon insolvency, unless the asset collateral is underwater. With such provisions, the highest rating levels are available to such asset "pledged" securities. An insolvency of the originating institution may cause an acceleration of the securities, but such acceleration will not constitute untimely payment since the original terms of the securities provided for acceleration upon insolvency.

Many investors prefer not to be exposed to the reinvestment risk that would result from accelerated repayment upon the insolvency of the insured institution. This problem can be solved by the thrift or bank selling the assets to a special purpose vehicle utilizing the previously described elements of separateness. The insured institution must also adopt certain resolutions and obtain certain opinions approving the fairness of the transaction. Such a properly structured "true sale" to the special purpose vehicle will enable the asset-backed securities to be issued without the risk of acceleration in the event of the insolvency of the originator.

Legal Forms of Special Purpose Vehicles

As discussed, the recent development of securitized credit products has fundamentally changed corporate finance by developing structures that insulate holders of asset-backed securities from the credit risk of the originator. These structures typically employ a special purpose vehicle to purchase the assets from the originator and to issue the asset-backed securities. The special purpose vehicles used for credit securitization generally take the legal forms of corporations or trusts, although such vehicles may also be partnerships.

A corporation is simply a legal entity created under the laws of one of the states. A corporation has an existence independent of its shareholders. It has the power to make contracts, to sue or be sued, to own property and to commit crimes. It is responsible for its own debts, and the liability of its shareholders for corporate actions is limited to their investment. The corporation is capable of perpetual existence, and its management is centralized in a board of directors and officers.

A trust is an unincorporated entity generally created under state law by a depositor contributing property to be held by a trustee pursuant to a written trust agreement between the depositor and the trustee. The depositor may be the beneficial owner of the trust property, or the ownership of the property may be conveyed to third parties. The trustee is responsible for managing the trust property on behalf of the beneficial owners.

A third possible legal form is that of a partnership. A typical partnership essentially is an association of two or more persons who engage in business as co-owners. Each partner may bind the other partners, and each partner has the right to participate in management. A partner is exposed to unlimited personal liability and he may not transfer his partnership interest without the consent of the other partners. Alternatively, a partnership may be structured to have both general partners (like those described above) and limited partners. Limited partners have no personal liability and have much more limited management rights than general partners.

Impact of Federal Income Tax Considerations

Federal income tax considerations establish important structural characteristics of securitized credit products. As we have noted, structured securitized credit typically requires a legal entity (the special purpose vehicle) to purchase the assets that form the basis for the asset-backed securities. Since the special purpose vehicles are legal entities, they may become subject to federal income taxation. From a federal tax perspective,[14] income tax on the special purpose vehicle can be minimized in one of two ways, either by choosing a vehicle that is not subject to tax or by having the vehicle issue "debt" the interest on which is tax-deductible, either by the vehicle itself as a taxpayer or by the owners of the vehicle. It is essential that any such purported "debt" securities qualify as debt from a federal tax point of view so that the tax deduction for interest payments may be obtained.

There are generally three types of issuers to consider from a tax perspective: (1) grantor trusts that typically issue pass-through certificates; (2) issuers of debt securities typically termed pay-through securities; and (3) REMICs. Each type of issuer has important advantages and limitations in the overall designing of securitized credit products. It is essential to look at those advantages and limitations in order to understand the reasons for the varying characteristics of the asset-backed securities described in the various individual transaction descriptions in Chapter 3.

---

[14] Special purpose vehicles are potentially subject to state income taxes in addition to federal income tax. We will only address the federal tax aspects of these structures since the state tax classifications will vary from state to state. However, state tax problems can generally be addressed by locating the vehicle in a low or no tax state.

Grantor Trusts

The first relevant tax classification is that of grantor trust. The grantor trust classification is extremely important since the very popular "pass-through" asset-backed securities are generally structured to qualify as participations in grantor trusts. The pass-through structure is one in which the principal payments on the receivables are directly passed through the grantor trust special purpose vehicle to the holders of the pass-through certificates. Interest payments, too, are passed through at the interest rate established for the certificates.

The term "grantor trust" comes from the Internal Revenue Code. As further described next, a grantor trust is a type of fixed investment trust that is essentially ignored for tax purposes. Owners of interests in such a trust are taxed as if they were the direct owners of their shares of the trust assets. A grantor trust is legally created by a contract between a depositor and an independent trustee. This contract is known as a Trust Agreement or a Pooling and Servicing Agreement. Typically, this contract will provide for:

- The appointment of the trustee
- The pooling and deposit of certain assets by the originator into the trust
- The issuance by the trust back to the originator/depositor of certificates of beneficial interest in the trust
- The appointment of the originator as the servicer of the assets
- The designation of the trustee as the representative of the certificate holders
- The trustee's remedies in the event of default.

A typical grantor trust structure is shown in Figure 2.5. Pursuant to a Pooling and Servicing Agreement, Originator A creates a grantor trust and appoints a trustee (Bank X) to act as a fiduciary for the investors with respect to the receivables. The originator deposits the receivables into the trust in exchange for pass-through certificates which the originator then sells to investors through an

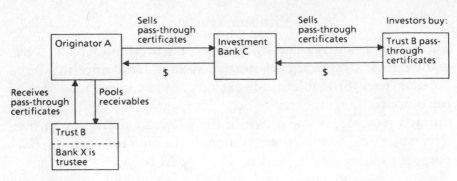

Figure 2.5.   Typical asset-backed security grantor trust structure.

investment bank. The pass-through certificates represent undivided ownership interests in the receivables pooled into the trust.

As shown in Figure 2.6, the monthly receivables payments are collected by Originator A as servicer on behalf of the certificate holders, and then remitted to the Trustee net of a servicing fee. The Trustee then forwards the monthly principal collections to the certificate holders, together with the monthly interest payments at the certificate interest rate. In most cases, the interest rate on the receivables will be significantly higher than the pass-through interest rate on the certificates. In such cases, Originator A has captured the value of its origination by raising the servicing fee to the appropriate level or by selling the receivables net of a retained yield. Alternatively, Originator A may pass-through a greater amount of interest and sell the pass-through certificates at a premium to face value. In any event, Bank X, as trustee for the

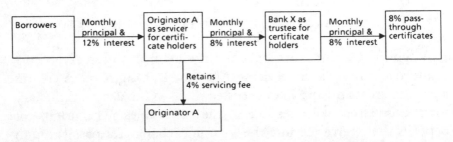

Figure 2.6.   Typical asset-backed security grantor trust structure (payment stream).

certificate holders, monitors the monthly cash flows to ensure that the investors are receiving payments to which they are entitled. If at any time Originator A were to default on its servicing obligation to collect the receivables or to remit payments for the investors, Bank X would take the appropriate corrective legal actions on behalf of the investors.

The grantor trust structure works as a conduit for outright sales of assets to investors. The trust is essentially ignored for tax purposes. Thus the exchange of receivables for pass-through certificates is a nonevent for tax purposes; a sale of those certificates is treated as a sale of a corresponding interest in the underlying receivables, and the trust itself is not taxed. Instead, the certificate holders are treated as owners of their respective shares of the trust's assets. Essentially, the Internal Revenue Code permits grantor trusts to function as nontaxable conduits so long as two conditions are met: (1) The trustee does not have the power to purchase new assets or substitute assets (except for substituting new receivables for defective receivables during an initial period) or any other power to reinvest monies in the trust, and (2) with limited exceptions, the trust has only a single class of pass-through certificates.[15] The passive nature of the grantor trust results in the name "pass-through" being commonly applied to such structures.

If a trust structure has prohibited reinvestment powers or multiple ownership classes, then the trust might be treated for tax purposes as an association taxable as a corporation. Such a characterization could have disastrous tax consequences since the interest income to the trust from the receivables would be fully taxable, while the payments from the trust to the certificate holders could be deemed nondeductible distributions to equity holders. As a result, the trust would have a substantial tax liability, and the certificate holders would receive yields substantially less than those they had anticipated.

---

[15] The prohibition against multiple classes is imposed under the IRS' so-called "Sears" regulations which were proposed in 1984 and finalized in 1986. Those regulations include an exception that allows multiple classes of ownership in two situations: (1) where the only difference between the classes is that one is subordinated to another in the event of defaults in trust assets (senior/junior); and, (2) where each class represents "stripped" interests in the underlying receivables (i.e., rights to identified principal or interest payments on identified receivables).

Because of these tax considerations, special purpose vehicles using the grantor trust structure have three common characteristics:

- Little or no alteration of cash flows
- No additions to trust assets after the initial asset pool is acquired (except for substitutions for defective assets in an initial period)
- Very limited interim investment of payments collected by the trust pending the regularly scheduled investor distribution dates.

The grantor trust structure has been used extensively for a number of years. GNMA, for example, guarantees pass-through certificates backed by government-insured mortgage pools which are then frequently sold as securities to numerous investors.

A structured asset-backed financing using a grantor trust has several advantages over an unstructured straight asset sale. A grantor trust structure permits assets to be pooled together, credit enhanced, and then sold to investors as highly rated, liquid securities. Thus lower-rated credits may directly access the securities market at the highest rating levels. Moreover, the use of the grantor trust tax classification permits the structured financing using a grantor trust as the special purpose vehicle (SPV) to realize these advantages without incurring any taxation at the SPV level.

There are, though, significant limitations to the pass-through securities created by the grantor trust structure. The first involves payment patterns. By its very nature, the grantor trust simply passes through to investors the principal and interest payments made by the borrowers. Thus investors in grantor trust securities receive principal repayments whenever made by the borrowers, as well as interest payments. This payment feature differs from that of a straight corporate bond which typically pays only interest until principal is repaid at the final maturity or calling of the bond. Accordingly, when comparing the yields of a straight corporate bond and a pass-through security, investors look to the "weighted average life" of the pass-through security. The "weighted average life" is the weighted average time to principal repayment. Ordinarily, the longer the weighted average life, the higher the yield must be to attract investors to place their investments for a longer period of time.

However, investors in grantor trust pass-through certificates usually cannot be sure that the weighted average life of their certificate will be that which they had anticipated from the terms of the underlying receivables. Most consumer loan contracts permit prepayment of principal at any time. As a result, home loan borrowers tend to prepay their mortgages upon the sale of their houses, and auto loan borrowers often prepay their auto loans upon the purchase of a new car. Moreover, prepayment rates for some types of receivables, especially residential mortgages, may vary over time. When interest rates are low, some borrowers may prepay their loans at a faster rate than originally expected (e.g., many homeowners will refinance their homes). These faster prepayments will result in a shorter weighted average life with the result that investors get their money back sooner than they anticipated.

Thus investors in pass-through certificates may be exposed to the risk that they may get their principal repaid at a time when reinvestment opportunities are relatively unattractive. This risk is particularly acute for mortgage pass-throughs since these securities are likely to prepay when interest rates are low, causing homeowners to refinance their mortgages. This prepayment risk of certain passthroughs is manifested in different forms in different economic environments. For example, another common type of prepayment risk occurs if an investor buys mortgage pass-through securities in a relatively low interest rate environment expecting their weighted average life to be 10 years. If interest rates rise over time, prepayments may be less than anticipated and the weighted average life of the security will rise to 15 years. Since the yield curve generally establishes higher interest rates for longer maturities, the investor will have suffered a loss by initially accepting a lower interest rate appropriate for 10-year securities, only to later discover them to be 15-year securities.

Another limitation of pass-through certificates is that holders of the certificates may not have different rights to the timing by which they receive principal payments on the pool of receivables. Thus it is not possible to allocate principal payments to different classes of certificates and thereby to create securities of differing maturities out of the pool of receivables in a grantor trust.

This limitation necessarily restricts originators of pass-throughs to marketing their certificates to that segment of the investor population that can tolerate the particular maturities of the assets underlying the pass-through certificates. It may be the case that the originator of the pass-through would have been able to obtain a lower all-in cost of funds by dividing the cash flow from the asset pool into a series of securities of different maturities—a mechanism that from a tax point of view cannot be accomplished by pass-through certificates. However, it should be noted that as a credit enhancement device, the originator of pass-through certificates usually may retain (but not transfer) a subordinated participation in the asset pool.

Debt Securities

The next important tax category is that of debt. Asset-backed securities may be structured to take the form of debt of the issuer, rather than the ownership interests represented by pass-through certificates.

The debt approach has been frequently used to create "pay-through" securities, which overcome the single maturity limitation of pass-throughs. The pay-through structure permits the issuer to restructure receivables' cash flows and offer a range of investment maturities to interested investors. These asset-backed securities originally developed in the mortgage-backed securities market, where they are called collateralized mortgage obligations (CMOs). CMOs developed as an alternative to mortgage pass-through certificates, particularly after 1984 when the IRS proposed the so-called "Sears Regulations" which were intended to clarify the existing law by prohibiting tax-exempt grantor trust status for issuers that restructured cash flows to create securities of maturities differing from that of the underlying asset pool. (See Note 15.)

Typically, pay-through securities will be issued by an entity which may be a corporation or an "owner trust." The entity acts as a special purpose vehicle to purchase assets and then issue several tranches of varying maturity asset-backed securities. These securities will be structured to qualify as debt under the Internal Revenue Code. Since the interest paid by an issuer of debt securities is fully tax-deductible, special purpose vehicles that issue debt are able to minimize taxation.

Figure 2.7 illustrates the operation of this structure. In order to securitize a group of its receivables with a 10-year average life, Originator A creates Limited Purpose Finance Corporation (LPFC) B.[16] Originator A then sells its receivables to LPFC B. LPFC B raises the funds to purchase the receivables by issuing three tranches of debt securities with varying maturities (5 years, 10 years, and 15 years). This ability to tailor cash flows to meet particular investor demands regarding maturity permits originators and their investment bankers to take advantage of the yield curve[17] to secure the lowest possible blended yield to investors. In contrast, certificates issued by a grantor trust necessarily are limited to precisely reflecting the maturity of the receivables whose payments are passed through the trust.

Issuers of asset-backed debt are thus freed from the limitations imposed by the grantor trust tax classification which simply provides a tax-exempt conduit for sales of ownership interests in the receivables. By contrast, in a debt structure, the issuer typically owns the receivables and simply sells debt that is backed by the assets. As a result, the issuer of debt is free to restructure the cash flow from the receivables into payments on several debt tranches with varying maturities.

The interest income from the receivables is taxable income to the issuer, if it is a corporation, or to the owners of the issuer if it is

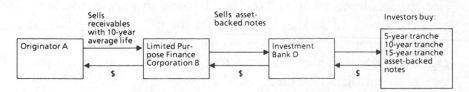

Figure 2.7. Typical asset-backed security corporate debt structure.

---

[16] B is structured as a limited purpose corporation in order to be bankruptcy remote from the risk of Originator A's bankruptcy, as discussed earlier in this chapter.

[17] This means taking advantage of the differing rates paid to investors at a given time for investments of different maturities. Properly managed, several tranches of securities of different maturities may be designed that produce a lower weighted average interest rate than the interest rate that investors would receive for a single maturity instrument.

classified as a partnership or trust. However, this taxable income is largely offset by the tax deduction from the interest expense on the debt that it issues. This expense for interest payments to debtholders is fully deductible for tax purposes.

From a tax perspective, it is essential that the asset-backed securities qualify as debt instruments in order to obtain this interest tax deduction. If the IRS viewed the securities as equity investments, payments on these securities would not be tax-deductible. In that event, the interest income from the receivables would be fully taxable and the interest payments to the noteholders would not be tax-deductible. As a result, the government would extract a great deal of value from the transaction through taxation.

To assure tax treatment as debt, structurers incorporate several features into limited purpose issuers. Thus while these issuers may be highly leveraged, they must contain some additional real layer of equity to distinguish the asset-backed debt notes from equity securities. To further guard against an IRS judgment that the holders of the asset-backed notes were direct equity owners of the underlying receivables, structurers create economic differences between the receivables collateral and the investors' debt securities. Such differences may include: payment frequencies on the debt securities that differ from those of the receivables; overcollateralization of the debt securities; optional call provisions on the debt securities; and maturity and interest schedules on the debt securities that differ from those of the receivables.

In summary, SPVs have the potential of issuing multiple maturity debt tailored to "play" the yield curve to permit the lowest possible weighted average coupon. On the other hand, while this debt pay-through tax structure has this potential economic advantage over the pass-through structure, the pay-through structure presents four difficulties not posed by pass-throughs.

1. In order for debt to be recognized as debt for tax purposes, there must be a real equity layer in the issuer and a mismatching of the cash flows on the receivables and the asset-backed debt. This equity layer may require fairly high returns and would not be created but for the tax requirement. Thus the need to create the equity layer can represent an additional economic cost of the debt structure.

2. Pass-through securities backed by mortgage assets are particularly attractive to thrifts and Real Estate Investment Trusts (REIT) since they qualify as real estate investment units approved for thrift and REIT investment. Debt, on the other hand, is not a qualifying real estate unit for thrifts and REITs which can somewhat limit the potential investor market for mortgage-backed debt securities (but see the section on REMICs).

3. A third difficulty created by the debt structure can arise from the accounting treatment of the issuer. Assume that the issuer is a Limited Purpose Finance Corporation (LPFC). If the originator owned all or most of the equity of this LPFC, Generally Accepted Accounting Principles (GAAP) may require the wholly owned LPFC to be consolidated onto the balance sheet of the originator parent. In the past, the Financial Accounting Standards Board (FASB) has generally required such consolidation for parents whose businesses are similar to that of the LPFC. Thus financial institutions generally would have to consolidate an LPFC. FASB has recently determined that such consolidation of majority-owned subsidiaries will generally be required of all businesses in the future. Consolidation would add back all of the asset-backed debt to the originator's consolidated balance sheet and thereby can eliminate the improvement in financial ratios that resulted from off-balance-sheet treatment.

4. If the issuer of the asset-backed debt securities is a Limited Purpose Finance Corporation or any other entity taxable as a corporation, another disadvantage can result. As a corporation, its earnings will be subject to taxation.[18] While much of the taxable income to that corporate issuer from interest income on the receivables will be offset by the tax deductions for the interest payments to investors on the asset-backed debt, usually some net taxable income

---

[18] The regular corporate tax rate is 34 percent. However, dividends paid to shareholders that are themselves corporations are eligible for a dividends paid tax deduction potentially equal to 70 percent of the dividends if the shareholder owns less than 20 percent of the equity, 80 percent of the dividends if the shareholder owns at least 20 percent and less than 80 percent of the equity, and 100 percent if the shareholder owns at least 80 percent of the equity.

remains.[19] Thus taxation can extract value from a taxable pay-through structure at the corporate issuer level, unless the corporate issuer is 80 percent or more owned by a parent corporation. In that event, the parent corporation can file a consolidated tax return with the issuer and eliminate any additional tax burden from the existence of the issuer as a separate corporation. However, if this 80 percent ownership test is satisfied, then it will not be possible to avoid GAAP consolidation with the parent.

The desire to solve the problems of additional taxes and the problem of GAAP consolidation led in 1986 to the structuring of some SPVs as owner trusts, rather than corporations.

Owner Trusts

The use of an owner trust as an issuer of debt rather than a corporation has the important advantage of avoiding an additional layer of federal income tax at the entity level. Instead, each item of income, gain, loss, deduction, and credit generated by the assets passes directly through to the trust owner for tax purposes. The deductions allocated to the owners include their proportionate share of the interest tax deduction for payments to the asset-backed debtholders and any other tax deductible expenses of the SPV. In short, the investors in the trust will receive the residuals without those residuals having been previously taxed at the SPV level. Thus, double taxation (first at the SPV level and secondly when the "owner" receives the residuals) has been avoided.

An owner trust is a business trust established in a manner similar to the previously discussed grantor trust. The originator (often called the "depositor") contributes assets to a trust by entering into a deposit trust agreement with a trustee. Typically, the owner trust then issues debt securities collateralized by the assets. These debt securities are structured to be of varying maturities, and create

---

[19] This net income may result from the relatively conservative cash flow assumptions necessary to obtain high credit ratings on rated pay-through structures. Also, some taxable balance may be created by the mismatching of cash flows or residuals in order to help establish the equity layer necessary for the issuer to issue debt.

residuals. These residuals belong to the owners of the owner trust. The owners are investors who have purchased the ownership of the owner trust's assets from the originator. The residuals flow through to the owners without SPV level taxation so long as the owner trust has been properly structured under the Internal Revenue Code.

To be properly structured, an owner trust will be structured for tax purposes either as a grantor trust or as a partnership. Typically, an owner trust that issues asset-backed securities will be used to issue multiple maturity debt securities and so will not qualify as a passive grantor trust. Instead, the owner trust will be structured to be taxable as a partnership. In order to qualify as a partnership, rather than as an association taxable as a corporation, the entity must possess less than a majority of the following four corporate characteristics: (1) continuity of life; (2) centralization of management; (3) limited liability; and (4) free transferability of interests. Accordingly, the owner trust structure typically provides that:

- The owners, acting by majority vote, retain a right to exercise management authority.

- The owners are typically jointly and severally, personally liable for liabilities of the trust such as legal and accounting expenses (but not the payments on the debt).

- The owners may not freely transfer their interests in the trust without the consent of the trustee and a number of fellow owners.

In summary, a number of issuers have used owner trust/debt structures in order to escape the limitations of the pass-through certificates and corporate debt structures. Unlike a pass-through certificate, debt of an owner trust can be issued in multiple maturities. Unlike a limited purpose finance corporation, an owner trust is free from income taxes at the entity level. Also, the use of an owner trust largely owned by outside investors solves the consolidation problem posed by limited purpose finance corporations owned by the originator.

However, the use of the owner trust structure may create some different limitations. Personal liability for trust expenses is not particularly attractive to investors. Nor, for that matter, do restrictions upon the transferability of interests enhance investor appeal. Investments in such owner trusts may also not be permissible for some state or federally regulated institutions (like banks, thrifts, insurance companies, or state pension funds) since partners may be deemed to be direct owners of the underlying assets, and such direct ownership may be restricted on a regulatory basis. Also, an originator may prefer to keep all of the residual (equity) interest, but if it does so it will be required to consolidate for GAAP purposes and show the asset-backed debt on its books. Finally, the cost still exists of having to create a meaningful equity residual interest in order for the debt to be recognized as debt for tax purposes.

Real Estate Mortgage Investment Conduits (REMICs)

In order to overcome the disadvantages of the previous tax classifications for issuers of mortgage-backed securities, Congress created a new tax classification called REMIC (Real Estate Mortgage Investment Conduit) which became effective as of January 1, 1987. Congress enacted the REMIC legislation largely in order to enable issuers to issue multiclass and multiple maturity securities without tax-related, structural constraints. Essentially a REMIC allows a mortgage security issuer to issue multiclass securities of different maturities and to enjoy flow-through tax treatment, so that no tax is imposed at the REMIC level. REMICs cannot be used for nonmortgage collateral.

The REMIC tax classification is available to issuers of mortgage-backed securities, irrespective of the legal form of the issuer or of the security. Thus an issuer may take the legal form of a corporation or a trust, and still elect to enjoy the benefits of the REMIC tax classification. A REMIC can even be a designated pool of mortgages that is not a separate legal entity. A REMIC can be more efficient than the debt tax classification previously used by many issuers of CMOs since the REMIC need not maintain the equity layer required to obtain the tax deduction for debt. Since equity is much more expensive than debt, the REMIC will be a more economic vehicle.

While eliminating the tax-related reason for holding equity in an issuer of CMOs, REMICs may not totally eliminate CMO residuals. Some residuals may remain because of the very conservative cash flow assumptions necessary for the highest credit ratings. Another advantage of REMIC is that it permits a more efficient sale of such residuals than an owner trust. Like an owner trust, REMIC allows the residuals to flow to ultimate investors without any SPV level taxation. However, while the investors in owner trust residuals typically must assume some personal liability and must agree to limits to their ability to subsequently resell their interests in the residuals, REMIC permits investors greater freedom to resell their interests in an issuer of mortgage-backed securities, and to have ownership interests in such an issuer without assuming any personal liability. Moreover, the REMIC legislation also established that REMIC interests would be further favored by being treated as: (1) qualifying assets for the purposes of allowing bad debt reserve treatment and other tax benefits for thrifts; (2) qualifying assets for Real Estate Investment Trusts; and (3) partially providing tax-exempt income for pension plans in certain circumstances.

These advantages of REMIC are also available to senior/junior subordinated structures. In such a multiclass structure, the junior class of debt securities provides credit support to the senior class. While the originator of a grantor trust could retain a junior class of securities, the originator could not transfer those junior securities. REMIC, on the other hand, permits the junior securities to be freely transferred. Thus REMIC permits an issuer of both multiple maturity and multiclass securities to structure in an efficient manner that reduces the amount of residuals, eliminates entity level taxation on any such residuals, and enhances the marketability of the residuals. Also, REMIC further simplifies multiple maturity issues by permitting the payment characteristics of the security issue to match those of the underlying assets.[20] This was frequently

---

[20] The payment characteristics of multiple-maturity CMOs have generally been structured to differ from those of the underlying assets in order to obtain corporate debt tax treatment. Thus, for example, payments on mortgage assets are typically collected on a monthly basis, but most CMOs have been structured to pay interest and principal on a quarterly basis in order to help demonstrate that the mortgage-backed securities are debt, rather than equity. REMIC permits the creation of monthly pay mortgage-backed securities, free from the tax-related constraint of establishing a different payment pattern for the securities from that of the collateral.

not possible previously, as in order to avoid double taxation, multiple maturity asset-backed securities had to be debt; and in order to qualify as debt, the payment frequency on the receivables often could not closely match the payment characteristics of the receivables. Moreover, REMIC permits issuers of such multiclass debt securities the option of treating the transaction as a sale for accounting purposes by creating securities that are sold to investors as pass-through certificates even if they are economically debt. As previously discussed, the non-REMIC debt structure generally did not permit such sale accounting by the issuer for the mortgage collateral. Also, REMIC permits issuers to obtain sale treatment for tax purposes and no sale for accounting purposes by issuing REMIC securities as debt.

While REMIC tax status is often desirable for CMO-type issues, the REMIC classification may even be elected by trusts that issue pass-through securities. The pass-through securities issuer might elect to be a REMIC in order to take advantage of particular tax or accounting aspects of the REMIC. In short, REMIC is a new tax classification available for a wide variety of mortgage-backed securities.[21]

Summary of Tax Considerations

For nonmortgage assets, we have seen that tax considerations often require a choice between a grantor trust that issues pass-through certificates and an issuer of pay-through debt securities.[22] Generally, the grantor trust structure has the advantage of eliminating taxation of the issuer of the asset-backed certificates, but the limitation that it cannot issue multiple maturity certificates tailored to investor demand. Issuers of debt securities typically have the advantage of being able to issue multiple maturity securities, but must have an expensive equity layer. Also, if the issuer of

---

[21] However, until June 1987, REMIC status was not yet being widely used for CMOs. Market conditions had established that CMOs with a floating rate tranche were highly attractive for issuers. However the REMIC legislation provided that such floating rate REMICs could only be created after the IRS issued appropriate regulations. These regulations were not issued until June, and as a result, issuers of floating rate CMOs were still using the older tax classifications in spite of their limitations.

[22] Recently, a few transactions have also been structured as issues of receivables-backed preferred stock.

debt securities is a corporation or an entity taxable as a corporation, there may either be some tax liability at the issuer level or an unattractive requirement that the assets and liabilities of the issuer be consolidated for accounting purposes with those of the originator. If the issuer of debt securities is an owner trust or other entity taxable as a partnership, such tax liability at the issuer level may be avoided, but at the cost of limiting the liquidity of the ownership interest in the issuer and related limitations. For mortgage assets, the creation of the REMIC tax category now allows issuers to essentially realize the structural flexibility of the pay-through structure, while realizing the tax transparency of the pass-through structure.

The above tax considerations played an important role in the structuring of each of the asset-backed securities transactions described in Part 2. The tax treatment of each of these transactions was determined by the economic characteristics of that transaction. The originator and structurer designed the economic characteristics of the transaction to obtain a desired tax treatment. Of course, the IRS has the right to challenge the claimed tax treatment, and any dispute would ultimately be decided by the courts.

Impact of the Federal Securities Laws

We have previously discussed the Securities Act of 1933, the Securities Exchange Act of 1934, and the Trust Indenture Act of 1939 in connection with traditional securities. These federal securities laws are equally applicable to structured asset-backed securities. An asset-backed issue must normally be registered under the 1933 Act if it is to be a public offering. An issuer of such publicly offered asset-backed securities usually must file regular reports of condition under the 1934 Act. Also, the issuer of an asset-backed debt security typically must retain an independent trustee under the 1939 Act. (See the discussion of these Acts earlier in this chapter for a more detailed discussion of the 1933, 1934, and 1939 Acts.)

However, there is a fourth federal securities-related law that is especially important for issuers of asset-backed securities. That law is the Investment Company Act of 1940 (1940 Act).

The 1940 Act was enacted to protect investors who entrust their savings to companies who invest and manage pools of such savings. The archetypal investment company is a mutual fund. Since such investment companies have large amounts of cash and negotiable securities, Congress believed that they might be subject to management abuse in the absence of federal regulation. What do investment companies have to do with credit securitization?

The answer is that, as we have already seen, most asset-backed securities are issued by special purpose vehicles that purchase financial assets and issue securities backed by those assets. Unfortunately, such SPVs are issuers that fall within the 1940 Act's definition of an investment company since they are largely in the business of issuing securities. Equally unfortunately, compliance with the 1940 Act's substantive requirements is completely impractical for issuers of asset-backed securities. The 1940 Act is extremely complex, and it would go beyond the scope of this book to thoroughly explain why compliance with each of the 1940 Act's registration categories would be impractical. But one illustration of the impracticality of 1940 Act registration should suffice. In order to comply with the substantive requirements of the 1940 Act provision seemingly most feasible for issuers of asset-backed securities, the issuer would have to maintain an asset/debt ratio of at least 3/1. Such a ratio would not work, since a major advantage of asset-backed securities is that they permit the issuer to virtually completely fund the assets with debt.

The bottom line on the 1940 Act is that the issuer of asset-backed securities must find an applicable exemption from the 1940 Act's registration requirements. As noted above, the 1940 Act is complex and a prospective issuer would be well advised to consult its attorneys concerning the availability of a 1940 Act exemption. Examples of such exemptions likely to be relevant to an asset-backed issuer include the following. First, the 1940 Act has a version of the private placement exemption. The 1940 Act exempts certain private offerings, sold to no more than 100 holders, each of whom purchases less than 10 percent of any class of the offering. This exemption is much more restrictive than the private placement exemption under the 1933 Act, which permits sales to an unlimited number of accredited investors.

A second relevant 1940 Act exemption is the one that has been generally applied to most asset-backed securities. The exemption provides that entities who engage in certain types of business are not investment companies. These exempted businesses include purchasing mortgages and other interests in real estate, and purchasing notes and accounts receivable representing the sale price of merchandise, insurance, and services. This exemption generally applies to issuers of securities backed by mortgages and many receivables. These special purpose issuers are in the business of purchasing assets that are exempt from 1940 Act coverage. There remain asset classes for which no asset-specific 1940 Act exemption is clearly applicable—like general purpose commercial loans. Hence, the 1940 Act poses a potential obstacle to some types of asset-backed securities. However, a 1940 Act exemption may also relate to the nature of the issuer. For example, properly structured issuers that solely issue asset-backed commercial paper may also escape the 1940 Act limitations. Also, a prospective issuer of an asset-backed security who cannot find a specific 1940 Act exemption may apply for the third sort of exemption. Such an issuer may apply to the SEC for a transactional exemption from the 1940 Act for the issuer's proposed issue of asset-backed securities.

All in all, the federal securities laws play an important role in the design of securitized credit products. The originators and structurers of such financings must weigh the comparative advantages and disadvantages of public versus private offerings under the securities laws. In addition, the Investment Company Act of 1940 imposes further constraints upon some types of structured asset-backed securities, depending upon the nature of the assets, securities, and structures involved.

Accounting for Transfers of Receivables with Recourse

Even as tax, bankruptcy, and securities law considerations play important parts in the structuring of securitized credit, so, too, do accounting considerations. Of course, companies have been selling their assets for many years without any particular difficulty in accounting for these sales. Such traditional asset sales in which the seller sells the assets to the buyer without any recourse back to the seller can be accounted for in a straightforward manner. The assets are removed from the seller's balance sheet and transferred to the balance sheet of the purchaser.

However, modern credit securitization usually involves structuring that includes the originator transferring assets to a SPV that ultimately issues the asset-backed securities. Investors in such asset-backed securities typically require some form of credit enhancement so that the investors are protected against the credit losses inherent in the assets. To a large extent, the federal government provided the credit enhancement that supported the securitization of residential mortgages. However, no such governmental credit enhancement is available for nonresidential mortgage assets or even for some types of residential mortgages. As a result, credit enhancement for these assets is frequently at least partially provided by some form of recourse to the originators of these assets.[23]

It is this recourse feature of credit securitization that raises questions about whether a transfer of assets from an originator to a special purpose vehicle constitutes a true sale of the assets, rather than a loan secured by receivables. If a transfer with recourse qualifies as a sale, then the assets and their supporting liabilities will both go off the originator's balance sheet. The originator is then likely to be able to realize significant equity cost savings in the manner described next. Also, the less debt on the originator's balance sheet, the more flexibility the originator has to borrow without violating existing lending agreements. On the other hand, if a transfer with recourse is accounted for as a receivables-backed loan, the receivables will remain an asset on the originator's balance sheet and the obligation to pay proceeds from the receivables to the SPV will be a liability on that balance sheet. Equity cost savings are not likely to be available since the assets and liabilities have remained on the originator's balance sheet.

For most originators, a transfer with recourse qualifies as a sale if it meets the conditions laid out by Generally Accepted Accounting Principles (GAAP). However, banks must also be concerned about Regulatory Accounting Principles (RAP). Both types of accounting criteria, and some of their implications for

---

[23] Indeed, we believe that a sound and economic credit securitization system usually requires some credit support by the originator. The originator is in the best position to assess the creditworthiness of the borrower. Also, the retention of credit risk by the originator will help to ensure that the originator retains an incentive to continue to originate quality assets, rather than sticking investors and third-party credit enhancers with uneconomic assets.

both the balance sheets and the income statements of originators, are laid out next.

GAAP

GAAP treatment of receivables transfers with recourse is controlled by the Statement of Financial Accounting Standards No. 77 which was issued by the Financial Accounting Standards Board in December 1983. In relevant part, FAS 77 essentially provides that a transfer of receivables with recourse shall be recognized as a sale if all the following conditions are met:

- The transferor surrenders control of the future economic benefits of the sold receivables. Surrender of control ordinarily means that the transferor may not have an option to repurchase the receivables. The only exception to this is that a transferor may be permitted or required to make a "clean-up" call of the receivables when their outstanding amount is relatively minor.
- The transferor cannot be required by the transferee or any other entity to repurchase the receivables except pursuant to the recourse provisions.
- The transferor's obligation under the recourse provisions can be reasonably estimated.

If a transfer with recourse meets the FAS 77 requirements and qualifies as a sale, then the transferor must account for its recourse obligation in accordance with FAS Statement No. 5, Accounting for Contingencies. FAS Statement No. 5 essentially requires the transferor to reserve the total amount of the reasonably expected loss resulting from the recourse provision at the time of the transfer. Suppose, for example, a transferor sold receivables with 3 percent recourse, 4-year maturity, and 25bp expected annual loss. In that event, the transferor might create a maximum 1 percent capital reserve against the aggregate expected loss over the 4 years.[24] The transferor would not be required to reserve or hold

---

[24] It is not clear whether GAAP would permit a transferor to create a slightly smaller reserve by discounting the 25bp 4-year annual expected loss down to its present value at the time the reserve was created.

capital against the 2 percent of recourse that was in excess of its reasonably anticipated loss. This remaining 2 percent recourse could simply be reported in a note to the transferor's financial statement.

An example of the proper GAAP accounting for such receivables sales with recourse is provided by a major finance company. That company's annual report for 1986 reported at Note 5:

> The Company sold net retail finance receivables aggregating approximately $8.8 billion in 1986, compared with approximately $526 million in 1985. . . . The Company's recourse liability under the limited guarantees is generally 5 percent of the outstanding balances in the pools. The amount recorded for this potential liability amounted to $87 million at December 31, 1986, and $5 million at December 31, 1985.

Thus the company reserved approximately 1 percent of its receivables sold with recourse, even though it had a maximum 5 percent recourse obligation. The 1 percent reserved by the company seems reasonable since its receivables typically had weighted average lives of slightly over 2 years and expected losses of no more than approximately 0.4 percent.

In fact, the amount that the company had reserved to cover losses on receivables on its balance sheet was also approximately 1 percent of their net amount as of December 31, 1986. Therefore, sales of receivables with recourse did not significantly change the amount of capital that had to be reserved against the expected credit losses on the company's receivables. However, the asset sale with recourse does remove the assets and their associated liabilities from the company's balance sheet.

Such an off-balance sheet accounting treatment that results from a sale bears several advantages. First, an originator's financial ratios (like its debt/equity ratio) are likely to be improved. As a result, an originator may be able to satisfy covenants with lenders that otherwise might be under pressure. Most importantly, though, the removing of the assets and associated debt from an originator's balance sheet raises the possibility that the originator may be able to realize significant equity cost savings.

For example, the finance company described above actually held approximately 7 percent equity capital against its balance sheet assets in order to satisfactorily cover the risks associated with the assets in a prudent manner consistent with its high credit rating.[25] If the assets sold with recourse had remained on its balance sheet, the company might hold approximately 7 percent equity against the assets. By removing the assets from the balance sheet, the company was able to preserve this 7 percent equity/asset ratio without raising additional (and relatively expensive) equity. Of course, if the fundamental economics of the transaction do not justify this equity savings, then investors may disregard the sale accounting for the transaction and require some equity to be held against the "sold" assets. However, for the reasons discussed in Appendix A, we believe such equity cost savings to be real.

Thus pursuant to FAS 77 and FAS 5, GAAP accounting permits a transferor to sell assets with recourse, to remove them from its balance sheet, and to simply reserve the capital necessary to cover the expected credit losses on the assets.

A sale of receivables with recourse affects not only the originator's balance sheet, but also its income statement. FAS 77 states that the difference between the sales price (adjusted for expected net credit losses, late payment costs, and estimated effect of prepayments) and the net receivables amount shall be recognized as a gain or loss at the time of sale. If the receivables are sold with servicing retained and the stated servicing fee differs from a normal servicing fee, the sales price shall be increased by the present value of excess servicing fees.

An example of an income gain effect of such a sale of receivables is as follows. Suppose that a seller has $100 in receivables which yield 15 percent with a 4-year maturity. The expected loss on the receivables is 1 percent over the 4-year period. The seller might sell the receivables to a special purpose vehicle for $120 and retain a reasonable 1 percent servicing fee. The special

---

[25] This is a book ratio since no market price is available for the finance company's equity as it is a subsidiary of another company. Nonetheless, a book ratio is likely to be relatively close to market since the finance company's assets are all relatively shorter term (4 years or less), financial assets. If anything, the 7 percent ratio may be slightly conservative since it does not add any additional value for the finance company franchise itself.

purpose vehicle would fund the receivables purchase with a sale of asset-backed notes to investors. In this case, the seller would realize $20 in income from the receivables sales, minus the $1 loan loss contingency. The seller would take the reasonable 1 percent servicing fee into income as it was received over the 4-year period. Alternatively, the seller might sell the $100 in receivables for $100 and retain a 7 percent servicing fee. In that event, the seller would be required by FAS 77 to increase for income accounting purposes the $100 sale price by the present value of the 6 percent component of the servicing fee that was in excess of a reasonable servicing fee.

On the other hand, a seller might have an income loss from an asset sale with recourse if he had $100 of "underwater" assets yielding a below market yield of 3 percent. Suppose the seller sold those receivables to a special purpose vehicle for $85. In this case, the seller would recognize a $15 loss on the receivables at the time of sale. The seller would not have had to realize such a loss for accounting purposes if the assets had not been sold. As a result, some sellers may be reluctant to securitize underwater assets and thereby trigger the accounting realization of the loss on those assets.

In summary, GAAP provides one important foundation for the development of securitization. Pursuant to FAS 77, originators of financial assets may engage in sales of assets and retain first loss obligations through recourse provisions. As a result of accounting for receivables transfers with recourse as sales, originators remove the assets and associated liabilities from their balance sheets, and may then realize substantial equity cost savings.[26] Income accounting, too, is an important factor in the development of securitization. To the extent that a securitized credit transaction results in an accounting profit or at least a revenue neutral transaction, origina-

---

[26] However, it is important to note that the Financial Accounting Standards Board is currently broadly reconsidering the whole area of financial instruments and off-balance sheet accounting. FASB 77 is under review since it has been fairly controversial within the accounting profession. That review process is likely to last at least 2 years. Presumably at some point in 1989, FAS will conclude its review of receivables sales with recourse and related matters.

    As the accounting for asset-backed securities transactions is quite complex, you should consult with an accounting firm about the possible accounting implications of any particular transaction.

tors are likely to be more inclined to securitize. To the extent that a securitized credit deal could result in an accounting loss of income, some potential originators may be more cautious.

RAP

GAAP accounting is generally relevant to most originators of securitized assets. Company annual reports and many other financial statements are prepared using GAAP accounting. However, banks and certain other regulated institutions may be primarily concerned with another form of accounting—Regulatory Account Principles or RAP. For example, the federal banking regulators require banks to hold a certain percentage of equity capital against all bank assets, with the amount of such assets being determined by RAP. Therefore, even if a bank can prepare its annual report to shareholders using GAAP, as a practical matter the bank must also be able to account for an asset sale with recourse as a sale under RAP, if the bank is to realize any equity savings from the transaction. Of course, different regulators have developed different Regulatory Accounting Principles to apply to different types of regulated institutions. While it would be beyond our scope to consider RAP for each type of regulated institution, we will now look at RAP as it is applied by the federal banking regulators to commercial banks for asset sales with recourse.[27]

While the federal banking regulators normally follow GAAP for regulatory accounting purposes, the banking regulators decided to adopt a different standard for sales of assets with recourse. In December 1985, the Federal Financial Institutions Examination Council[28] decided that for the purposes of reporting to bank supervisory agencies and for the determination of capital adequacy, a transfer of assets would generally qualify as a sale only if the transferring bank retained no risk of loss or obligation for the

---

[27] This area of regulatory accounting tends to develop particularly rapidly, and the reader should consult with qualified attorneys and accountants concerning such developments.

[28] The FFIEC includes the Board of Governors of the Federal Reserve System, the Federal Deposit Insurance Corporation, the Office of the Comptroller of the Currency, the Federal Home Loan Bank Board, and the National Credit Union Administration.

payment of principal or interest. Thus an asset transfer with recourse generally only amounts to a borrowing by the transferor for bank RAP purposes. As a result, a bank that engages in an asset sale with recourse must continue to hold the full amount of regulatory capital against the asset. Currently, the federal banking regulators effectively require about 7 percent capital in order for a bank to be free from capital-related close regulatory supervision.[29]

There are two major relevant exceptions to the banking regulators' prohibition of "sales" with recourse for RAP purposes. The first applies to sales of participations in pools of residential mortgages. The bank call report instructions specify that a commercial bank may report as a sale transfers of participations with recourse in pools of residential mortgages so long as the bank does not retain any "significant risk of loss." The question of how much recourse back to an originating bank would amount to "significant risk of loss" is an open question on which the three federal banking regulators may not agree. The present consensus seems to be that more than 10 percent recourse would be significant, and that some lesser amount is not significant.

In the event that a bank were to "sell" assets without recourse to the bank, but with recourse to its holding company or another holding company subsidiary, then the holding company would report the transaction as a memorandum item on the consolidated holding company report to the Federal Reserve. The Federal Reserve can then treat the asset for capital adequacy purposes at the consolidated holding company level in the same manner as if recourse had been back to the originating bank. Thus any form of recourse can cause the asset to be included for capital adequacy purposes at the holding company level, except for less than "significant risk of loss" on participations in residential mortgages.

However, there is a second generally applicable exception to the banking regulators' prohibition of "sales" with recourse for RAP purposes. That exception is the so-called "spread account" structure.

---

[29] The current actual minimum capital requirement is 5.5 percent primary capital and 6 percent total regulatory capital.

Essentially, a spread account works in the following manner. An originating bank might sell assets yielding 12 percent to a SPV, which would then issue 7 percent asset-backed certificates. The 5 percent spread (the difference between the 12 percent yield on the assets and the 7 percent yield on the certificates), less a servicing fee, would be accumulated in the spread account, which is simply a type of escrow account, up to a stated level. After the spread account achieved the stated level, any excess spread would be immediately paid to the originating bank. The funds in the spread account would provide credit support for the asset-backed certificates. After those certificates were completely paid off, the funds remaining in the spread account would revert back to the originating bank. However, the bank would not take the spread account funds into income until that time. Therefore, the regulators determined that the use of the spread account to cover payment defaults would not result in a loss to the bank. As a result, the banking regulators determined that asset sales with spread accounts do qualify as sales under RAP since the funds in the spread account had not yet been taken into bank income. Hence, according to the regulators, the spread account arrangement does not constitute the sort of "recourse" that they had ruled against.[30]

SUMMARY

We have now generally looked at the legal and accounting issues that affect the structures used for securitization. The direct structure for traditional debt securities including notes, bonds, and commercial paper, simply amounts to a contract to pay principal and interest to investors. Investors are exposed to the risk of late payment or loss in the event of a bankruptcy of the issuer of such notes, bonds, and commercial paper. The traditional direct structure for loan sales also amounts to a contract by the borrower to pay investors' principal and interest. The loan or loan participation purchased by the investor may be secured by valuable collateral. However, in the event of the borrower's bankruptcy, the investor

---

[30] For a more detailed description of a spread account, see the transaction description for the California Credit Card Trust 1987-A in Chapter 4.

may still experience a prolonged interruption of timely payments of interest and principal.

In response to these limitations of the traditional structures, new structures emerged to create securitized credit products whose credit is independent of the originator. Special purpose vehicles were created to purchase assets from originators. Securities issued by these SPVs would be sold to investors in order to fund the purchase of these assets. The securities issued by these SPVs were supported by the SPVs' assets and were insulated from the risk of the originator's bankruptcy. Separated from the originator's credit risk, the SPVs' securities were easily credit enhanced to the highest rating levels.

As we have seen, legal and accounting issues strongly affect credit securitization. Structures are created that are affected by securities laws, the Bankruptcy Code, regulatory and insolvency considerations, tax classifications and accounting rules. Structuring decisions on each of these issues necessarily result in different advantages and limitations accruing to the originators, structurers, credit enhancers, and investors in securitized credit products.

In Part 2, we analyze a number of credit securitization transactions to see the impact of these legal and accounting decisions upon the participants in the transactions. We will then specifically examine the economic and other benefits the participants derived from these transactions. This chapter has provided the underlying analytical framework for understanding the structuring options available to each of these transactions, as well as the inherent economic advantages and limitations of the particular structure selected for the transaction.

Part 2

Securitized Credit Transactions

Originators, credit enhancers, structurers, placers, servicers, and investors can all benefit from credit securitization. Originators may enjoy lower all-in financing costs, improved asset/liability management, broader access to the capital markets, and increased returns on equity. Third party credit enhancers, structurers, placers, and servicers earn very attractive fee income. Investors receive pleasing combinations of yield, maturity, credit risk, and credit transparency.

As shown in the figure II.1, most residential mortgage assets eligible for credit enhancement through the U.S. government-related guaranty programs are securitized. The securitization of these assets was greatly simplified by programs which provided inexpensive, government-related, payment guaranties covering as much as 100 percent of the principal and interest payments due to investors. We will not discuss the governmentally assisted securitization of such "conforming" residential mortgages. Instead, we will examine, in detail, new and innovative securitized

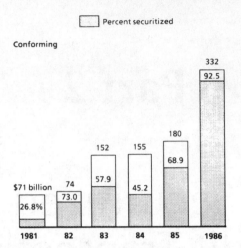

Source: Mortgage Banking Association; FNMA; Financial World Publications.

Figure II.1.   Residential mortgage originations (1981–86) (percent securitized).

credit transactions involving the asset classes in which securitization is just beginning. By looking at transactions in these asset classes that are undisturbed by implicit governmental subsidies, we are able to see the economic power and flexibility of the credit securitization technology. We will trace the development of fundamental economics and structures of transactions in the following asset classes:

1. Vehicle loans
2. Credit card loans
3. Lease receivables
4. Commercial mortgages
5. Nonconforming residential mortgages
6. Receivables-backed commercial paper programs.

For several of these asset classes, we describe more than one transaction in order to illustrate the range of structures. Each transaction description has three sections:

- *Introduction*—summarizing the circumstances that led to the transaction
- *Structure*—describing what was done in the origination, structuring, credit enhancement, placement, trading, and servicing elements of the business system to complete the transaction. This portion of each transaction's description also contains a discussion of the tax, accounting, bankruptcy, and other legal aspects of structuring the transaction. A familiarity with these concepts from Chapters 1 and 2 is helpful, though not essential, in understanding this portion of the transaction structure.
- *Benefits*—giving our interpretation of the economic and other benefits of the transaction. These estimates are generally based on our analysis of publicly available information.

3

Vehicle Loans

While the first public securitized transaction of nonmortgage assets in March 1985 involved computer leases, the second transaction, and many after that, involved vehicle loans. Overall, 47 of the 63 nonmortgage public SCP transactions in the period from 1985 to December 1987 involved automobile/truck receivables (excluding receivables-backed commercial paper and preferred stock). These transactions resulted in the public issuance of approximately $17.6 billion in receivables-backed securities, approximately 79 percent of the $22.4 billion total. Originators of these securities included auto finance companies like General Motors Acceptance Corporation, Chrysler Finance Company, and Nissan Motor Acceptance Corporation, as well as commercial banks and thrifts like Marine Midland Bank, Home Federal Savings and Loan, Western Financial Savings Bank, Bank of America, and First National Bank of Boston. In addition, a significant volume of auto receivables-backed SCPs were issued through private market loan sales by major auto finance companies, including both Ford Motor Credit and Chrysler Finance Company.

In the transactions by different originators, we have seen several different approaches to securitizing auto loans. We will now look in detail at the following three transactions in order to see these varying approaches:

- Asset-Backed Securities Corporation, Asset-Backed Obligations Series I (GMAC pay-through structure)
- GMAC 1986—G Grantor Trust, Certificates of Participation (GMAC pass-through structure)
- Chrysler Finance Corporation, Auto Loan Sale.

ASSET-BACKED SECURITIES CORPORATION
ASSET-BACKED OBLIGATIONS, SERIES 1

The largest single domestic corporate debt issue to date was a $4 billion issue in October 1986 by Asset-Backed Securities Corporation (ABSC). (See ABSC Term Sheet, Figure 3.1.) The proceeds from this issue were used by a special vehicle, ABSC, to purchase $4,248,485,000 in automobile and light truck receivables from GMAC. The loans were originated by General Motors dealers in the Fall of 1986 under special low-interest rate sales programs.

GMAC has been an active issuer of debt securities in recent years in part to finance the increased dollar volume of lending generated by several reduced-rate programs offered on General Motors vehicle sales. Overall, in 1986, GMAC's U.S. operations raised more than $26.6 billion on a net basis in the capital markets. Approximately $17.8 billion was short-, medium-, and long-term GMAC debt, and approximately $8.8 billion was from sales of receivables-backed securities collaterized by automobile and light truck receivables. In fact, prior to the ABSC Series 1 issue in October 1986, GMAC had already completed six separate public issues of vehicle loan securities, all of which were structured as grantor trust pass-throughs.

However, when the special low-interest rate incentive programs generated a significant surge in volume in the Fall of 1986, GMAC and one of its investment bankers, the First Boston Corporation, decided to utilize a new securitized credit structure that would among other purposes appeal to investors as not representing GMAC credit risk for portfolio diversification purposes.

Issue	Asset Backed Obligations, Series 1 6.25% Class 1-A notes 6.90% Class 2-B notes 6.95% Class 1-C notes
Issuer	Asset Backed Securities Corporation
Offering date	October 15, 1986
Rating (S&P, Moody's)	AAA/Aaa
Principal amount	$2,095,000,000 Class 1-A 585,000,000 Class 1-B 1,320,000,000 Class 1-C
Collateral	New GM vehicles
Average life (years)	1.05 for Class 1-A 2.20 for Class 1-B 3.07 for Class 1-C
Yield to average life (CBE)	6.30% for Class 1-A 6.96% for Class 1-B 7.27% for Class 1-C
Payment frequency	Quarterly
Spread to treasuries at offering	69 b.p. for Class 1-A 75 b.p. for Class 1-B 80 b.p. for Class 1-C
Recourse (amount/provider)	5% GMAC Limited Guaranty, 1% ABSC
Credit enhancement	6% Letter of Credit/Credit Suisse
Managing underwriter	The First Boston Corporation

Source: SEC Registration Statement; McKinsey analysis.

Figure 3.1. Asset-Backed Securities Corporation, Asset-Backed Obligations, Series 1.

Structure

The structure of this transaction is summarized in Figures 3.2 and 3.3, and explained next.

Origination. GMAC identified $2,334,549,000 in 2.9 percent loans with 36-month scheduled maturities, and $1,913,936,000 in 4.8 percent loans with 48-month scheduled maturities. These loans were originated by GM at lower-than-market interest rates.

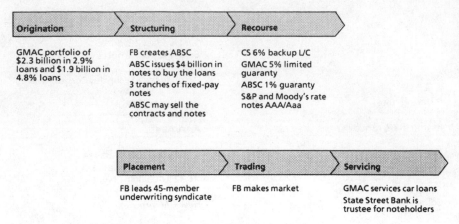

Source: SEC Registration Statement; McKinsey analysis.

Figure 3.2. Asset-Backed Securities Corporation, Asset-Backed Obligations, Series 1.

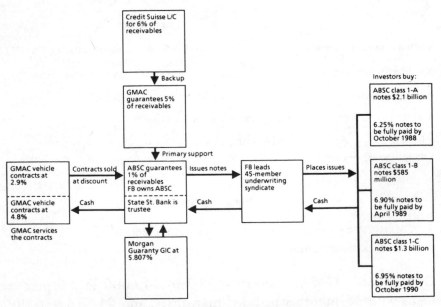

Source: SEC Registration Statement; McKinsey analysis.

Figure 3.3. Asset-Backed Securities Corporation, Asset-Backed Obligations, Series 1.

To compensate GMAC for the below-market returns on these loans, GM may have made cash payments to GMAC.

Structuring

1. *Creation of Special Purpose Vehicle.* As described in Chapter 2, in the typical asset-backed security structure, the originator establishes a special purpose vehicle (SPV) to which the originator sells its assets. The SPV issues securities collateralized by the underlying assets that the SPV then owns. However, if GMAC as the originator had owned the SPV that issued these securities, some investors would have essentially viewed them as GMAC securities for portfolio diversification purposes. At the time the transaction was being contemplated, First Boston determined that the securities could be placed at an optimal cost of funds if some insitutional investors did not have to view the asset-backed securities as GMAC paper for portfolio diversification purposes. Accordingly, in May 1986, First Boston established ABSC as a wholly-owned, limited purpose finance corporation subsidiary of First Boston Securities for the purpose of issuing securities collateralized by automotive receivables and other assets. Any issue of ABSC notes would be viewed as securities of ABSC, rather than that of the originator of the receivables. Thus, the ABSC Series 1 notes would not be viewed as GMAC debt for portfolio diversification purposes.

The selection of a limited-purpose finance corporation structure was integral to this financing strategy. Since ABSC was a limited-purpose finance corporation, First Boston was able to capitalize this wholly-owned subsidiary with significant equity and to appoint First Boston personnel as ABSC's directors and executive officers. These corporate characteristics of ABSC were sufficient to make ABSC the legal issuer of the notes and eliminate the concerns of investors about diversifying their portfolios.

2. *Tax/Accounting Structure of the Transaction.* As discussed in Chapter 1, the decision to use a limited purpose finance corporation structure usually has tax-related consequences. One advantageous consequence is that the issuer may structure tranches of notes of different maturities to minimize its blended cost of funds. Another consequence is that the limited-purpose finance corporation

is subject to federal income tax. This tax liability may be directly payable by the limited purpose finance corporation or consolidated with that of a parent that owns 80 percent or more of the finance corporation. In this transaction, income to ABSC from the vehicle contracts is treated as taxable income. In order to minimize taxation, the notes issued by ABSC had to be treated as corporate debt rather than equity, so that ABSC's interest payments would qualify as tax-deductible expenses. Cadwalader, Wickersham & Taft, counsel to ABSC, provided an opinion that the ABSC notes would be treated as corporate debt, in part because ABSC was originally structured with a significant layer of stockholders' equity ($39,658,000 total) and because the ABSC notes were clearly differentiated from the auto loan receivables by both terms (quarterly pay versus monthly pay) and maturities (notes are fixed amortization with three different maturities while the receivables are prepayable).[1]

Of course, as discussed in Chapter 1, such debt treatment for ABSC's notes only minimized taxation. Over the 4-year life of the issue, the income to ABSC from payments on the vehicle loans would somewhat exceed ABSC's tax-deductible interest payments to noteholders. This excess "residual" was created to make sure the notes were debt for tax purposes, to satisfy certain very conservative rating agency assumptions concerning payment flows and collateral value, and to provide a profit for ABSC.

From an accounting perspective, the sale of the vehicle loans by GMAC to ABSC had qualified as a true sale under Generally Accepted Accounting Principles (GAAP), since GMAC's liability under the recourse provision could be reasonably estimated; ABSC could not "put" the loans back to GMAC; and GMAC could not "call" the loans back from ABSC.[2] As ABSC was then issuing corporate debt to investors, rather than selling equity participations in the vehicle loans, the vehicle loans and the $4 billion in ABSC debt would have had to both remain on ABSC's balance sheet.

---

[1] See the discussion of federal income taxation in Chapter 1 for further explanation of the structuring of securities to get corporate debt tax treatment.

[2] See Chapter 1 for a discussion of Financial Accounting Standards Board Statement 77, which establishes the GAAP standard for asset sales with recourse.

GAAP would then have required First Boston to consolidate ABSC's assets and liabilities into First Boston's consolidated balance sheet at year-end for financial reporting purposes. First Boston preferred not to have this $4 billion in ABSC debt remain on its consolidated balance sheet. Therefore, First Boston decided that after the public issue of $4 billion in ABSC notes, ABSC would resell the auto loan receivables to an owner trust [3] which would also assume the obligation to pay the ABSC notes. As a result of the resale, First Boston was able to eliminate the $4 billion in debt and assets from its consolidated balance sheet.

3. *Payment Characteristics of the Notes.* The decision to use a limited-purpose finance corporation structure also enabled the cash flows to be carved up so that the maturities of the securities could be tailored to particular investor preferences. In the ABSC transaction, First Boston detected a great deal of investor demand, particularly from money market funds, for notes with maturities shorter than the 36-month and 48-month maturities of the underlying vehicle contracts. Money market funds are typically prohibited from investing in any security whose ultimate maturity was greater than 2 years. First Boston also detected a great deal of demand from banks for notes with an average life of slightly over two years and from insurance companies for three year average life notes.

As a result, the ABSC Series 1 notes were structured in three tranches: a $2,095 million 2-year tranche with a 1.05-year weighted average life; a $585 million 2.5-year tranche with a 2.2-year weighted average life; and a $1,320 million 4-year tranche with a 3.07-year weighted average life. Interest is payable on the notes of each tranche on a quarterly basis, and principal is payable quarterly in series so that all principal is paid to the first tranche before principal payments to the second tranche. This multiple maturity structure was designed to produce the lowest cost of funds.

The ABSC Series 1 notes were unusual in that they were fixed-maturity notes with fixed-amortization schedules. They will not subject the investors to the prepayment risk that accompanies many

[3] See Chapter 1 for a more detailed explanation of owner trusts.

asset-backed financings, and which typically leads investors to require a yield premium. Prepayment risk results from the fact that some vehicle owners will repay their loans prior to maturity, typically because they are selling the vehicle. The rate of such prepayments is not totally predictable. The rating agencies usually limit special purpose vehicles issuing debt to reinvesting principal prepayments essentially at a risk-free rate. This reinvestment rate is usually much lower than the interest rate paid by borrowers on the outstanding loans. Because of the uncertainty about the prepayment rate and the relative unattractiveness of an SPV reinvesting prepayments, a limited-purpose finance corporation is usually not able to efficiently establish a fixed schedule of principal payments to investors. Instead, as with most collateralized mortgage obligations, principal payments are paid through to noteholders whenever they are received.

As a result, noteholders of some collateralized securities, particularly mortgaged-backed securities, may be exposed to the prepayment risk that principal may be repaid faster than expected at a time when relative reinvestment opportunities are unattractive, or that principal may be repaid slower than anticipated and so have earned a yield below that for other paper of similar maturity. Securities backed by nonmortgage assets tend to have less prepayment risk as the payment patterns of such assets may be quite predictable. The ABSC Series 1 issue was able to entirely eliminate prepayment risk by issuing fixed-maturity notes that did not permit prepayments. This fixed-maturity schedule was possible because of the combination of the low interest rates on the incentive-rate vehicle loans together with a guaranteed investment contract (GIC) provided by Morgan Guaranty. Since the 5.807 percent rate on the GIC was higher than the interest rate on the vehicle contracts, prepayments by the vehicle purchasers could only increase the interest earnings available to pay the ABSC noteholders (see Figure 3.4). Thus, by definition, ABSC could maintain a fixed-maturity payment schedule irrespective of the rate of principal payments.

4. *Protection against Bankruptcy Risk.* As discussed in Chapter 1, one of the major advantages of securitized credit is that it

Payment stream

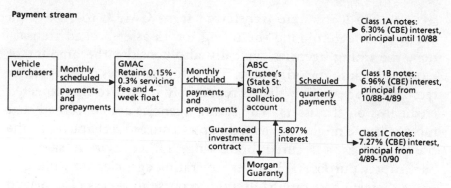

Source: SEC Registration Statement; McKinsey analysis.

Figure 3.4.   Asset-Backed Securities Corporation, Asset-Backed Obligations, Series 1.

enables originators to access the securities market at rating levels higher than their own general credit. In order to attain such higher credit levels, the rating agencies require that the transaction be structured to eliminate the risk that a bankruptcy of the originator would interfere with timely payments on the notes. The ABSC Asset Backed Obligations obtained AAA/Aaa ratings from Standard & Poor's and Moody's as a result of such structuring.

The use of a special purpose vehicle was important in obtaining AAA/Aaa ratings for an asset-backed transaction originated by GMAC, a AA+/Aa1 credit. As a result of selling the assets to the special purpose vehicle, investors could be protected from the automatic interruption in payments that would result from GMAC's bankruptcy if GMAC had owned the assets. In order to properly establish the ABSC notes as AAA/Aaa securities, ABSC had to be "bankruptcy remote" from the risk of a GMAC bankruptcy and also structured so that ABSC's own activities could not lead to bankruptcy.[4] In order to be protected from a GMAC bankruptcy, the transfer of the vehicle loans from GMAC to ABSC was clearly documented as a sale in the legal documents and accounted for as a sale, and the security interests in the vehicles

---

[4] In addition, of course, the ABSC asset-backed issue had to receive AAA quality credit enhancement as discussed in the next section.

securing the loans were transferred from GMAC to ABSC. In addition, in determining the rating for an asset-backed transaction, the rating agencies typically also consider the amount of recourse back to the originator. The rating agencies often look for recourse in an amount that is reasonably related to the expected credit loss on the assets. The rating agencies are concerned that more recourse might lead a bankruptcy court to recharacterize the transaction as a secured borrowing, rather than a sale, for bankruptcy purposes. However, the rating agencies are willing to grant their highest ratings despite recourse in excess of expected loss if other credit and structuring factors are satisfied. In the ABSC Series 1 transaction, the 5-percent limited recourse back to GMAC was higher than the less than 1-percent maximum expected loss on the assets. However, the overall bankruptcy-remote structuring of the transaction and the credit support level was so strong that the rating agencies decided to permit this recourse level.

In order to obtain AAA/Aaa ratings, investors in ABSC also had to be protected against the possibility that ABSC could go bankrupt and thereby interrupt timely payments on the notes. Accordingly, ABSC itself was constructed as a bankruptcy-remote entity. As mentioned earlier, ABSC was incorporated as a limited-purpose finance corporation solely for the purpose of issuing receivables-backed debt and related activities. ABSC was also restricted with respect to incurring additional debt. Thus investors in the notes were protected from ABSC taking business risks or incurring any future debt that was not of AAA/Aaa credit quality.

Credit Enhancement.   The ABSC Series 1 notes were rated AAA by Standard & Poor's and Aaa by Moody's as a result of several levels of credit enhancement. The first level was a first-loss limited guaranty by GMAC for 5 percent of the aggregate amount of the auto receivables. In addition, ABSC provided a limited guaranty equal to an additional 1 percent of the amount of the receivables. This 1 percent ABSC guaranty was supported by the equity in ABSC. Both of these limited guaranties were supported by a 6-percent "back-up" Letter of Credit issued by Credit Suisse, which is rated AAA by Standard & Poor's and Aaa by Moody's.

The 6 percent total first loss credit enhancement on the ABSC issue more than amply covered any reasonably anticipated credit losses. The historical net credit loss experience (after liquidation of the auto collateral) on GMAC vehicle loans over the last 5 years did not exceed 0.36 percent per year. Since the weighted average life of the ABSC vehicle loan collateral was approximately 2 years, credit losses on the ABSC loans are anticipated to be well under 1 percent.

The ABSC Series 1 issue received AAA/Aaa ratings from the rating services because: (1) the credit enhancement of the issue provided multiple coverage of expected credit losses; and (2) the credit enhancement was ultimately supported by an AAA/Aaa credit—Credit Suisse. Both the multiple expected loss coverage and the ultimate recourse to an AAA credit enabled the rating agencies in order to grant their highest ratings. By virtue of the structuring and credit enhancement, the ABSC issue attained a rating higher than the AA+/Aa1 rating of GMAC, the originator of the assets, and higher than the A rating of First Boston, the ultimate parent of ABSC.

Placement.   First Boston was the lead manager for a syndicate of 45 underwriters for the issue. As lead manager, First Boston actually underwrote approximately 53 percent of the $4 billion issue. Investor demand for the ABSC issue was very strong—so strong that the size of the issue was increased from the $3.2 billion amount listed in the Preliminary Prospectus Supplement of October 10, 1986, to $4 billion in the final Prospectus Supplement 4 days later. One money market fund by itself purchased more than $750 million of the shortest maturity tranche. Banks were large purchasers of the middle tranche, and insurance companies of the longest maturity tranche. Investor demand was strong because of the AAA/Aaa ratings, a yield premium to similar average life AAA/Aaa corporate notes that we estimate may have been as much as 20bp, the high quality of the receivables, and the fact that these asset-backed securities were fixed maturity without prepayment risk.

Trading.   Investor demand for the ABSC notes has continued to be strong, and First Boston continues to make a market in the ABSC Series 1 notes.

Servicing.   GMAC remains the servicer for the vehicle loans sold to ABSC. As servicer, GMAC is still responsible for collecting the monthly payments on the vehicle loans, and for repossession and resolution of any defaulting loans. As a result of integral GMAC controls, neither the individual borrowers nor the branch employees handling the servicing of the accounts are aware that the loans are no longer owned by GMAC. We estimate that GMAC receives a servicing fee of between 15bp and 30bp.

Benefits

GMAC.   Through the ABSC structured financing, GMAC was able to achieve its primary goal of removing over $4 billion of assets and their related liabilities, from its balance sheet, at a time when its debt-to-equity was near the upper end of the band in which the ratio is managed. Thus, the ABSC issue provided GMAC with an attractive alternative source of funds for its auto finance business.

Moreover, by engaging in the ABSC financing, we estimate that GMAC was able to fund the auto loans in a significantly more economic manner than match-funded traditional debt financing. As shown in Figure 3.5, we estimate that on an annual basis, GMAC may have saved as much as 1.30 percent annually over the cost of match-funded traditional finance. This estimate is made in accordance with the methodology described in Appendix A. We are not privy to the particular nonpublic financial details of the transaction, so we have made reasonable approximations where necessary. Let us now look at the estimated comparative costs to GMAC of funding the auto loans by an off-balance sheet sale to ABSC, compared to match-funding the auto loans with traditional GMAC debt and equity capital. For the purposes of

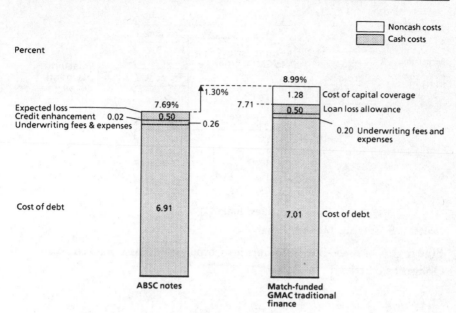

Source: McKinsey analysis; GMAC Annual Report.

Figure 3.5.   Asset-Backed Securities Corporation, Asset-Backed Obligations, Series 1, comparative annualized pretax financing costs (October 14, 1986).

this comparative analysis we have assumed that all costs of the ABSC Series 1 issue are ultimately borne by GMAC. We realize that the actual level of GMAC's costs was determined by the price level at which the auto loans were sold to ABSC.

The first element of cost for the ABSC notes was the 6.91 percent cost of debt which represents the blended corporate bond equivalent yield[5] on the three tranches of asset-backed obligations weighted by the relative size and average lives of each tranche.

The next element of cost is the 26bp annualized cost for underwriting fees and expenses. This includes $15,942,500 in underwriting fees and a further $1,450,000 in other issuance expenses (Figure 3.7). This $17.4 million in total expenses over the life of the issue has been annualized over the 1.9 years blended

---

[5] Corporate bonds typically pay interest semiannually. The yield on the ABSC notes (which pay interest quarterly) has been adjusted to a corporate bond equivalent in order to compare this yield to that of ordinary GMAC notes.

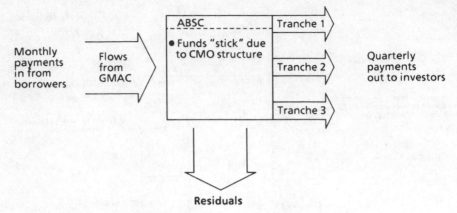

Residuals

Source: Prospectus; McKinsey analysis.

Figure 3.6. Asset-Backed Securities Corporation, Asset-Backed Obligations, Series 1.

SEC registration fee (2 b.p.)	$800,000
NASD filing fee	5,100
Trustee's fees and expenses	100,000
Printing and engraving	100,000
Legal fees and expenses	250,000
Accounting fees and expenses	50,000
Rating agency fees	120,000
Miscellaneous	24,900
Total	**$1,450,000**

Source: SEC Registration Statement.

Figure 3.7. Expenses of ABSC, Asset-Backed Obligations, Series 1, issue.

weighted average life of the ABSC notes to produce a 26bp annual cost when spread over the full $4 billion issue.[6] The next element of cost is the 2bp annualized credit enhancement fee paid to Credit Suisse for its letter of credit covering 6 percent of the issue. We estimate Credit Suisse's annual fee to be approximately 3/8 percent on the 6 percent amount that was guaranteed, which amounts to 2bp annually when spread out over the full $4 billion issue.

The last cost element to GMAC in the ABSC financing is the expected loss. This cost arises from the 5 percent limited recourse back to GMAC. As a result of this recourse, GMAC will incur credit losses on the vehicle loans up to the 5 percent level of the limited guaranty even though the loans are no longer on its balance sheet. As mentioned earlier, GMAC's actual losses on automotive loans have been under 40bp annually for several years. Nonetheless, we are using a 50bp expected annualized loss figure since that is approximately the amount that we estimate GMAC to reserve against the loans.[7]

The above cost elements combine to produce a 7.69 percent total all-in annual pre-tax financing cost to GMAC of financing the vehicle loans through a sale to ABSC.

This 7.69 percent financing cost compares to an estimated 8.99 percent all-in cost of traditional GMAC balance sheet financing. The first element of this traditional cost is the estimated 7.01 percent yield that GMAC would have to pay on matched maturity

---

[6] Since this $17.4 million represents up-front fees, we should cost it over the 1.9 year average life in order to get a present value of $17.4 million. However, we have not made any such adjustment since it would be virtually perfectly offset by a comparable adjustment to the underwriting fees in the traditional finance column.

Also, please note that the transfer price for the receivables between GMAC and ABSC may have been one that resulted in a gain for ABSC. Any such gain would flow to the benefit of First Boston as the owner of ABSC.

[7] While the 50bp expected loss on the loans is technically not a financing cost, we have included it in order to show that pursuant to the controlling Financial Accounting Standards Board rules, GMAC must reserve its expected loss pursuant to its recourse obligation. This reserve is a cost since GMAC reasonably anticipates its loss. Pursuant to GAAP, GMAC need not reserve any further capital against the recourse obligation. We also believe that as a practical matter GMAC need not hold any further equity against the recourse obligation. Both Moody's and Standard & Poor's have indicated that as of the ABSC transaction, they would not require GMAC to reserve any further capital against that recourse obligation. (See the Appendix for a more detailed discussion of this point.)

notes. This yield is slightly higher than the 6.91 percent yield on the ABSC notes because GMAC notes would issue at only a AA+/Aa1 rating level, while the ABSC issue was credit-enhanced to AAA/Aaa. Our 7.01 percent estimate for the GMAC notes is likely to be conservative, since GMAC would have had to offer a premium to sell $4 billion in GMAC notes all at one time.

The second cost element to traditional financing would be the underwriting fees and expenses in connection with issuing such notes. We estimate this expense to be 20bp. In addition, GMAC would incur any credit losses on the vehicle loans, and we again use a 50bp loan loss allowance in connection with the loans.

There remains one additional cost element to traditional GMAC financing—the cost of capital coverage. The cost of capital coverage represents the cost increment over the cost of debt necessary to reflect equity costs. Thus, the cost of capital coverage is equal to the weighted average cost of capital (WACC) minus the cost of debt. In calculating the cost of capital coverage, we are adjusting the funding costs to allow for the fact that GMAC funds its assets with both debt and equity. We therefore impute an equity cost to the financing in an amount that is directly proportional to GMAC's overall ratio of debt and equity.

A detailed description of the methodology by which we calculated cost of capital coverage is set forth in Appendix 1. In GMAC's case, we calculated the cost to be 1.28 percent. We used the Capital Asset Pricing Model (CAPM) to calculate a 25.2 percent cost of equity from a 6.1 percent risk-free rate, a beta of 1.0, a market premium of 7.5 percent, and a tax rate of 46 percent. Also, we applied GMAC's estimated 14.2/1 leverage ratio of assets to equity. We then derived the 1.28 percent pretax cost of capital coverage as follows:[8]

$$\frac{25.2\% \text{ (pretax cost of equity)} - 7.01\% \text{ (cost of debt)}}{14.2 \text{ (leverage)}} = 1.28\%$$

In summary, we estimate that GMAC achieved an all-in pre-tax annual financing cost advantage of 1.30 percent by engaging in

---

[8] See Appendix A for an explanation of this calculation.

the structured ABSC financing. This cost advantage essentially results from equity cost savings that result from GMAC's selling of the vehicle loans and thereby largely eliminating the equity costs of balance sheet financing.

In addition, GMAC also eliminated the prepayment risk and the interest rate risk that would have resulted from traditional balance sheet financing. Of course, we performed the above financing cost comparison on a match-funded basis by comparing the ABSC notes with a GMAC financing of a comparable maturity. Nonetheless, there is a major interest rate risk difference between the two forms of finance. In the ABSC financing, GMAC has completely eliminated any asset-liability mismatch risk (prepayment risk) by selling the vehicle loans to ABSC. If the vehicle loans prepay at an unexpected rate, any such prepayments are absorbed by the ABSC structure. GMAC is indifferent to the prepayment rate. On the other hand, if GMAC had kept the vehicle loans and funded them with liabilities matched to their expected average life, GMAC might still incur interest rate risk from asset-liability mismatch. The vehicle loans might prepay at an unexpected rate that did not conform to the maturity of the supporting fixed-maturity GMAC liabilities. In short, structured credit securitization inherently matches cash flows in a manner that traditional finance does not.[9]

First Boston.   The ABSC transaction generated substantial revenues for First Boston. The underwriting discount was 35bp on the $2,095,000,000 Class 1-A Notes, 40bp on the $585,000,000 Class 1-B Notes, and 47.5bp on the $1,320,000,000 Class 1-C Notes, resulting in a total of $15,942,500 in underwriting fees. As lead manager, First Boston actually underwrote 53 percent of

---

[9] We must also note that not only did GMAC match-fund through the ABSC financing at an economic rate, but also GMAC retained a portion of the income from the receivables for continuing to act as the servicer. GMAC received a monthly servicing fee we estimate at an annual rate of 0.15 percent on the outstanding $2,334,549,000 in 2.9 percent auto loans and at an annual rate of 0.3 percent on the $1,913,936,000 in 4.8 percent loans. In addition to this servicing fee, GMAC, as servicer, also receives the float on each month's auto loan payments for an average period of 4 weeks. This servicing income did not represent a further advantage to GMAC, since GMAC would have serviced the loans and retained the float even if it had used traditional financing.

the total issue and received approximately that proportion of the underwriting fees. In addition, as noted earlier, First Boston was the sole owner of the special purpose vehicle used for this financing. As a result, First Boston may have earned additional income depending upon the price at which it purchased the receivables from GMAC.

Equally importantly, the ABSC Series 1 transaction was an important milestone in the development of the asset-backed securities market and of First Boston's presence within that market. The acceptance of a $4 billion issue by the asset backed market represented a broad investor acceptance of the such securities that thereafter resulted in tighter spreads of asset-backed securities to comparable corporates. By lead managing this and a large number of other issues (see Appendix B), First Boston secured a powerful role in this growing asset-backed securities market.

Credit Suisse. As the third-party credit enhancer, Credit Suisse earns an annual fee which we estimate to be about ³⁄₈ percent on the 6 percent of the outstanding auto loan principal which it guaranteed. This translates into only about 2 basis points of the total amount of the transaction, a fee which First Boston determined to be well justified by the difference in yield required investors for AAA/Aaa as opposed to lower rated securities.

Investors. The ABSC transaction proved very popular with investors. The ABSC notes were extremely attractive since they were AAA rated notes that were of fixed maturities ranging from about 2 to 4 years. Such high quality notes are particularly appealing since they are relatively scarce in that maturity spectrum. In fact, some institutional investors essentially thought they were getting AA yields on AAA notes.[10]

Afterword. As we previously noted, securitized credit has become a major new funding source for GMAC. After its initial use of the technology in December 1985, GMAC went to the public market with securitized issues on a somewhat regular basis in 1986 (see Figure 3.8). In fact, GMAC sourced $8.5 billion through sales of

---

[10] The notes traded so well that a second ABSC issue was issued 2 months later.

GENERAL MOTORS ACCEPTANCE CORPORATION ISSUES OF ASSET BACKED CERTIFICATES 1985–86

Issue	Date	Expected average life	Spread to treasury	Size of issue
GMAC 1985-A	12/12/85	1.91	65	$ 524,683,826.53
GMAC 1986-A	1/23/86	1.87	64	423,552,152.85
GMAC 1986-B	4/16/86	1.97	85	1,049,490,815.89
GMAC 1986-C	6/20/86	2.05	95	755,074,360.85
GMAC 1986-D	8/19/86	1.50	80	354,749,616.18
GMAC 1986-E	8/19/86	2.10	97	725,069,040.16
GMAC 1986 Euro-A	9/19/86	N/A	N/A	276,330,000.00
GMAC 1986-F	11/18/86	1.91	71	326,962,356.49
GMAC 1986-G	12/17/86	1.91	75	444,857,394.44

GENERAL MOTORS ACCEPTANCE CORPORATION SALES OF RECEIVABLES TO ASSET BACKED SECURITIES CORPORATION 1985–86

Sale	Date	Expected average life	Pool rate	Size of sale
2.9% Pool	10/14/86	N/A	2.75%	$ 2,334,549,000
4.8% Pool	10/14/86	N/A	4.50	1,913,936,000
2.9% Pool	12/02/86	N/A	2.75	89,122,000
4.8% Pool	12/02/86	N/A	4.50	106,519,000

ASSET BACKED SECURITIES CORPORATION ISSUES OF ASSET BACKED OBLIGATIONS COLLATERALIZED BY RECEIVABLES PURCHASED FROM GENERAL MOTORS ACCEPTANCE CORPORATION 1985–86

Issue		Date	Weighted average life	Spread to treasury	Size of issue
ABSC Class	1-A	10/14/86	1.05	69	$2,095,000,000
	1-B		2.20	75	585,000,000
	1-C		3.07	80	1,320,000,000
ABSC Class	2-A	12/02/86	1.09	49	95,000,000
	2-B		2.24	55	25,050,000
	2-C		3.13	58	60,176,000

Source: McKinsey analysis.

Figure 3.8.

97

receivables in 1986, as compared to $12.8 billion through debt with greater than 1-year maturity and $5.0 billion (net of debt repaid) in commercial paper. Thus, securitized credit became a major source of funds for GMAC, although it has not been active in the market since August of 1987.

In looking at Figure 3.7, the issues entitled GMAC A-G and GMAC Euro-A are all "pass-through" issues, as opposed to the two "pay-through," CMO-type issues of ABSC. We describe one of these GMAC pass-through structures in our next transaction description.

GMAC 1986-G GRANTOR TRUST 6.85 PERCENT ASSET-BACKED CERTIFICATES

After selling a significant portion of its below market rate loans from the fall 1986 incentive rate programs through ABSC, GMAC returned to the grantor trust pass-through structure. One example of that structure is the GMAC 1986-G Grantor Trust, which went to market in December 1986 (see Figure 3.9, Term Sheet).

Structure

The structure of this transaction is summarized in Figures 3.10 and 3.11, and explained below.

Origination.   GMAC pooled together 38,944 vehicle loans with $444,857,394.44 in receivables. The pool had a weighted average annual percentage rate of 11.82 percent, and a weighted average maturity of 53.6 months. We estimate that the expected average life of the receivables was 1.9 years. The vehicle receivables were broadly geographically distributed throughout the U.S. Each receivable represented a loan on a new automobile or light truck, the first payment on which was due in December 1986.

Structuring

1. Creation of Special Purpose Vehicle. GMAC conveyed the receivables and security interests in the vehicles to a trust, created

Issue	6.85% Asset Backed Certificates, Series 1986-G
Seller/servicer	General Motors Acceptance Corporation
Offering date	December 17, 1986
Rating (S&P, Moody's)	AA/Aa1
Principal amount	$444,857,394.44
Collateral	Primarily new GM vehicles
Expected average life (years)	1.91
Yield to average life (CBE)	7.03%
Payment frequency	Monthly
Spread to treasuries at offering	75 b.p.
Recourse (amount/provider)	5% GMAC Limited Guaranty
Credit enhancement	None
Managing underwriter	The First Boston Corporation

Source: SEC Registration Statement; McKinsey analysis.

Figure 3.9. GMAC 1986-G Grantor Trust.

by GMAC, under a pooling and servicing agreement with Morgan Guaranty Trust Company of New York. In return for the receivables, GMAC received $444,857,394.44 in asset-backed certificates which it then sold to the underwriters for placement with investors.

2. Tax/Accounting Structure of the Deal. The GMAC 1986-G Grantor Trust was structured to qualify for tax-exempt, grantor trust status under the Internal Revenue Code. Accordingly, the GMAC 1986-G Grantor Trust was structured with a single class of certificates which simply entitles purchasers to receive a pro-rata share of interest and principal on a monthly

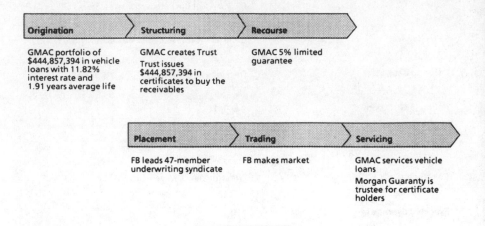

Source: SEC Registration Statement; McKinsey analysis.

Figure 3.10.   GMAC 1986-G Grantor Trust, 6.85% Asset-Backed Certificates, Series 1986-G.

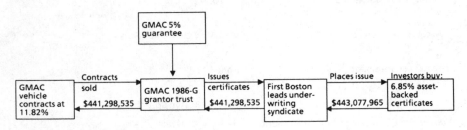

Source: SEC Registration Statement.

Figure 3.11.   GMAC 1986-G Grantor Trust, 6.85% Asset-Backed Certificates, Series 1986-G.

basis as it is received by the trust. The assets of the trust were fixed as of the effective date of its creation, and cannot be added to during the life of the trust. Also, the trust cannot engage in active reinvestment of the receivables, since the interest and principal received by the trust is distributed each month. For all of these reasons, the attorneys for GMAC, Sutherland, Asbill & Brennan, provided a legal opinion that the trust qualified as a grantor trust exempt from federal income taxation under the Internal Revenue Code. For tax purposes, each certificate holder will be treated as the owner of a pro-rata undivided interest in each of the receivables in the trust.[11]

From an accounting perspective, the transaction was structured as a true sale of the vehicle receivables. As discussed in Chapter 1, FAS 77 provides that a transfer of receivables with recourse is a sale if the transferor surrenders control of the future economic benefits of the sold receivables, if the transferor's liability under the recourse obligation can be reasonably estimated, and if the receivables cannot be "put" back to the transferor except for a minor clean-up call. In this case, GMAC met all three conditions and so accounted for the transaction as a sale under GAAP. GMAC had surrendered control of the economic benefits in that any increase in the value of the certificates due to a decline in interest rates would accrue to the certificate holders. The amount of GMAC's liability under the 5-percent limited recourse provision could reasonably be estimated to be no more than 1 percent over the life of the receivables based upon GMAC's prior net loss experience.[12] Finally, certificate holders do not have a right to "put" their certificates back to GMAC, though GMAC retained the right to make a clean-up call when the outstanding principal amount in the trust was 5 percent or less of its original balance. Since this transaction qualified as a sale under FAS 77, the vehicle receivables were removed from GMAC's balance sheet.

3. *Payment Characteristics of the Certificates.* The decision to use a grantor trust structure necessarily meant that monthly principal payments on the $444,857,394 amount financed under the vehicle contracts would be directly passed through to the certificate holders. (See Figure 3.12.) Principal payments collected each month were to be paid on a distribution date on or about the fifteenth day of the following month. Certificate-holders would also receive their monthly pro-rata share of their 6.85 percent per annum interest from the vehicle finance charge collections on such distribution dates.

---

[11] See Chapter 1 for a more detailed discussion of grantor trusts.

[12] As a result of such recourse obligations, in 1986 GMAC actually reserved approximately 1 percent for this and similar asset sales with recourse.

Payment stream

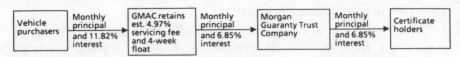

Source: SEC Registration Statement.

Figure 3.12. GMAC 1986-G Grantor Trust, 6.85% Asset-Backed Certificates, Series 1986-G.

The vehicle purchasers have the right to prepay their loans at any time, and such prepayments of principal would be passed through to certificate holders. As a result of expected prepayment characteristics, the expected average life of the certificates was 1.9 years, substantially shorter than the 2.48 years scheduled average life assuming no prepayments. Certificate-holders are exposed to some risk that the actual average life of the certificates may vary from the 1.9-year expected average life because of unexpected prepayment rates. However, any such variance was likely to be minor because of the relatively short average life of these assets and their relative insensitivity to interest rate levels.

4. Protection against Bankruptcy Risk. As discussed in Chapter 1, a true sale to a bankruptcy-remote special purpose vehicle is important in structuring most asset-backed transactions for originators that are subject to the Bankruptcy Code. This structuring allows the credit of the asset-backed issue to be stepped up above that of the originator. Without such structuring, a bankruptcy of the originator could cause the automatic stay provision of the bankruptcy code to interfere with the timely payment of interest and principal to the investors.

It is important to note that while the GMAC 1986-G Grantor Trust was structured as a sale to a bankruptcy-remote special purpose vehicle, GMAC did not seek to raise the rating of the issue above GMAC's AA/Aa1 rating[13] by obtaining a back-up-guaranty from a AAA/Aaa credit. Credit enhancement for the issue was only provided by limited recourse to GMAC as

---

[13] GMAC's Standard & Poor's rating was reduced in November 1986 to AA from the AA+ rating referred to in the preceding ABSC deal description.

described in the next section on credit enhancement. If the issue had been credit-enhanced in order to obtain a rating above GMAC's, the rating agencies would have generally required compliance with their bankruptcy-remote criteria which include that: (1) the documents of the transaction describe the transfer of assets from the originator to the Trust as a sale; (2) both the originator and the Trust account for the transaction as a sale; (3) recourse back to the originator be limited to an amount reasonably related to expected loss; (4) the Trust's ownership of the receivables be perfected by appropriate filings under the Uniform Commercial Code; and (5) this perfection not be jeopardized by commingling receipts from the receivables with the originator's general receipts.[14]

While the GMAC 1986-G Grantor Trust was structured to comply with most of the above criteria, the amount of recourse to GMAC was substantially in excess of expected loss and the receivables receipts were commingled with GMAC funds prior to the monthly distribution date. It is not clear whether the rating agencies would have permitted these structural features and still rated the GMAC 1986-G certificate as AAA/Aaa assuming a third party, rated AAA/Aaa, provided the ultimate credit enhancement. The rating agencies could have reasoned, as in the previously described ABSC transaction, that the overall creditworthiness of the structure and credit enhancement for it were sufficient to permit such recourse and commingling. However, the rating agencies did not have to reach that issue, since GMAC did not seek to step up the Grantor Trust Certificates rating to AAA/Aaa.

Credit Enhancement.   As we just noted, the certificates received an AA/Aa1 rating from Standard & Poor's/Moody's. The certificates were credit-enhanced by the 5 percent first loss recourse to GMAC in the form of a limited guaranty. This limited guaranty represented a multiple of historic credit losses over the life of the issue.[15] Without a third party guaranty provided by a AAA credit,

---

[14] See Chapter 1 for a more detailed account of protection against bankruptcy risk.

[15] GMAC's net credit losses had never been more than 36bp over the last 5 years (500bp limited guaranty/36bp × 1.9-year average life = 7.2 × loss coverage).

the overall rating on the certificates could not be higher than that of GMAC. Therefore, the certificates were limited to GMAC's AA/Aa1 senior-debt ratings.

Placement. First Boston was the lead manager for a forty-seven-member underwriting syndicate. First Boston and its co-managers (Merrill Lynch Capital Markets, Morgan Stanley & Co., and Salomon Brothers, Inc.) each underwrote 10 percent of the issue.

Servicing. GMAC is the servicer for the vehicle loans sold to the trust. As servicer, GMAC is responsible for collecting the monthly payments on the vehicle loans. Typically, GMAC receives payments throughout a calendar month and commingles them with its other income. On the fifth business day of each month, GMAC notifies the trustee, Morgan Guaranty, of the amount collected in the previous month that will be payable to the certificate holders (i.e., principal payments together with the 6.85 percent annual interest on the certificates). On the fifteenth day of the month, GMAC transfers the funds payable to certificate-holders to a certificate account maintained by the trustee. Upon receipt of the funds, the trustee distributes the monies to the certificate-holders.

As servicer, GMAC also advances monies to the certificate account in respect of any delinquent payments, and recovers any such advances upon receipt of the actual payments. In the event of a default, GMAC repossesses and sells the vehicle. Of course, GMAC's loss exposure is limited to its 5 percent limited guaranty.

Benefits

GMAC. By selling the vehicle loans into the 1986-G Grantor Trust, GMAC was able to remove the vehicle loans and their supporting liabilities from its balance sheet in a manner that resulted in perfect match-funding and the elimination of all of the interest-rate risk.

Moreover, we estimate that the 1986-G Grantor Trust allowed GMAC to fund the auto loans in a significantly more economic manner than match-funded traditional debt financing. We estimate that on an annual basis, GMAC saved approximately 1.05 percent in its all-in pre-tax financing costs (see Figure 3.12). This estimate is our best approximation from publicly available information made in accordance with the methodology described in Appendix A.

The 7.79 percent estimated cost to GMAC of funding the vehicle loans through the Asset Backed Certificates was calculated by considering: (1) the 7.03 percent corporate bond equivalent yield on the certificates; (2) the 26bp annualized underwriting fees and issuance expenses consisting of $1,779,430 in underwriting discounts and $390,000 in registration, legal, printing, rating agency, and trustee fees spread over the $444,857,391 issue's 1.9-year average life; and (3) an estimated 50bp annualized expected loss on the loans.[16]

The second bar in Figure 3.12 represents the annual cost to GMAC of match-funding using traditional financing. We estimate that a 2-year note issued in the public market would have required a field of approximately 6.85 percent. In addition, we estimate that the annualized underwriting fees and expenses of such an issue may have cost 20bp. The loan loss allowance that would be used up by credit losses on the vehicle loans we again estimate at 50bp. Finally, GMAC would have a cost of capital coverage of approximately 129bp. This cost represents the additional incremental cost attributable to funding with equity as well as debt. In calculating this cost of capital coverage we used a 6.24 percent risk-free rate, a beta of 1.0, a marginal tax rate of 46 percent, and a leverage ratio of assets/equity of 14.2/1.[17]

Therefore, as shown in Figure 3.12, GMAC realized an all-in annual pretax financing cost savings of about 1.05 percent as a result of using the 1986-G Grantor Trust structure.

It is essential to note that the above financing cost savings represents the complete all-in cost advantage of the GMAC 1986-G

---

[16] While the expected loss on the loans is technically not a financing cost, we have included it in order to show that pursuant to FAS 77, GMAC must reserve its expected loss over the life of the sold assets that would accrue from the recourse obligation.

As we previously noted, GMAC's actual annual credit loss experience had not been greater than 36bp annually in recent years. Nonetheless, we estimate that GMAC created a reserve of roughly 1 percent for expected losses, and this 1 percent amounts to approximately 50bp annually.

[17] See Appendix A for a treatment of the general methodology of calculating cost of capital coverage.

Grantor Trust. As would be the case in a traditional debt financing, GMAC would retain the spread revenue between the 11.82 percent yield on the receivables and the 6.85 percent interest rate paid to the certificate-holders or note-holders, as the case may be (see Figure 3.13). GMAC termed the bulk of this spread a pool servicing fee, and it termed 4bp of the spread a guaranty fee. Thus, GMAC actually receives and retains the spread above its financing costs.

Another advantage realized by GMAC through the securitization was that GMAC completely eliminated its prepayment risk and its interest-rate risk. It is nearly impossible to *perfectly* match-fund auto installment loans, and eliminate both prepayment risk and interest rate risk, using traditional types of on-balance sheet financing. Because, as noted earlier, auto installment loans prepay at rates that are not perfectly predictable. However, funding auto loans with a combination of short-term floating rate debt and fixed rate term debt can eliminate a great deal of the prepayment risk, but does not eliminate interest-rate risk. Thus, perfect on-balance sheet match-funding, which eliminates both prepayment risk and interest-rate risk, is not possible.

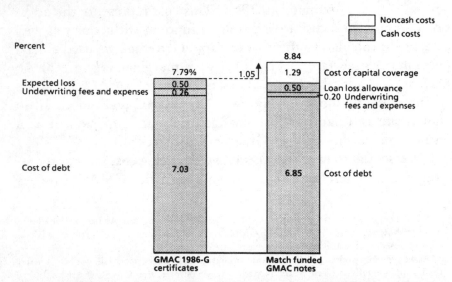

Source: SEC Registration Statement; McKinsey analysis; GMAC Annual Report.

Figure 3.13. GMAC 1986-G Grantor Trust comparative annualized pretax financing costs (Asset-Backed Certificates, Series 1986-G).

First Boston. The GMAC 1986-G Grantor Trust generated substantial revenues for First Boston, the lead manager, and its underwriting syndicate. The gross underwriting discount was 40bp, which produced $1,779,430 in total underwriting discounts and commissions.

Investors. Investors, too, were pleased with the asset-backed certificates which sold at an attractive 75bp spread over Treasuries.

CHRYSLER FINANCIAL CORPORATION $1.2 BILLION AUCTION OF RETAIL AUTOMOTIVE RECEIVABLES

In early November 1986, the Corporate Finance Officer responsible for the Chrysler relationship at Morgan Guaranty Trust Company of New York (Morgan Guaranty) learned that Chrysler Financial Corporation (CFC)[18] wanted to arrange a billion dollar asset-backed financing and to conclude it before year end.

Morgan Guaranty decided to offer a competitive private financing structure to CFC for the billion dollar issue. In order to get this business, Morgan Guaranty had to deliver a financing at an all-in cost of funds that would be competitive with the public market alternative. CFC was well aware of the public market alternative since it had previously originated one such public issue of $250 million in July 1986, underwritten by Salomon Brothers. CFC also had available an undrawn Receivables Purchase Facility from a group of commercial banks.

In contrast to its investment bank competitors that proposed a public issue of asset-backed securities, Morgan Guaranty proposed to run a private auction of the car loans to interested institutional bidders, primarily banks. In this auction, Morgan Guaranty would act as an auction agent. At the same time, Morgan Guaranty would be able to assure CFC of financing at a fixed maximum ceiling cost by agreeing, if necessary, to purchase all of the receivables for Morgan Guaranty's own account at a certain price.

---

[18] CFC is a subsidiary of Chrysler Corporation.

Thus, Morgan Guaranty's loan auction alternative offered financing at an attractive maximum price—a structure competitive in cost to Chrysler to a public market issue of securities. Morgan Guaranty believed that it could offer a maximum all-in cost to Chrysler comparable to that available from investment banks competing for the Chrysler business. After reviewing the various financing proposals, Chrysler decided to conduct the transaction through the Morgan Guaranty loan auction (see the Term Sheet, Figure 3.14).

Structure

The structure of this transaction is summarized in Figures 3.15 and 3.16, and explained next.

Issue	Retail Automotive Receivables Auction
Parent/seller	Chrysler Financial Corporation/ Chrysler Credit Corporation
Servicing bank	Morgan Bank (Delaware)
Offering date	December 15, 1986 (50%) December 29, 1986 (50%)
Principal amount	$1,200,000,000 (face amount) of vehicle receivables
Collateral	New contracts for Chrysler vehicles
Average life (years)	1.75
Payment frequency	Monthly
Recourse (amount/provider)	7.50% holdback
Placement agent	Morgan Guaranty Trust Company of New York

Source: Offering Documents; Morgan Guaranty Trust Company of New York.

Figure 3.14. Chrysler Financial Corporation.

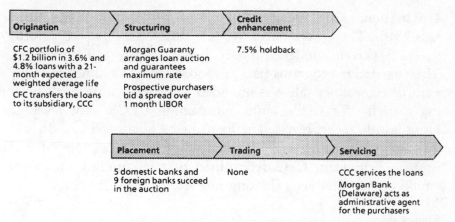

Origination	Structuring	Credit enhancement
CFC portfolio of $1.2 billion in 3.6% and 4.8% loans with a 21-month expected weighted average life	Morgan Guaranty arranges loan auction and guarantees maximum rate	7.5% holdback
CFC transfers the loans to its subsidiary, CCC	Prospective purchasers bid a spread over 1 month LIBOR	

Placement	Trading	Servicing
5 domestic banks and 9 foreign banks succeed in the auction	None	CCC services the loans
		Morgan Bank (Delaware) acts as administrative agent for the purchasers

Source: Offering Documents; Morgan Guaranty Trust Company of New York.

Figure 3.15. Chrysler Financial Corporation, $1.2 billion Auto Loan Auction.

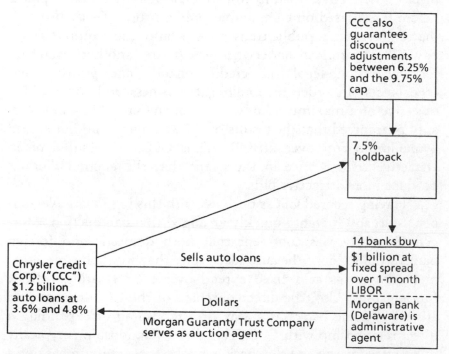

Source: Offering Documents; Morgan Guaranty Trust Company of New York.

Figure 3.16. Chrysler Financial Corporation, $1.2 billion Auto Loan Auction.

Origination. CFC identified $1.2 billion in newly originated auto loans. These were "incentive rate" loans issued at 3.6 percent and 4.8 percent under Chrysler incentive rate sale programs. These incentive programs had produced record volumes for CFC and the receivables sale was intended to provide additional funding capacity for CFC, while maintaining CFC's debt leverage ratios within target levels. The loans being auctioned had 36 and 48-month maturities, and a pooled weighted average anticipated life of 21 months. CFC determined that its funding objectives would be best met via a floating rate sale of the receivables.

Structuring

1. Obtaining the Business. It was estimated that a public issue of floating rate asset-backed notes through an investment bank coupled with an interest rate swap would require the issuer to pay an effective floating cost of LIBOR plus 20 basis points before fees. Based on comparable public issues, it was also estimated that such a public transaction would also require CFC to pay 40bp upfront in underwriting fees, and another several bp for registration, legal fees, credit enhancement, printing, and other costs. In order to obtain the business and meet CFC's objective of a maximum known cost of the sale, Morgan Guaranty guaranteed that the results of the auction would not exceed a maximum cost over LIBOR. Thus CFC was assured of an attractive ceiling price in the event that the auction did not produce more attractive bids.

Having secured CFC's business with this bid in late November, Morgan Guaranty quickly arranged the loan auction. Morgan Guaranty was confident that both domestic and foreign banks would bid for the auto loans since they would be interested in buying loans at a fixed spread over their floating LIBOR funding rate. Also, the direct purchase of the CFC loans would appeal to some banks as a way of establishing or expanding a direct relationship with CFC. This direct relationship is typically more attractive to the purchasing banks than the purchase of a typical loan participation in which the seller might never learn of the bank's purchase.

2. The Auction Process. On November 21, 1986, CFC and Morgan Guaranty sent an offering memorandum to the existing financial institution participants in CFC's credit facilities, and to a number of other interested financial institutions. The memorandum set an auction date of December 10, 1986, and a preferred minimum bid size of $25 million. The potential purchasers would be bidding to buy percentage ownership interests in $1.2 billion face amount of auto sale installment contracts. Potential purchasers would bid a spread over the 1-month LIBOR rate. If a prospective purchaser's bid was successful, the purchaser would receive interest at the spread it had bid over the LIBOR rate. The LIBOR rate would be adjusted monthly, but would never exceed a maximum of a 9.75 percent. Thus, the purchaser's rate was capped at 9.75 percent plus the spread over LIBOR successfully bid by the purchaser in the auction.

The auction was conducted on December 10, 1986. The auction process was structured so that each of the bidders knew that CFC would see all of the bids—this CFC oversight was intended to encourage bidders desiring to enhance their relationship with CFC to bid at the level of their minimally required yield, rather than submitting speculative high-spread bids.

For organizational reasons, CFC preferred that the actual seller of the loans should be one of its subsidiaries, Chrysler Credit Corporation (CCC). Therefore, CFC transferred the loans immediately prior to the sale. Accordingly, we will refer to the originator as either CFC or CCC, as appropriate. CFC also preferred for cash management reasons to receive the proceeds of the auction sale in two installments. Thus the sale of the first 50 percent of the receivables settled on December 15, and the second 50 percent settled on December 29. CFC required that the sale be completed before the end of the year so that the sale would be effective for its year-end consolidated balance sheet.

3. Accounting Structure of the Deal. For accounting purposes, the loan auction was a true sale of the auto receivables under GAAP, since: (1) CCC could not "call" back the receivables except for clean-up call when less than 5 percent of the principal remained outstanding; (2) CCC's liability under its recourse agreement could be reasonably estimated (see credit enhancement below), and (3) purchasers could not "put" the receivables back to CCC. Since the loan auction was a GAAP true sale, CCC was able to remove the sold loans from its balance sheet.[19]

4. Payment Characteristics of the Purchased Loans. CCC auctioned a total of about $1.2 billion face amount of car and light truck loans (auto loans). These loans were incentive rate loans yielding 3.6 percent or 4.8 percent that had been generated by Chrysler Motors incentive sales programs. CCC ultimately received approximately $1 billion from the buyers of the loans after the $1.2 billion face amount had been discounted by the 7.5 percent holdback (described in the following section on credit enhancement) and by an initial discount rate of 6.25 percent.

Buyers of ownership interests in the pool of auto receivables received monthly payments consisting of principal together with a buyer's rate of return. The monthly buyer's rate of return would be the prior month's 1-month LIBOR rate plus the applicable spread over LIBOR. In the event that the applicable monthly rate of return fell below the initial 6.25 percent discount rate, then CCC would be paid any such difference from the auto contract collections. In the event that the monthly rate of return rose above the 6.25 percent discount rate, CCC agreed to pay any such difference to the buyers up to the 9.75 percent maximum interest rate cap on LIBOR, plus the buyers' applicable spreads.

As originally structured, the expected weighted average life of the pooled auto loans was 1¾ years based on the scheduled maturities of the loans. Of course, the borrowers could prepay their loans. Because principal repayments by the borrowers would be passed through to the buyers in proportion to the buyers' allocable share of the pool, the buyers might be repaid their principal at a rate quicker than they had originally anticipated. However, because the purchasers received a floating rate, they generally were protected from the price risk of a movement in the level of interest rates.

5. Protection against Bankruptcy Risk. The auto loan auction was a private loan sale in the inter-bank market. This

---

[19] See Chapter 1 for a more detailed description of GAAP accounting.

structure does not entirely insulate purchasers from Chrysler's general credit. However, the buyers did receive title to the auto receivables from CCC. CCC marked the computer records of the auto loans that had been sold, and CCC also filed Uniform Commercial Code Financing Statements reflecting the sale. The exposure to CFC arises because, while the amount of credit enhancement provided by CCC in the form of a holdback (as described below) was far in excess of expected losses, collections on the sold receivables were commingled with CCC's other funds. As a result, a CCC bankruptcy might affect the buyer's entitlement to some of the receivables and/or the holdback. Such exposure should not exceed 1 month's worth of collections because the purchasers could appoint a new servicing agent immediately upon CFC or CCC default. Finally, additional exposure to CFC/CCC arises because the buyers first look to CCC for adjustments to the purchase price when required rates of return float in excess of the initial 6.25 percent discount rate. Should it be necessary, the holdback could be dedicated to support any such rates of return.

Credit Enhancement. Auto receivables, of course, are subject to credit losses and to delinquent payments as a result of tardy purchaser payments. Accordingly, credit enhancement was provided by a 7.5 percent "holdback" whereby the purchasers withheld 7.5 percent of the purchase price at the closing. Amounts set aside by means of this holdback were available to cover credit losses as they are charged off and discount adjustments resulting from late payments. To the extent that such losses or adjustments do not equal or exceed 7.5 percent of collections (calculated on a cumulative basis), CCC will receive monthly distributions from the purchasers which reduces the holdback to 7.5 percent of the unpaid balance of the contracts. Typically, such distributions will be netted against amounts due the purchasers. Over the life of the transaction, the amount of the holdback will not exceed 7.5 percent of the unpaid balance on the contracts, with a minimum floor equal to 3 percent of the original contract balances.

Investors considered the 7.5 percent holdback more than adequate to cover any reasonably anticipated losses or discount adjustments resulting from late payments. According to publicly available statistics, CFC had an extremely high quality vehicle receivables portfolio. For the prior 12 months, CFC only experienced a 0.22 percent annual credit loss on its outstanding auto receivables. Thus, the 7.5 percent holdback provided ample coverage of the anticipated credit losses over the life of the receivables.

In addition to the credit enhancement provided through the holdback, purchasers of the loans were, of course, provided credit support through their security interest in the underlying vehicles and additionally through recourse to the originating dealers on 40 percent of the loans. Also, purchasers of the loans were protected against geographic risk since the receivables were widely geographically distributed. Finally, CFC represented that all contracts sold were originated in the same manner with the same credit standards that CFC normally follows for contracts which are not sold.

The 7.5 percent holdback of this pool of secured receivables, when viewed against the good credit quality of the receivables, was sufficient to satisfy the purchasers of the creditworthiness of their purchase. In this context, it is worth noting that a 7 percent backup L/C enabled Chrysler's July 1986 public offering of auto receivables-backed certificates to receive an AAA rating from Standard & Poor's.

Placement.   Ultimately, 27 financial institutions placed bids in the receivables auction. Fourteen of these institutions had their bids accepted. Listed by the relative size of their purchases from the largest to the smallest, the successful bidders were five domestic and nine foreign banks as follows:

- Morgan Guaranty Trust Company of New York
- The Mitsui Bank, Ltd.
- The Bank of New York
- Union Bank of Switzerland
- Banco di Roma
- Bankers Trust Company
- The Northern Trust Company
- National Bank of Detroit

- Societe Generale
- The Yasuda Trust and Banking Company, Ltd.
- Berliner Handels-und Frankfurter Bank
- Credit Commercial de France
- Daiwa Bank Trust Company
- Kredietbank International Group.

Approximately 50 percent of the receivables went to the foreign banks and 50 percent went to the smaller group of domestic banks, who tended to purchase larger shares. The purchasing banks had the right to assign their interests to financial institutions and other institutional investors satisfactory to CCC, and to grant participations.

Servicing. CCC remained as the collection agent for the auto contracts. Morgan Bank (Delaware) was appointed as administrative agent representing the purchasers. As administrative agent, Morgan Bank (Delaware) had the right to remove CCC as collection agent if so instructed by the majority of purchasers.

CFC typically received the monthly vehicle contract payments through a network of domestic bank lock-boxes. Collections for the sold contracts would be made through this normal collection network. CCC would then identify the funds due to purchasers on a daily basis, but not segregate the collections. As noted in the previous section, this blending of funds might cause any funds collected by CCC, but unpaid to the purchasers, to remain part of CCC's estate in the event of its bankruptcy. However, in the ordinary course of events, CCC will remit to Morgan Bank (Delaware), as the servicing bank, the purchasers' share of collections for the previous month on the 20th day of the following month. Morgan Bank (Delaware) will then make payments to the individual purchasers.

Benefits

CFC.[20] Through the auto receivables auction, we estimate that CFC was able to realize substantial financing cost savings over a

---

[20] We are treating the benefits to CFC and its CCC subsidiary as benefits to CFC.

traditional "on balance sheet" loan. Although we could not confirm the economics of this private market transaction with CFC, we estimate that on a pretax basis CFC saved as much as 2 percent in all-in financing costs over a straight debt financing (see Figure 3.16). We arrive at this conclusion starting with the premise that CFC wanted to engage in a floating-rate financing. We estimate that the total annual financing costs of the loan sale above LIBOR were a 30bp premium paid to the buyers, a further 12bp in administrative fees and expenses, and a 22bp expected loss on the holdback. Thus we believe that the financing cost to CFC was about 64bp above the 1-month LIBOR rate.[21]

In contrast, the second bar in Figure 3.17 shows the cost to CFC of a traditional floating rate financing. We estimate that CFC floating rate notes would have sold at about a 50bp spread to LIBOR. In addition, the underwriting fees and expenses of such an issue would have cost about 25bp. The loan loss allowance that would be used up by credit losses on the vehicle loans we again estimate at 22bp. Finally, CFC would have a cost of capital coverage of approximately 1.84 percent. This cost represents the additional incremental cost attributable to funding with more expensive equity in addition to debt. In calculating this cost of capital coverage, we used a pretax cost of equity of 25.4 percent. We derived this equity cost using CAPM from a 6.24 percent risk-free rate, a beta of 1.0, a market premium of 7.5 percent, and a 46 percent tax rate. We then applied CFC's leverage ratio of 10.3/1 to calculate the cost of capital coverage.[22]

Therefore, the all-in traditional pretax financing cost to CFC would have been 2.81 percent over LIBOR—a rate 2.17 percent in excess of the comparable financing cost of the loan auction.

Moreover, through the auto receivables auction, CFC also achieved its goal of reducing its balance sheet debt financings. CFC had a target debt leverage ratio which was under pressure from a surge in vehicle financings resulting from the August through October incentive rate programs. An indication of this

---

[21] Since the CFC loan auction was a private deal, we do not have access to precise information on these costs. However, we do believe that our cost estimates are directionally correct.

[22] See Appendix A for a description of the general methodology for this calculation.

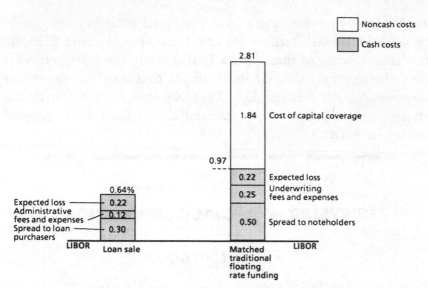

Source: Morgan Guaranty Trust Company of New York; McKinsey analysis.

Figure 3.17. Chrysler Financial Corporation, $1.2 billion Auto Loan Auction, comparative annualized pretax financing costs.

potential leverage problem may be roughly estimated from CFC's balance sheet as of September 30, 1986, which had risen to a 9.33 debt/equity ratio, well above the company's approximately 8/1 year-end 1985 ratio. The impact of the approximately $1 billion in loan auction proceeds on this ratio may be seen, since it would have enabled CFC to bring the ratio down from 9.3 to 8.8 if it had occurred on that September 30 date. Thus CFC was able to access the capital markets to obtain the capped floating rate debt that it desired, through a sale that improved its balance sheet ratios without obtaining expensive equity capital from its parent, Chrysler Corporation.

Morgan Guaranty Trust Company.   Morgan Guaranty received a fee for structuring the transaction. While less than the 40bp underwriting fee often charged by investment banks, the fee was substantial, particularly since the amount of the transaction was so large. Morgan Guaranty also received further income from Morgan Bank (Delaware)'s role as administrative agency for the purchasers.

Purchasers. The purchasing banks received relatively high quality, credit-enhanced, receivables at a fixed spread above LIBOR. In addition, some of these banks (particularly the foreign banks) were able to report to their head offices that they had entered a relationship with a major U.S. borrower and that a tombstone advertising this relationship appeared in the *Wall Street Journal* (see Figure 3.18).

CHRYSLER FINANCIAL CORPORATION

$1,200,000,000

Auction of retail automotive receivables

FUNDS PROVIDED BY:
MORGAN GUARANTY TRUST COMPANY OF NEW YORK
THE MITSUI BANK, LTD.
NEW YORK BRANCH
THE BANK OF NEW YORK
UNION BANK OF SWITZERLAND
BANCO DI ROMA
CHICAGO BRANCH
BANKERS TRUST COMPANY
THE NORTHERN TRUST COMPANY
NATIONAL BANK OF DETROIT
SOCIETE GENERALE
THE YASUDA TRUST AND BANKING CO., LTD.
NEW YORK BRANCH
BERLINER HANDELS-UND FRANKFURTER BANK
CREDIT COMMERCIAL DE FRANCE
DAIWA BANK TRUST COMPANY
KREDIETBANK INTERNATIONAL GROUP

SERVICING AGENT:
MORGAN BANK (DELAWARE)

The undersigned structured and arranged this transaction

Morgan Guaranty Trust Company *of New York*

This announcement appears as a matter of record only   December 1986

Figure 3.18.

4

Credit Card Loans

Credit card loans are just beginning to be securitized. Indeed, at first glance, credit card loans have some characteristics that would appear to make securitization difficult. The loans are for relatively small amounts (usually less than $3000), for relatively short and unpredictable periods (typically repaid in from 1 to 12 months), and vary dramatically in credit loss experience (from 1 to 5 percent), even within an individual institution's portfolio. As a result, until recently the securitization of these loans mainly resulted from limited sales of credit card loan portfolios between banks since their credit departments possessed the necessary skills to appraise the credit quality of these portfolios.

However, in 1986, Salomon Brothers applied the emerging securitization technology to credit card loans in a manner that allowed these loans to be structured, credit enhanced, and sold to the broader investor community. Subsequent credit card loan-backed transactions underwritten by First Boston, Goldman Sachs, Morgan Guaranty, and Salomon Brothers evidence the potential for the further securitization of this asset class.

In this section, we describe the following credit card receivables transactions:

- Banc One (CARDS™)
- RepublicBank Delaware (Credit Card-Backed Notes)

- Bank of America (California Credit Card Trust 1987-A)
- Maryland National Bank Credit Card Loan Auction.[1]

BANC ONE CORPORATION CERTIFICATES FOR AMORTIZING REVOLVING DEBTS (CARDS™)

The first issue of a credit card receivables-backed security was the private placement of a $50 million CARDS issue in March 1986 by Salomon Brothers for Banc One (see Term Sheet, Figure 4.1). The CARDS issue represented an important landmark in the development of credit securitization. Prior to CARDS, proposals had been submitted to the federal banking regulators for a number of other transactions involving bank assets. However, other transactions had not met the regulators' standards for a sale of nonmortgage assets. A structure was developed for the CARDS that, for the first time, satisfied the standards of the banking regulators for a sale for regulatory accounting purposes (RAP). The structure, developed in the Banc One transaction, provided the basis for all future credit securitization of nonmortgage bank assets.

Banc One had been a particularly active originator of credit card assets. Banc One had experienced rapid growth of these credit card assets, and it was interested in credit securitization as a new source of funds since rapid asset growth was putting pressure on its traditional sources of funds.

Please note that the following description of the Banc One transaction is less complete than the subsequent descriptions of the RepublicBank Delaware and Bank of America credit card transactions. The Banc One transaction was a private placement, so we were not able to obtain the same level of information as for some other transactions.

Structure

The structure of this transaction is summarized in Figures 4.2 and 4.3, and explained below.

---

[1] The description of this transaction is a summary since it was a private transaction on which little information is available.

Issue	8.35% Certificates for Amortizing Revolving Debts (CARDS)
Parent/seller	Banc One Corporation
Offering date	March 31, 1986
Rating (Fitch)*	A
Principal amount	$50,000,000
Collateral	Credit card loans
Weighted average life (projected)	2.2 years
Yield to average life	8.35%
Payment frequency	Monthly
Spread to treasuries at offering	125 b.p.
Recourse (amount/provider)	Spread account
Managing underwriter	Salomon Brothers, Inc.

*Subsequent to issue.
Source: Salomon Brothers, Inc.

Figure 4.1. Banc One Corporation, Certificates for Amortizing Revolving Debts (CARDS).

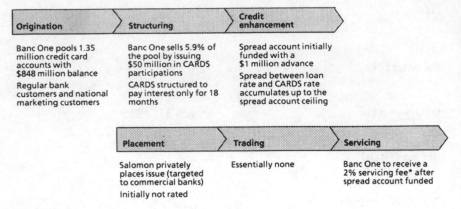

*Estimate.

Source: Salomon Brothers, Inc.

Figure 4.2.   Banc One—Certificates for Amortizing Revolving Debts (CARDS).

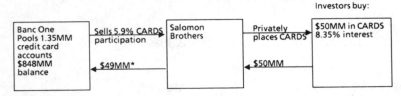

*Estimate.

Source: Salomon Brothers, Inc.

Figure 4.3.   Banc One—Certificates for Amortizing Revolving Debts (CARDS).

Origination.   Banc One determined that it wanted to sell approximately $50 million in credit card receivables. Recognizing that the credit quality of credit card loans can vary—and understanding that investors would want assurance of the quality of the assets being securitized—Banc One identified a static pool of 900 thousand credit card accounts with a total balance of $848 million, yielding 21.6 percent, and decided to sell a $50 million participation in that pool. This structure was designed to assure investors that they were receiving a representative sampling of the portfolio, rather than a substandard portion of it.

Structuring

1. No Special Purpose Vehicle. As discussed in Chapter 1, a major purpose of structured finance is to protect investors against the risk of the originator's bankruptcy. Banks, however, are not subject to the Bankruptcy Code. While a special purpose vehicle may assist a company subject to the Bankruptcy Code in structuring an asset-backed security, banks have more latitude to structure without a special purpose vehicle. In the CARDS transaction, Banc One chose not to establish a special purpose vehicle. Instead, Banc One simply offered investors participations in a pool of receivables in credit card accounts; investors purchased ownership of an undivided portion of the pool.

Since the CARDS transaction did not have a special purpose vehicle, it had a relatively simple structure. The CARDS participations were sold by Banc One to Salomon Brothers, which in turn offered the CARDS to investors.

2. Tax/Accounting Structure of the Transaction. As noted earlier, a primary goal of Banc One was to get the $50 million in credit card loans off its books for banking Regulatory Accounting Purposes (RAP), as well as for GAAP purposes. At the time of the CARDS issue, the federal banking regulators had determined that if there were any direct recourse back to an originating bank for credit losses, the assets would remain on the originating bank's books for regulatory accounting and capital adequacy purposes. As a result, the bank would have to hold capital against these assets. Since Banc One's purpose was to engage in a true sale that would remove the credit card loans from its books for regulatory purposes, Salomon Brothers and Banc One developed the spread account structure described next. By using this spread account, the CARDS transaction was accounted for as a sale that removed the loans from Banc One's books under RAP.

Salomon Brothers, with the assistance of Booth & Baron, its special bank regulatory counsel, designed a spread account to provide investors with protection against credit losses. The spread account was an escrow account available to protect CARDS investors. The spread account would receive the approximately

13.25 percent income spread between the 21.6 percent effective interest[2] rate actually paid by the credit card borrowers and the 8.35 percent interest rate paid to the CARDS holders. This spread account would be available to pay to investors to cover credit losses.

Although funds received in the spread account could be reported as income under GAAP, the regulators agreed that there should be a separate RAP rule under which funds in the spread account would not be reported as income until such funds were no longer available to cover defaults on the CARDS. As a result, recourse against the spread account was not viewed by the regulators as recourse against the bank, and the receivables underlying the CARDS were removed from the bank's balance sheet.

The CARDS transaction also was a sale of the credit card assets under GAAP since: (1) Banc One could not "call" back the receivables with the possible exception of a minor clean-up call; (2) the amount of Banc One's ultimate liability under the spread account could be reasonably estimated; and (3) investors could not "put" the CARDS™ back to Banc One.[3] Accordingly, Banc One was able to remove the $50 million in credit card assets and supporting liabilities from its balance sheet for financial reporting purposes.

For tax purposes, Banc One elected to treat the CARDS as debt of the bank. Thus the transaction was essentially viewed as a borrowing by the bank, rather than a sale, for tax purposes. Interest payments to the CARDS investors were to be fully tax-deductible by Banc One. Of course, ultimately the Internal Revenue Service and the federal courts are the final arbiters of tax treatment. As a result, the CARDS were structured to qualify for a fall-back tax treatment in the event they were not treated as debt of Banc One. In that event, the transaction was structured

---

[2] The effective interest rate represents the actual yield on the credit card portfolio after the nominal rate is reduced to take account of "convenience users" who completely pay their credit card bills without incurring finance charges.

[3] See Chapter 1 for a more detailed discussion of RAP and GAAP accounting.

to qualify for partnership tax treatment in which Banc One was in a position analogous to that of a general partner in the asset pool and the investors in a position analogous to that of limited partners. (See the California Credit Card Trust 1987-A for a more detailed description of this sort of tax structure.)

3. Payment Structure of CARDS. A significant hurdle to structuring the Banc One transaction was the relatively quick paydown rate on outstanding credit card loans. A typical credit loan frequently repays within an 8-month period. However, Banc One wanted to arrange an asset sale that would get the loans off its books for more than 8 months. Accordingly, Banc One and Salomon Brothers agreed to structure the transaction as the sale of $50 million principal participation in a pool of receivables in particular accounts, rather than a sale of individual loans.

As a result, the CARDS investors could purchase a $50 million share of the receivables in the overall 900 thousand credit card accounts throughout an 18-month revolving period. While individual loans to these accounts might repay in 8 months, borrowers would typically borrow new money from the accounts. During the revolving period, the CARDS investors would continue to own a $50 million participation in the overall pool whose size might vary from time to time. Also, during the revolving period, investors would receive monthly interest-only payments at the 8.35 percent annual rate (see Figure 4.4).

Principal would be reinvested in the pool by relending the principal to the same cardholders. After the 18-month period, the CARDS investors would receive their pro rata share of principal repayments on the portfolio. Because principal paydown rates are fast on credit card accounts, the expected average life of CARDS was only about 2.2 years. The CARDS mature when the outstanding CARDS principal declines to $2.5 million or after 5 years, whichever occurs earlier. At that time, the spread account is used to retire the issue.

4. Protection against Bankruptcy Risk. As noted previously, the CARDS transaction was structured without a special purpose

Payment stream

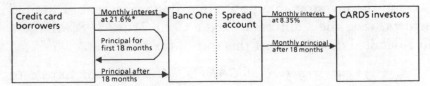

* Estimated effective rate (after convenience use).

Source: Salomon Brothers, Inc.

Figure 4.4.   Banc One—Certificates for Amortizing Revolving Debt (CARDS).

vehicle. While structures of bank transactions need not protect against bankruptcy risk by using a special purpose vehicle, the structures do need to assure investors of continued timely payments and perfected ownership of the receivables. Banc One filed the necessary filing statements under the Uniform Commercial Code and appropriately marked its computer general ledger account to reflect the CARDS investors' ownership of a portion of the accounts so that the insolvency of the bank would not impair timely payment of proceeds on the receivables to the investors.

Credit Enhancement.   The monies in the spread account were available to protect investors from credit losses on their CARDS investment. Protection against credit loss is especially important for credit card receivables-backed securities, since net charge-offs tend to be relatively high. Bank credit cards charge-off rates have averaged between approximately 2 to 4 percent in the last few years, and individual portfolios may experience substantially higher rates depending on credit underwriting standards.

Therefore, credit enhancement was particularly important for this first issue of a credit card receivables-backed security. One potential weakness of the spread account structure was that at the issuance of the CARDS, there would be little or no monies accumulated in the spread account, and hence little credit loss protection. Accordingly, Banc One advanced approximately \$1 million into the spread account. The spread account would repay that \$1 million loan to Banc One after sufficient monies had accumulated in the account. In any event, the $1 million loan would be repaid to Banc One prior to any repayment of the investors' principal. It should be noted that the size of the spread account was capped, and that any excess would be paid to Banc One. Also, after the retirement of the CARDS, the balance in the spread account would be paid to Banc One.

However, notwithstanding the innovative spread account structure, the credit enhancement structure of the CARDS transaction was not alone sufficient to obtain a very high investment grade rating by the rating agencies. The yield on the revolving credit card loans and, therefore the spread, might drop during the life of the issue, thereby leaving less protection for investors. Moreover, a high prepayment rate could shorten the life of the CARDS, thereby reducing the size of the spread. Therefore, additional third-party credit enhancement would be necessary to secure a very high rating. Banc One chose not to purchase any such additional third-party credit enhancement, and the issue was placed without being rated by Standard & Poor's or Moody's. In fact, the only rating the Banc One CARDS obtained was a single A Fitch rating that emerged after the CARDS had been issued.

Placement.   Salomon Brothers was the sole underwriter for CARDS, which Salomon privately placed. The small amount of information available suggests that this innovative, but not AAA or AA rated security, may not have been easy to place. Investors may be reluctant to accept securities backed by new types of assets, unless the issues are structured and credit-enhanced to very high levels.

Trading.   Apparently, there has been little or no market in or trading of the CARDS. Since the issue was small in size ($50 million) and privately placed, it was relatively illiquid.

Servicing.   Banc One remained the servicer for the entire $848 million pool of credit card loans, including the $50 million

CARDS participation. As servicer, Banc One collects the monthly payments on the loans, and makes monthly distributions to the CARDS investors. There is a 2-week interval between the end of the monthly collection period and the distribution date to investors in the Banc One CARDS issue similar to the convention that exists in the mortgage market. Banc One was entitled to an approximate 3.5 percent monthly servicing fee together with the spread account balance at the maturity of the issue. However, Banc One was not entitled to collect the 3.5 percent ongoing servicing fee until after the spread account reached its maximum designated size.

Impact of CARDS™

Banc One. Through the CARDS issue, Banc One was able to achieve an off-balance sheet financing of $50 million in credit card loans for approximately 2 years. Thus Banc One was able to: (1) remove the assets from its balance sheet and free up expensive regulatory capital; (2) somewhat reduce its large credit card asset portfolio; and (3) at the same time retain essentially all of the yield on the credit card receivables in the form of servicing fees.[4]

Salomon Brothers. Since CARDS was privately placed, the underwriting fees for the issue are not available. Given the small size of the issue, it is unlikely that the transaction was very profitable for Salomon Brothers. However, Salomon Brothers accomplished its primary goal of structuring the first issue in the potentially large market of credit card receivables-backed securities. Salomon developed the experience, expertise, and models necessary for further securitization of this asset class. In fact, in 1987 Salomon Brothers acted as lead manager for three large public issues of CARDS credit card-backed securities, totaling $1.2 billion.

---

[4] We have not calculated the all-in financing cost advantage to Banc One of the CARDS™ transaction for two reasons. First, due to the private nature of the transaction, we lack certain critical information for performing this calculation. Second, we have performed this calculation for the public credit card receivables-backed transactions of Bank of America and RepublicBank Delaware. We believe that the Bank of America transaction, in particular, demonstrates such a comparative financing cost calculation for credit card-backed transactions.

REPUBLICBANK DELAWARE 7.15 PERCENT CREDIT CARD-BACKED NOTES, SERIES A

After a structure for the securitization of credit card receivables had been pioneered in the CARDS™ transaction, the way was clear for the further securitization of these assets. Indeed, in January 1987, RepublicBank Delaware issued $200 million in such credit

Issue	Credit Card Backed Notes, Series A
Parent/seller	RepublicBank Delaware
Offering date	January 16, 1987
Rating (S&P)	AAA
Principal amount	$200,000,000
Collateral	Credit card receivables
Expected average life (years)	3.0
Yield (CBE)	7.24%
Payment frequency	Monthly
Spread to treasuries at offering	90 b.p.
Recourse (amount/provider)	Spread account
Credit enhancement	5% Letter of Credit/ Union Bank of Switzerland
Lead manager	Goldman, Sachs & Co.

Source: SEC Registration Statement; Goldman, Sachs & Co.

Figure 4.5.   RepublicBank Delaware, Credit Card Backed Notes, Series A.

card-backed notes. (See Figure 4.5, Term Sheet.) The RepublicBank Delaware issue represented a further refinement in credit card-backed notes since the notes were credit-enhanced to Standard & Poor's highest quality level—AAA.

In July 1986, the RepublicBank Corporation, a banking holding company, established RepublicBank Delaware as a wholly owned, Delaware-chartered, consumer credit bank subsidiary. As a consumer credit bank, RepublicBank Delaware could make loans to natural persons and accept certain large deposits. RepublicBank Delaware began its operations by acquiring approximately $256 million in credit card receivables together with the underlying accounts from RepublicBank Dallas, N.A., another wholly owned subsidiary of RepublicBank Corporation.

RepublicBank Delaware funded the purchase of those credit card receivables largely with approximately $220 million in jumbo certificates of deposit (CDs) payable to RepublicBank Dallas. The jumbo CDs were to mature on July 25, 1988, and had an interest rate of 150bp over the U.S. Treasury Note rate.

In the late summer of 1986, RepublicBank Delaware decided to engage in a public offering of credit card receivables-backed notes in order to refinance at a lower cost of funds than the 150bp above the Treasury Note rate that RepublicBank Delaware was required to pay on its outstanding CDs. RepublicBank Delaware and its financial adviser, Goldman, Sachs & Co., believed that it could obtain lower cost funds through a public offering and use these funds to retire the CDs. However, as described next, RepublicBank Delaware decided to structure the transaction as an asset-backed financing on its balance sheet, rather than a sale of the assets.

Structure

The structure of the financing is shown in Figure 4.6, and described next.

Origination. RepublicBank Delaware pledged essentially all of its outstanding VISA and MasterCard accounts with outstanding balances as security for the $200 million in credit card-backed notes. The pledged accounts were screened to ensure that they

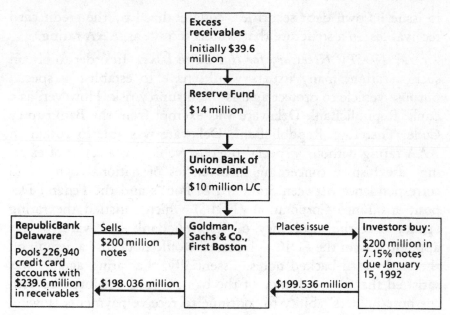

Source: Offering Documents; Goldman Sachs.

Figure 4.6. RepublicBank Delaware, Credit Card Backed Notes, Series A.

were not more than 34 days delinquent as of the January 6, 1987 cut-off date. The accounts held a total of $239,585,116 in receivables as of that cut-off date, with a weighted average annual interest rate of 16.85 percent. More than 99 percent of the receivables arose from credit card accounts assigned to RepublicBank Delaware by RepublicBank Dallas. Therefore, it is not surprising that more than 80 percent of the accounts had Texas billing addresses. The balance were new accounts originated by RepublicBank Delaware through associated banks and direct mailings.

Structuring

1. A Financing, Not a True Sale. As noted earlier, RepublicBank Delaware decided that it preferred to directly issue asset-backed debt rather than structure a true sale of the receivables. For a variety of reasons, RepublicBank Delaware decided that it preferred to keep the credit card assets on its books for regulatory accounting purposes. Thus RepublicBank Delaware simply sought to issue its own debt securities, collateralized by the credit card receivables, in a structure that would receive an AAA rating.

2. *No SPV Necessary for this Bank Issue.* In order to obtain such a rating, many issuers would have to establish a special purpose vehicle to protect against bankruptcy risk. However, as a bank, RepublicBank Delaware was exempt from the Bankruptcy Code. Therefore, RepublicBank Delaware was able to obtain an AAA rating without a special purpose vehicle as a result of existing case history concerning insolvencies of national banks and correspondence between Standard & Poor's and the Federal Deposit Insurance Corporation (FDIC) which satisfied the rating agency that the insolvency of RepublicBank Delaware, or the appointment of the FDIC as receiver, would not cause a default on the credit card-backed notes. Essentially, the rating agency was satisfied that an insolvency of the bank would not interfere with the note-holders' ability to continue to receive payments flowing from the credit card receivables.

3. *Revolving Period.* RepublicBank Delaware's credit card receivables repay principal at a rapid rate that typically would result in the repayment of principal in a 6- to 7-month period. If such principal payments were directly passed through to the investors, the investors would be completely paid off in that short period—a period much shorter than RepublicBank Delaware desired. To lengthen the life of the financing, a 32-month revolving period was structured into the transaction. During that revolving period, the investors would only receive interest payments. At the end of the revolving period, principal payments would be passed through to investors.

This revolving period also served a second function. Regulation D requires banks to reserve a certain portion of their deposits with the Federal Reserve System on an interest free basis. The Federal Reserve might view the $199.036 million that RepublicBank Delaware raised through this financing as reservable deposits. The present reserve rates are 12 percent on any deposit that a depositor can immediately withdraw on demand, 3 percent on any deposit that must be paid to a depositor within 7 days to 18 months, and 0 percent on any deposit that need not be repaid to a depositor for 18 months or more. A fixed 18-month revolving period during which no principal could be repaid could reduce the applicable reserve rate on this financing to the 0 percent level, thereby saving RepublicBank Delaware a substantial sum.

However, as discussed next, the revolving period for the RepublicBank Delaware Notes could be early terminated as a result of certain unlikely events. Consequently, RepublicBank Delaware may have established relatively small reserves calculated by applying the low percentage likelihood of early termination to the amount of principal that then would be repaid within 18 months at the applicable reserve rates.

4. *Payment Structure of the Notes.* As previously noted, purchasers of the notes would receive monthly interest-only payments at the annual rate of 7.15 percent during the revolving period. These interest payments would be payable on a distribution date on or about the fifteenth of each month. The corporate bond equivalent yield of this interest payment pattern was 7.24 percent. At the end of the revolving period, monthly principal payments would also commence on the distribution dates. At historical credit card loan payment rates, principal should be completely repaid in 6 to 7 months. RepublicBank Delaware had the right to completely pay off the notes after their outstanding principal amount declined to 10 percent of their original amount.

In order to obtain an AAA rating, certain standard payment pattern protections were built into the structure including provisions for on an early termination of the revolving period in the event of extraordinarily high charge-offs or in the event that the overall receivables pool size declined to an unhealthy level. Such events would terminate the revolving period and trigger principal repayments.

5. *Prepayment Risk.* Investors, of course, prefer not to be exposed to the prepayment risk that would result from an early termination of the revolving period. Such prepayment of principal could occur if the outstanding balances in the 226,940 pledged accounts ever fell below $200 million for a significant period. RepublicBank Delaware estimated that there would be some seasonal fluctuation in the account balances, but that such

fluctuations would be less than 20 percent. Accordingly, the bank over-collateralized the notes by pledging accounts containing $239,585,116 in receivables. In the event that the balance in the pledged accounts ever fell too low, RepublicBank Delaware agreed to pledge additional accounts, if available, in order to further protect against prepayment.

6. *Protection against Bankruptcy/Insolvency.* RepublicBank Delaware was exempt from the Bankruptcy Code and therefore able to obtain an AAA rating without using a special purpose vehicle to protect against the risk of delay in payment resulting from a bankruptcy filing. However, in order for the noteholders to be protected in the event of an insolvency, their security interest in the pledged credit card receivables had to be perfected by filing of appropriate financing statements under the Uniform Commercial Code.

7. *Accounting/Tax Structure of the Transaction.* The RepublicBank Delaware credit card-backed notes were structured to be debt securities of RepublicBank Delaware, that were simply secured by the credit card receivables. The federal banking regulators have declared that any form of recourse to a bank would cause a transaction to be viewed as a financing, rather than a sale, of receivables other than residential mortgage receivables. In this case, RepublicBank Delaware provided a form of recourse by over-collateralizing the notes since all $239,585,116 in pledged receivables were available to provide credit support for the $200 million in notes. Thus the credit card assets remained on the bank's books under RAP, and the bank had to continue to fully hold primary capital against those assets. Goldman, Sachs & Co. advised RepublicBank that the transaction could have easily been structured as a true sale of assets simply by relying on the spread account described in the next section on credit enhancement. However, RepublicBank preferred that the transaction be designed as a financing.

Since the credit card-backed notes were simply corporate debt securities of RepublicBank Delaware, they were treated as such for federal income tax purposes. Thus the interest payments to the noteholders were tax deductible from RepublicBank Delaware's income.

Credit Enhancement. The RepublicBank Delaware notes were rated AAA by Standard & Poor's as a result of three credit enhancement devices. First, a reserve fund (a form of the spread account described in the preceding Banc One transaction description) was established to provide credit support for the notes. The reserve fund was initially funded by the issuer with $2 million (1 percent of the principal amount of the issue). The reserve fund was designed to accumulate to a maximum amount of $14 million (7 percent of the principal). This reserve would accumulate as a result of the difference between the annual interest income of approximately 16.85 percent paid on the credit card loans and the 7.15 percent interest paid out on the $200 million in notes. The continuation of a substantial spread was protected by RepublicBank Delaware's agreement not to lower its annual interest rate on the loans below approximately 13 percent.

The second credit enhancement device was a $10 million L/C issued by Union Bank of Switzerland. This L/C could be drawn upon to cover interest and principal payments on the notes. The available amount under the L/C would be reduced by unreimbursed drawings upon it, but ample cash flow should be available to reimburse for any such drawings from the above reserve fund.

The third credit enhancement device was the initial over-collateralization resulting from the pledge of accounts containing $239,585,116 in receivables to collateralize $200 million in notes. This over-collateralization level, which initially was 20 percent, would change over the life of the issue due to seasonal variance in credit card account balances.

These credit enhancement devices were sufficient to obtain an AAA rating since the net loss experience of RepublicBank Delaware and RepublicBank Dallas (where most of the accounts originated) was under 3 percent annually. Since the reserve fund would contain $10 million to $14 million throughout most of the life of the issue and the L/C would provide an additional $10 million the noteholders would be well-protected with at least 10 percent to 12 percent loss coverage likely to be available at all times. Essentially, the large cash flow generated by the approximately 10 percent spread between the yield on the receivables and the yield to investors, together with the L/C from an AAA credit, enabled the issue to be AAA related. The provisions for trigger events to terminate the revolving period if necessary to protect credit quality also were important to the structuring of this credit.

Servicing.   RepublicBank Delaware remained the servicer for the pledged receivables and agreed not to charge any servicing fee with respect to the receivables. (However the bank, of course, would receive each month the entire substantial spread between the yield received on the credit card loans and the yield paid to noteholders, after the reserve fund was filled to the appropriate level.)

As servicer, RepublicBank Delaware established a servicing account for the pledged receivables. On a daily basis, RepublicBank Delaware would transfer receipts from the servicing account to a collection account established by the Bank of New York as trustee for the noteholders. In this manner, RepublicBank Delaware would transfer to the control of the trustee all monies necessary to make distributions to noteholders, fill the reserve fund, and reimburse Union Bank of Switzerland for any unreimbursed drawings on the letter of credit.

RepublicBank Delaware's responsibilities as servicer included the responsibility to make reasonable efforts to collect all payments due on the pledged receivables. In fulfilling this responsibility, RepublicBank Delaware subcontracted certain servicing functions. The Southwestern States Bankcard Association acted as a subservicer to provide data processing and billing and payment services, and RepublicBank Dallas was retained to perform special handling services on the accounts.

This servicing structure provided protection to the noteholders through the rapid transfer of their monies to an account controlled by the trustee and also allowed RepublicBank Delaware to subcontract servicing functions to take advantage of scale economies.

Benefits

RepublicBank Delaware.   Through the credit card-backed notes, RepublicBank Delaware achieved its primary goal of economically refinancing its credit card portfolio.

It was able to do so through this asset-backed financing at a time when the credit markets were not particularly receptive to the general debt of Texas institutions. By refinancing its credit card portfolio, RepublicBank Delaware was able to largely repay the $220 million in jumbo CDs payable to RepublicBank Dallas. This repayment allowed RepublicBank Dallas to source funds in an economical manner.

From the perspective of RepublicBank Delaware, we estimate that the credit card-backed notes allowed it to realize a substantial financing cost saving over the cost of the jumbo CDs payable to RepublicBank Dallas. The CDs were of 2-year maturity issued in July 1986 at a rate we estimate to have been about 8.11 percent. Therefore, the debt financing cost to RepublicBank Delaware of funding the credit card loans was still about 8.11 percent in January 1987 when the credit card-backed notes were issued. To this 8.11 percent cost of debt we add a 2.77 percent annual expected loss allowance on the credit card receivables to get an all-in annualized debt financing cost of 10.88 percent. (See Figure 4.7.)

Essentially, RepublicBank Delaware issued the credit card-backed notes in order to largely retire the outstanding jumbo CDs. The all-in annualized cost of the credit card-backed notes was about 10.32 percent. The first element of this 10.32 percent total

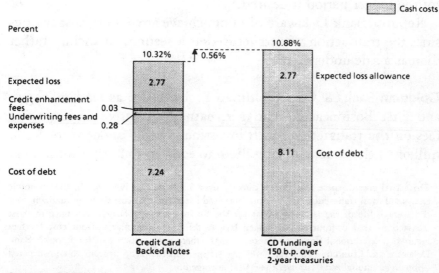

Source: McKinsey analysis.

Figure 4.7. RepublicBank Delaware, Credit Card Backed Notes, Series A comparative annualized pretax debt financing costs.

cost is the 7.24 percent (CBE) interest cost of the notes. The second cost element is the $1 million underwriting fees plus the $500 thousand other expenses of the issue which roughly totals to 28bp annually when spread over the full $200 million issue.[5] The third element of cost is the credit enhancement fee which we estimate at about 62.5bp annually on the 5 percent of the issue that was guaranteed, which amounts to about 3bp annually over the full issue amount. Finally, we add the 2.77 percent expected loan loss to come to a total 10.32 percent all-in debt financing cost.[6]

In summary, we estimate that, as shown in Figure 4.7, RepublicBank Delaware reduced its cost of debt by about 56bp on an annual pre-tax basis by issuing the credit card-backed notes to refinance its CDs. Of course, it should be noted that RepublicBank Delaware chose to structure the notes so that their average life was approximately 3 years, approximately running to January 1990. The CDs payable to RepublicBank Dallas would have matured on July 25, 1988. RepublicBank Delaware apparently chose to structure the notes to run longer than the CDs because it correctly anticipated a rise in interest rates. Thus the notes allowed RepublicBank Delaware to lock in a relatively lower cost of funds for the longer period it desired.

RepublicBank Delaware did not achieve any equity cost savings since the transaction was structured as a secured financing, rather than as a sale under RAP.

Goldman Sachs & Co.   Goldman Sachs & Co. as lead manager, and First Boston as co-manager, earned attractive underwriting fees on the transaction. Each investment bank underwrote $100 million of the issue, allowing them to earn up to $500 thousand in

---

[5] The actual cost of these fees spread directly over $200 million is 69bp. In the economic analysis of most transactions we have not bothered to step up that cost when annualizing over the average life of the issue to adjust for the upfront timing of such fees since in most transactions that upfront cost has been largely offset by a similar upfront cost for fees incurred in traditional financing. Here, though, there are no such fees for RepublicBank Delaware's CD funding. Therefore, we have stepped up the 69bp upfront to an estimated 28bp on an annualized basis over the 3 year average life.

[6] Please note that we have not considered equity costs in the comparative cost analysis of the credit card-backed notes with the CDs since in both cases the credit card assets remained on RepublicBank Delaware's balance sheet and therefore had to be fully supported with primary capital at a level above the minimum 5.5 percent level set by the banking regulators.

underwriting fees.[7] Equally importantly, the investment banks gained important leadership recognition for bringing to market the first public issue of credit card receivables-backed notes.

Union Bank of Switzerland. As the third-party credit enhancer, Union Bank of Switzerland (UBS) stands to earn approximately $187.5 thousand in fee income over the life of the transaction (62.5bp fee times the $10 million L/C times 3 years). This fee income comes to UBS in a transaction with extremely low credit risk because of the high cash flow through the reserve fund.

Investors. Investors, too, benefited from this transaction. They were able to purchase AAA rated, approximately 3-year average life notes at a 90bp spread to treasuries. Moreover, there was very little prepayment risk to these investors because of the over-collateralized pool and the quick paydown of principal after the revolving period.

Afterword. In early 1988, First RepublicBank experienced severe credit difficulties that ultimately required assistance from the Federal Deposit Insurance Corporation. As a result, as of March 31, 1988, debentures of First RepublicBank Corp. were trading at only 44 cents on the dollar as investors worried that they might receive less than full repayment of their principal. However, the AAA rating of the RepublicBank Delaware Credit Card-Backed Notes remained in place notwithstanding the deterioration of First RepublicBank's general credit situation. Moreover, the Credit Card-Backed Notes traded as of March 31, 1988 at about 98 1/4—a spread to treasuries of only about 85 bp. While some other credit card offerings traded as tight as 70 bp over treasuries, the fundamental point is that the investor market accepted the continuing high credit quality that resulted from the structuring of the Credit Card-Backed Notes.

CALIFORNIA CREDIT CARD TRUST 1987-A

In late 1986, Bank of America decided that it would be advantageous to shrink its balance sheet. Bank of America had recently

---

[7] The investment banks would earn 50bp on the notes they placed directly with institutional and retail purchasers, and 20bp on notes sold to securities dealers for resale.

experienced some substantial write-offs arising out of its loan portfolio, and the bank decided that it could most efficiently meet its regulatory capital requirements by reducing the assets on its balance sheet and thereby improving its capital/assets ratio. Accordingly, the bank decided to engage in a $400 million structured sale of its credit card receivables.

From a structural perspective, Bank of America succeeded in combining the best elements of the earlier Banc One and RepublicBank credit card receivables transactions. As in the.Banc One transaction, the Bank of America transaction (California Credit Card Trust) was designed as a true sale of the credit card assets so that the banking regulators would not require expensive capital to continue to be held to support the assets. As in the RepublicBank transaction, California Credit Card Trust was structured and credit-enhanced in a manner that allowed the issue to attain the highest possible AAA/Aaa ratings issued by the rating agencies (see Figure 4.8, Term Sheet).

Structure

The structure of the Bank of America transaction is shown in Figure 4.9, and described next.

Origination. Bank of America conveyed 836,659 "Classic VISA" credit card accounts to the California Credit Card Trust. These accounts contained $655,097,130 of principal receivables and $7,533,581 of finance charge receivables. According to the terms of the pooling and servicing agreement between Bank of America and the Trustee (Manufacturers Hanover Trust Company of California), each of the accounts conveyed to the Trust must have been in existence for at least 24 months and must not be 30 or more days delinquent. The accounts were originated through the bank's branches, retail outlets, and direct mailings. Substantially all of the cardholders had California billing addresses.

Structuring

1. Type/Creation of Special Purpose Vehicle. As noted earlier, Bank of America established a trust as the special purpose

Issue	6.9% Asset-Backed Certificates
Parent/seller	Bank of America
Offering date	February 25, 1987
Rating (S&P, Moody's)	AAA/Aaa
Principal amount	$400,000,000
Collateral	Credit card receivables
Expected average life (years)	1.9
Yield to average life (CBE)	6.95%
Payment frequency	Monthly
Spread to treasuries at offering	65 b.p.
Recourse (amount/provider)	Spread account
Credit enhancement	15% Letter of Credit/ Union Bank of Switzerland
Lead manager	The First Boston Corporation

Source: SEC Registration Statement; McKinsey analysis.

Figure 4.8. California Credit Card Trust 1987-A.

vehicle for this transaction. Bank of America created the trust by entering into a pooling and servicing agreement with the designated trustee, Manufacturers Hanover. Bank of America then conveyed the credit card accounts to the Trust. The Trust initially consisted of approximately $662 million of receivables arising under 836,659 accounts. The trust then sold $400 million in 6.9

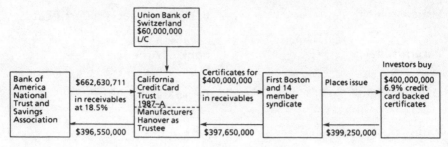

Source: SEC Registration Statement; Bank of America.

Figure 4.9.   California Credit Card Trust 1987-A, 6.90% Asset-Backed Certificates.

percent Asset-Backed Certificates, each of which represented a fractional undivided interest in $400 million of trust principal. Bank of America received the net proceeds of this sale of $400 million in receivables, together with a certificate of ownership of the excess receivables in the trust above the $400 million sold to investors. The amount of such excess principal receivables initially retained by Bank of America was approximately $255 million.

2. The Revolving Period.   Cardholders typically repay the outstanding balances in their accounts in a relatively rapid manner— usually in a little over a year in Bank of America's experience. If such principal payments were directly passed through to the investors, the investors would be completely paid off in that period— a period shorter than Bank of America desired. To lengthen the period, an 18-month revolving period was structured into the transaction. During that revolving period, the investors would only receive interest payments (see Figure 4.10). At the end of the revolving period, principal payments would be passed through to the investors.

The decision to set an 18-month revolving period was also influenced by the requirements of the Federal Reserve System. Regulation D requires banks to place a certain portion of their deposits with the Federal Reserve System on an interest-free basis. These regulatory reserves are obviously somewhat costly to banks since the banks would otherwise be earning income on the amounts reserved. The current reserve rates are 12 percent on any

Payment stream

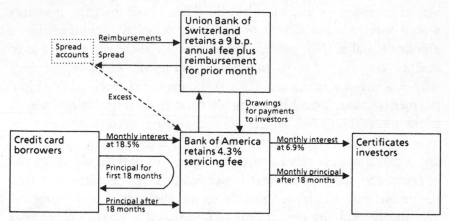

Source: SEC Registration Statement; Bank of America; McKinsey analysis.

Figure 4.10.   California Credit Card Trust 1987-A, 6.90% Asset-Backed Certificates.

deposit that a depositor can immediately withdraw on demand, 3 percent on any deposit that must be paid to a depositor within 7 days to 18 months, and 0 percent on any deposit that need not be repaid to a depositor for 18 months or more. It is possible that the Federal Reserve would view the proceeds from the sale of certificates as reservable deposits. In that event, the revolving period would substantially reduce the amount reserved. The applicable reserve rate could be as low as 0 percent since the 18-month revolving period, if strictly adhered to, would mean that depositors (the investors) could not receive their deposits back for 18 months.[8]

3. Payment Structure of the Notes. Purchasers of the certificates would receive monthly interest-only payments at the annual rate of 6.9 percent during the 18-month revolving period. These interest payments are to be paid on a distribution date which would usually be the fifteenth day of the month following the month in which the receivables were collected. The corporate bond equivalent yield of this interest payment pattern was 6.95 percent. At

---

[8] Alternatively, if the 18-month revolving period could be shortened as a result of some extraordinary event, Bank of America might be able to reserve a relatively small amount.

the end of the revolving period, monthly principal payments would also commence on the distribution dates. Each month, investors would receive a proportion of collected principal payments in an amount equal to their percentage ownership of the receivables as of the last day of the revolving period. Thus principal repayments would occur at a faster rate than if the investors received principal payments at a declining rate in proportion to their declining balance of the receivables pool. At the point that the investors' share of the overall pool declines to $20 million (5 percent of the initial balance), Bank of America becomes obligated to make a clean-up call to completely pay-off the certificate-holders. It was estimated that the investors would be completely repaid their investment after the 18-month revolving period plus an additional 5.5 to 6.5 months of principal payments.

4. Prepayment Risk. Investors, of course, prefer not to be exposed to substantial prepayment risk. Prepayment of the investors' principal could occur if the outstanding balance of the receivables in the Trust ever fell below $400 million during the revolving period. Bank of America estimated that in order to protect $400 million in credit card balances against seasonal variance (e.g., the balances are relatively high at the time of this issue just after Christmas), it needed to structure at least a 10 to 15 percent excess cushion into the pool of accounts. In fact, Bank of America more than amply protected against this variance by conveying a pool of principal receivables totalling $662,630,711 in receivables. Thus even if the new borrowings by credit card holders during the revolving period were less than their principal repayments, the overall pool of accounts was sufficiently large to protect against any foreseeable prepayment risk.[9] Also, in order to further guard against any such substantial diminishment of the receivables held by the trust, Bank of America retained the right to convey additional Classic VISA accounts to the trust.

---

[9] This $662 million pool size greatly exceeds the amount of cushion that Bank of America decided it needed to protect against net repayments. In part, this extra large pool size resulted from the tax-related need discussed in the next section to assure that the pool size did not fall below $500 million. In the unlikely event that repayments so far exceeded new borrowings by the credit card holders so as to drive the pool below $500 million, the revolving period could be terminated, and payments of principal to investors could begin.

5. *Protection against Insolvency of Bank of America.* As a bank, Bank of America was exempt from the bankruptcy code and thus would not need to use a special purpose vehicle to protect against the risk of bankruptcy. Nonetheless, perhaps to afford investors a clear-cut separation from Bank of America in the event of its insolvency, the Trust was created as a special purpose vehicle to hold the credit card accounts. In order to protect the certificate holders in the event of an insolvency, appropriate financing statements had to be filed under the Uniform Commercial Code (UCC) in order to perfect the Trust's claim to the receivables. Also, Bank of America's computer files were marked to indicate that the receivables had been conveyed to the Trust, and the Trustee received a record identifying the accounts and receivables. The perfection of this claim protects the Trust's and the certificate-holders' claim to the receivables in the event of an insolvency of Bank of America.

6. *Accounting/Tax Structure of the Transaction.* The California Credit Card Trust was structured in a manner that permitted the $400 million in credit card assets sold to investors to be removed from Bank of America's balance sheet for regulatory accounting purposes. Consequently, the Bank was relieved of the obligation to hold expensive primary capital against those assets.[10] Bank of America achieved such off-balance sheet treatment by setting up a structure in which there was no recourse back to Bank of America. Credit enhancement was exclusively provided by a spread account and a third-party credit enhancer. This structure satisfied the banking regulators' position that "true-sale" treatment under RAP would be blocked by any recourse back to an originating bank. (See Chapter 1 for a more detailed explanation of regulatory accounting.)

The sale of the credit card receivables also qualified as a true sale under GAAP since the three requirements of FAS Statement #77 were satisfied as: (1) Bank of America could reasonably

[10] The federal banking regulators require a minimum of 5.5 percent primary capital to be held against bank assets. In practice, even more capital must be held in order for a bank to escape close regulatory oversight. For example, Bank of America's target ratio was approximately 7 percent capital to assets. Primary capital consists of equity, reserves, preferred stock, and certain other items.

estimate its losses on the spread account; (2) the certificate holders could not "put" the certificates back to the bank; and, (3) the Bank of America could not "call" the certificates except for a small clean-up call. (See Chapter 1 for a more detailed explanation of GAAP accounting.)

For tax purposes, Bank of America obtained an opinion from its tax counsel, Orrick, Herrington, & Sutcliffe, that the certificates should be treated as corporate debt of the bank. The opinion letter stated that while the transaction was structured in a manner that resulted in a true sale of the assets under both RAP and GAAP; nonetheless, from a tax perspective the transaction should be viewed as a borrowing by the bank secured by the receivables. The opinion letter stated that the economic substance of the transaction should govern its tax classification. Accordingly, Orrick, Herrington & Sutcliffe argued that the transaction did not transfer risk of loss from the bank to the certificate holders since the notes were highly credit-enhanced. Therefore, transaction should be viewed as a borrowing by the bank, rather than a sale, for tax purposes. The certificates should be treated as debt obligations of the bank, and interest payments to the certificate-holders should be fully tax-deductible by the Bank.

In the event that the certificates were not treated as debt for tax purposes, then the transaction was structured in a manner that Bank of America anticipated would cause the Trust to be treated as a partnership for tax purposes so that there would be no income tax payable at the Trust level.[11] In order to qualify for partnership tax treatment, the transaction was structured so that Bank of America would be in a position analogous to that of a general partner, and the noteholders would be in a position analogous to that of limited partners. As discussed in Chapter 1, partnerships are not taxable at the partnership level. However, in order to preserve this option of partnership tax treatment, Bank of America, as general partner,

[11] As noted in Chapter 1, an unincorporated business organization must lack at least two of the following four corporate characteristics in order to qualify for partnership tax treatment: continuity of life, centralization of management, limited liability, and free transferability of interests. Orrick, Herrington & Sutcliffe opined that the Trust lacked at least three of these characteristics: continuity of life, centralized management, and free transferability of interests (since Bank of America could not transfer its substantial interest). The law firm's opinion also suggested that the Trust might also lack the fourth characteristic of limited liability.

had to have a significant ownership interest in the Trust. Bank of America's tax attorneys advised that a minimum of 20 percent of the Trust should be owned by Bank of America. As a result, the permissible minimum size of the receivables in the trust initially was $500 million for tax reasons so that $400 million could be sold to investors. Therefore, the relatively large size of the $655,097,130 receivables pool resulted from a combination of tax reasons and a desire to protect noteholders against prepayment risk.

Credit Enhancement. The 6.9 percent Asset-Backed Certificates were rated AAA/Aaa by Standard & Poor's and Moody's respectively, due to their extremely strong capacity to repay principal and interest in a timely fashion. This capacity results from the nature of the assets and the credit enhancement supporting the assets.

As a preliminary matter, it should be noted that the credit card receivables were actually yielding approximately 18.5 percent on an annual basis from the monthly finance charges and the annual membership fees.[12] Thus after deducting the monthly servicing fee of 4.3 percent, approximately 14 percent in income on the receivables was actually available to cover the 6.9 percent certificate yield to investors. While credit card assets typically do generate such high yields, they also typically experience substantial credit losses. California Credit Card Trust utilized third-party credit support to guard investors against losses.

Union Bank of Switzerland provided a $60 million letter of credit (15 percent of the investor's principal) to provide for timely interest and principal payments to investors. Whenever credit losses or late payments caused the collections on the receivables to be insufficient to cover payments due to certificate-holders, the L/C would be drawn upon to fund the necessary payments. To the extent that the L/C was drawn upon, it could be replenished for credit support purposes from future cash flow into the previously described spread account.

---

[12] The actual interest rate paid on most accounts was approximately 19.8 percent and the bank also received additional annual membership fees. However, this yield is reduced to an 18.5 percent effective rate by "convenience use" by cardholders who fully pay their balances each month before incurring any finance charges.

The spread account was initially funded by a $4 million advance from Bank of America. Thereafter, the spread generated each month from the 18.5 percent annual income on the receivables, minus the 6.9 percent annual interest on the certificates, minus the 4.3 percent annual servicing fee, minus the 9bp annual L/C fee, was available to reimburse UBS for the prior month's drawings on the L/C. The excess would then be paid into the spread account. If this monthly cash flow was insufficient to reimburse UBS for the prior month's drawings on the L/C, then UBS would reimburse itself from the accumulated reserve in the spread account. The spread account was capped at $16 million—any excess accumulation over $16 million could be paid to Bank of America.

Thus the California Credit Card Trust issue was essentially structured to provide $60 million of credit support through the L/C supplied by a AAA/Aaa-rated bank. Moreover, this $60 million could provide more than $60 million of coverage since future cash flows could replenish the L/C during the life of the transaction for credit support purposes. This credit enhancement through the L/C was sufficient to obtain an AAA/Aaa rating since it provided credit support coverage of any foreseeable credit losses. The annual actual gross credit loss experience on the relevant overall Bank of America VISA portfolio had only been:

1986	1985	1984	1983
2.46%	2.31%	2.19%	2.76%

Moreover, the particular accounts actually in the Trust had been selected in a manner that should produce credit quality better than the above loss experience on the overall portfolio. The receivables in the Trust came from accounts that were all seasoned accounts (in existence 2 years or more) with relatively good payment records (none were 30 or more days delinquent). Thus the continuing $60 million (15 percent) credit support for the certificates would more than amply cover any reasonably expected credit losses over the 1.8 year average life of the certificates.[13]

---

[13] The total expected loss would have been less than 4.5 percent over the life of the issue.

Two further precautions were taken in connection with arranging the credit enhancement for the certificates. First, Bank of America agreed not to lower the finance charge on the receivables below a certain level for 6 months, and thereafter only to lower it if the bank lowered its finance charge on its overall VISA portfolio. Second, any reduction of the finance charge below a certain level would be defined by the prospectus as a pay-out event triggering principal repayments to the investors. Therefore, investors were assured of a large L/C and a floor rate on the receivables that would essentially terminate the issue in order to protect against the possibility of any default on regularly due payments.

Placing. The First Boston Corporation was the lead manager for the issue which was underwritten by a syndicate of 15 investment banks (see Figure 4.11). As lead manager, First Boston actually underwrote 46 percent of the $400 million in certificates. The underwriting discount for the issue was 0.40 percent.

Trading. First Boston announced in the prospectus that, at least initially, it intended to make a market in the certificates.

Servicing. Bank of America remains the servicer of the credit card receivables, for which it receives a 4.3 percent servicing fee per annum, calculated and paid monthly on the outstanding receivables principal. As servicer, Bank of America receives all payments of principal and interest by cardholders on behalf of the Trust. The certificate-holders' proportion of such payments are then separated from the bank's proportion of the receivables pool. The bank's proportion is then directly paid over to the bank. During the revolving period, the investors' proportion of principal payments is reinvested in card receivables. The investors' share of finance payments is deposited into a finance charge account. On or about the fourteenth day of each month, the Trustee withdraws all finance charge receivables collected in the previous month. The Trustee then transfers the amount necessary to pay monthly certificate interest (to the bank as paying agent) for distribution to the certificate-holders on the following day. The Trustee also pays the monthly letter of credit fee and servicing fee, and then pays the

Underwriting syndicate

Underwriters	Aggregate principal amount of certificates to be purchased
The First Boston Corporation	$184,000,000
Bear, Stearns & Co., Inc.	14,000,000
Donaldson, Lufkin & Jenrette Securities Corporation	14,000,000
Drexel Burnham Lambert, Inc.	14,000,000
E.F. Hutton & Co., Inc.	14,000,000
Merrill Lynch, Pierce, Fenner & Smith, Inc.	18,000,000
Morgan Stanley & Co., Inc.	18,000,000
Nomura Securities International, Inc.	14,000,000
Paine Webber, Inc.	18,000,000
Prudential-Bache Securities, Inc.	18,000,000
L.F. Rothschild, Unterberg, Towbin, Inc.	18,000,000
Salomon Brothers, Inc.	18,000,000
Smith Barney, Harris Upham & Co., Inc.	14,000,000
UBS Securities, Inc.	14,000,000
Dean Witter Reynolds, Inc.	14,000,000
Total	**$400,000,000**

Source: SEC Registration Statement.

Figure 4.11. California Credit Card Trust 1987-A, 6.9% Asset-Backed Certificates.

remaining balance to Union Bank of Switzerland to be held in accordance with letter of credit arrangements. After the revolving period, monthly principal payments on the investor portion are paid on or about the fifteenth day of the following month in a similar manner.

Benefits

Bank of America. Through the California Credit Card Trust transaction, Bank of America achieved its primary goal of obtaining off-balance sheet regulatory treatment for its sale of $400 million in credit card assets. As a result, Bank of America was no longer required to hold expensive primary capital against these assets. The bank thus improved its overall primary capital/assets ratio without needing to resort to the equity markets to raise expensive new capital.

The economic benefits to the bank are graphically illustrated in the accompanying Figure 4.12. This exhibit represents our estimate of the all-in cost savings of financing the credit card receivables through the Asset-Backed Certificates, rather than traditionally funding the receivables for the same period on Bank of America's balance sheet.

The first column in Figure 4.12 illustrates the cost to Bank of America of the Asset-Backed Certificates. The 6.9 percent certificates were sold at 99.8125 percent, and after an adjustment to reflect payment timing differences, this payment rate amounts to a 6.95 percent corporate bond equivalent yield to investors.[14] The next element of cost, 38bp in underwriting fees and expenses—consists of the $1.6 million in underwriting fees together with the

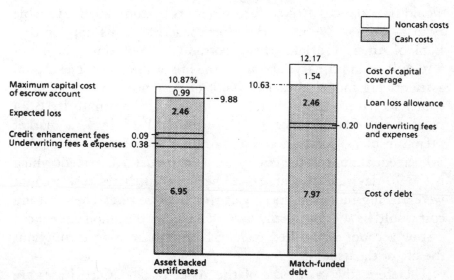

Source: Bank of America; McKinsey analysis.

Figure 4.12. California Credit Card Trust 1987-A comparative annualized pretax financing costs (percent).

[14] This 6.95 percent CBE rate was provided by First Boston.

$1.1 million in other issuance expenses associated with the certificates, stated as a proportion of the certificate principal amount. This cost has been annualized over the 1.8 year expected average life of the issue. The credit enhancement fee has been estimated to be ⁵⁄₈ percent annually on the letter of credit balance, which approximately equals 9bp over the entire $400 million issue. To this amount, we add the annual expected credit loss on the receivables of 2.4 percent, which Bank of America will incur as a result of the spread account. Thus the annualized cash costs of the certificate financing total to 9.88 percent.

However, we believe that the all-in financing costs of the certificates could require consideration of an additional non-cash cost. Money that is in the spread account cannot be taken into Bank of Americas' income for RAP purposes until after the certificate-holders are completely repaid in approximately 24 months. Assuming Bank of America had to establish a spread account to serve as first loss insurance in the amount of $16 million, Bank of America would have essentially lost the use of those funds that would have directly flowed through to its bottom line of available primary capital. We make the most conservative assumption that Bank of America suffered the opportunity cost of losing the use of $16 million in primary capital for the life of the issue. The capital asset pricing model estimates Bank of America's pre-tax cost of equity to have been 30 percent using a matched-maturity 6.24 percent risk-free rate, Bank of America's 1.33 beta, a market premium of 7.5 percent, and a tax rate of 46 percent. From that 30 percent annual cost of equity we then deduct 5.2 percent which is the 90-day risk-free rate since the funds in the escrow account were earning money essentially at the risk-free rate. The resulting cost would be 99bp annually over the full $400 million issue if the escrow account were filled to its $16 million ceiling throughout the life of the issue.[15]

Therefore, the cash costs of the Asset-Backed Certificates are estimated to be 9.88 percent, and the all-in costs including the equity cost of the escrow account, to be at most 10.87 percent.

---

[15] Of course, the actual cost would be somewhat less than this since it would be several months before the escrow account filled.

In contrast, the cash costs to Bank of America of financing $400 million in assets on its balance sheet for the same period are estimated to be 10.63 percent, and the all-in costs to be 12.17 percent, calculated as follows. We estimate that a 1.8-year, straight-debt financing would have cost Bank of America, a BBB credit, 7.97 percent, and we estimate the annualized underwriting fees and other expenses to be 0.20 percent. In addition, Bank of America would have also incurred a loan loss expense of about 2.46 percent on the receivables. Thus the cash cost of financing $400 million would have been 10.63 percent, if it had been financed exclusively with debt. However, as noted earlier, a bank is required by the banking regulators essentially to fund a proportion of assets with more expensive equity capital. The current absolute regulatory minimum is 5.5 percent, but Bank of Americas's target rate was about 7 percent. Pursuant to the previously described capital asset pricing model, this equity cost 30 percent. Therefore, the additional cost of capital coverage is about 1.54 percent to allow for this equity support. The all-in financing cost to Bank of America then amounts to 12.17 percent.

In summary, Bank of America realized significant savings as a result of its California Credit Card Trust transaction. These savings resulted in part from the equity cost savings of structuring this off-balance sheet financing. These savings also resulted from being able to access funds through the certificates at a AAA/Aaa rating, rather than at Bank of America's BBB rating. The savings developed through this rating difference substantially exceeded the structuring and credit-enhancement costs of the certificates.

First Boston.   First Boston and the 14-member underwriting syndicate earned up to $1.6 million in fee income from the 40bp underwriting discount. As lead manager, First Boston actually underwrote 46 percent of the total issue. Perhaps more importantly, by bringing to market the first public issue of bank-originated credit card receivables in a manner that qualified as a sale under RAP, First Boston gained important recognition that could generate substantial new business.

Union Bank of Switzerland. As the third-party credit enhancer, UBS charged approximately $5/8$ percent annually on its $60 million L/C. As a result, UBS stands to earn about $750 thousand in fees over the approximate 2-year life of the transaction. This fee income is significant since UBS is virtually totally protected against credit loss by the overall design of the transaction and the spread account.

Investors. Investors, too, benefited from the California Credit Card Trust transaction. They were able to purchase AAA/Aaa debt securities of a 1.8 year weighted average life at a 65bp spread to Treasuries.

MARYLAND NATIONAL BANK
CREDIT CARD RECEIVABLES SALE

In late 1986, Maryland National Bank engaged in a private sale of credit card receivables via Morgan Guaranty Trust Co. of New York using the spread account structure (described earlier in this chapter). Since little information is available on this private placement and since we have previously described other credit card transactions, this transaction description will be abbreviated. Nonetheless, we thought it important to include this summary description to indicate that a commercial bank, like Morgan Guaranty, can actively compete in securitization across asset classes. Further, this sale of credit card receivables is particularly interesting in that the receivables were sold on a floating rate basis.

Structure

Maryland National Bank had a $1.8 billion portfolio of credit card receivables. The receivables were of exceptionally high quality since Maryland National Bank's credit card losses averaged 1.15 percent in 1985, less than half the national average for MasterCard and VISA issuers. Maryland National Bank decided to sell $175 million of its MasterCard and VISA receivables in a manner that would enable the bank to secure medium term, floating rate funding that qualified as a true sale for both GAAP and regulatory accounting purposes.

Accordingly, Morgan Guaranty arranged to purchase and sub-participate the $175 million in receivables. This $175 million represented a percentage interest in a larger credit card receivables pool that was large enough to protect against early repayments of principal. Purchasers of the receivables would receive monthly interest payments during a 24-month revolving period, and then monthly principal payments. The weighted average life of the issue was expected to be 31 months, and the final maturity 45 months.

Participations were structured so that potential purchasers would receive a fixed spread above the 1-month LIBOR rate, and this LIBOR interest rate would be repriced monthly. Maryland National Bank's maximum funding cost was established on the loans by Morgan Guaranty's commitment to purchase the entire issue for a certain price (par).

Credit enhancement to protect investors against credit losses and late payments was provided through a spread account. The spread account was built up on a monthly basis from the difference between the approximately 17 percent effective annual interest rate on the credit cards and the floating interest rate on the sold loans, after a servicing fee was deducted.

The purchase and placement of Maryland National's credit card loans brought substantial benefits to all participants. Maryland National was able by the loan sale to shift the funding of these loans off its balance sheet, and thereby experience significant equity cost savings. Morgan Guaranty received an attractive fee for structuring the transaction, and was left with an attractive asset for its retained share of the transaction. Finally, the investors who purchased the loans (largely foreign banks) received high quality assets at a fixed spread above their basic LIBOR funding rate.

5
Lease Receivables

Lease receivables is a broad category that includes the contractual payment streams involved in any sort of lease arrangement. These receivables include computer leases, auto leases, airplane leases, equipment leases, and many other types of leased assets. Many lease receivables can be easily securitized, since they have stable payment flows of several years maturity, reasonably valuable collateral consisting of the leased equipment, and lessees who may well be investment-grade credits.

Computer lease receivables were the first to be securitized through publicly issued securities. Sperry Corporation originated the first such issue in March 1985, and later it (and its successor Unisys) followed with further issues in September 1985 and December 1986. Also in December 1986, Goldome Savings Bank originated a public issue of computer and telecommunications lease-backed notes. And, in 1987, Volkswagon auto lease receivables were securitized.

In this chapter, we will analyze the first public lease receivables transaction—Sperry Lease Finance Corporation, Series A.

SPERRY LEASE FINANCE CORPORATION, SERIES A

Sperry Corporation was one of the nation's best known computer companies.[1] The heart of its business was the production and marketing of electronic data processing systems, equipment, software, and services. While Sperry directly sold these products to customers, it also financed customer leases of computer equipment. However, unlike some other manufacturing companies, Sperry never established a finance company subsidiary to finance such leases. As a result, financing for customer leases was directly held on Sperry's balance sheet.

In 1984, Sperry made a corporate decision to focus its efforts and balance sheet capital on manufacturing and sales. Sperry decided that it did not want to continue to operate both a computer company and a finance company through its balance sheet. The computer business and the lease finance business required very different capital structures—the former operating at very low financial leverage ratios and the latter at much higher leverage. Accordingly, Sperry decided on a large sale of its computer leases which would: (1) eliminate this lease financing from its balance sheet, (2) eliminate interest rate risk on financing the leases, and (3) open up a new capital markets channel for the corporation at a credit level higher than Sperry's A/BBB+ rating (Moody's/Standard & Poor's).

Having reached this decision, Sperry considered the comparative advantages of a public or private sale, and ultimately decided that it would achieve more economic financing in the public market for any issue of over $100 million. Accordingly, Sperry decided to go to the public market for the large issue size it contemplated. It engaged First Boston to design and bring to market in March 1985 the first public structured issue of non-mortgage, asset-backed securities. (See Term Sheet, Figure 5.1.) The process of structuring and bringing the issue to market took approximately a year.

---

[1] Sperry Corporation merged with Burroughs Corporation in November 1986 to form Unisys.

Issue	11% Lease-Backed notes, Series A
Parent/seller	Sperry Corporation
Offering date	March 7, 1985
Rating (S&P,)	AAA
Principal amount	$192,455,000
Collateral	Computer leases
Maturity (years)	6
Average life (years)	2.07
Yield to average life (CBE)	11.24%
Payment frequency	Monthly
Spread to treasuries at offering	49 b.p.
Recourse (amount/provider)	5% Sperry Corporation, 15% Sperry Lease Finance Corporation
Credit enhancement (type/provider)	5% and 15% Letters of Credit/ Union Bank of Switzerland
Managing underwriter	The First Boston Corporation

Source: SEC Registration Statement.

Figure 5.1. Sperry Lease Finance Corporation.

Structure

Origination.   Sperry Corporation pooled $192,455,000[2] in electronic data processing equipment leases. The leases were with a total of 58 entities. Commercial customers generated 44 percent of the dollar amount of the leases; the federal government generated 37 percent; the State of Pennsylvania generated 12 percent; and nonprofit customers generated 7 percent. Sperry provided installation, servicing, and software to customers, in addition to the leased equipment. The lease contracts specified the particular leased equipment, the monthly charges, and the term of the lease. The lease contracts generally were not cancellable by the customers without cause, except those with the federal government were subject to cancellation for convenience or nonappropriation of funds.

Structuring.   The structure of this issue is shown in Figures 5.2 and 5.3 and described next.

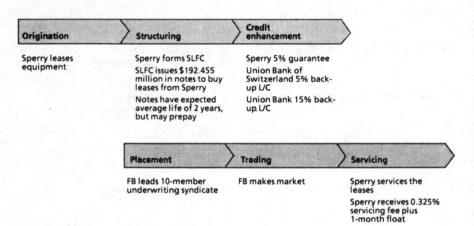

Source: SEC Registration Statement.

Figure 5.2.   Sperry Lease Finance Corporation, 11% Lease-Backed Notes, Series A.

---

[2] This figure equals the dollar amount of the lease receivables net of servicing fees discounted by the interest rate of the notes.

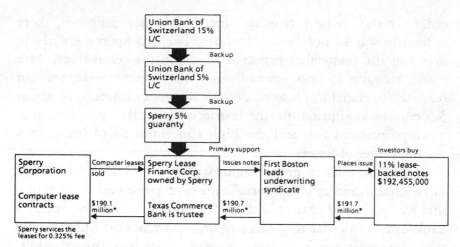

Source: SEC Registration Statement.

Figure 5.3.   Sperry Lease Finance Corporation, 11% Lease-Backed Notes, Series A.

1. Type/Creation of Special Purpose Vehicle. Sperry decided to establish a limited purpose finance corporation as the special purpose vehicle for this financing. Accordingly, Sperry Lease Finance Corporation (SLFC) was incorporated in Delaware on February 8, 1985. Sperry Corporation owned 100 percent of the shares of SLFC. The plan for the financing was that Sperry Corporation would sell the lease receivables to SLFC in return for the proceeds of the public offering of SLFC's asset-backed debt securities (the 11 percent lease-backed notes).

2. Protection against Bankruptcy Risk. SLFC, as the special purpose vehicle for the financing, had to be established in a manner that would eliminate the risk that a Sperry bankruptcy filing or other event could interrupt or otherwise impair payments to the noteholders. Accordingly, Sperry had to sell—as opposed to pledge—the leases to SLFC so that neither the leases nor the lease payments would be property of Sperry's estate in the event of its bankruptcy. Therefore, Sperry and SLFC executed a Sale and Assignment Agreement transferring the ownership of the lease receivables, and both parties accounted for the transfer as a sale. In order for this to be a true sale for bankruptcy purposes, there ordinarily should not be any recourse back to Sperry greatly in excess of the reasonably expected losses on the receivables. As a result, recourse to Sperry was limited to 5 percent—an amount reasonably related to a historic default rate we estimate to be about 3.5 percent as adjusted for the transaction-specific, governmental nonappropriation risk and the high concentration of leases in a small number of lessees.

Also, in order to protect against bankruptcy risk, SLFC had to be established as a separate "bankruptcy-remote" corporation that was protected against both the risk of its own and of Sperry's bankruptcy. In order to protect against the risk that SLFC would take a business action that could result in its bankruptcy, SLFC could not engage in any business other than the issuance of lease-backed notes and the purchase of leases. In order to protect against the risk that Sperry, in the event of its bankruptcy, would cause SLFC to file a voluntary bankruptcy petition, SLFC was required to have at least one director independent of Sperry and a unanimous vote of SLFC's Board was required for any such voluntary bankruptcy filing. Further, the Prospectus for the lease-backed notes had to disclose that Sperry, in the event of its bankruptcy, had no intent to cause SLFC to file a voluntary bankruptcy petition so long as SLFC was solvent. Finally, SLFC obtained an opinion from its counsel, Chadbourne, Parke, Whiteside & Wolff, that SLFC was structured in a manner that should insulate it from a Sperry bankruptcy.[3]

3. Accounting/Tax Structure of the Deal. Not only was the SLFC issue structured as a true sale for bankruptcy purposes, but it was also structured as a sale of the lease receivables from Sperry to SLFC for accounting purposes. The sale of the receivables satisfied the FAS 77 sale requirements that: (1) Sperry not be able to "call" the receivables back from SLFC, (2) that SLFC not be able to "put" the receivables back to Sperry, and (3) that Sperry be able to reasonably estimate its liability pursuant to its recourse obligation. Accordingly, the receivables were removed from

---

[3] For a further discussion of protection against bankruptcy risk, see Chapter 1.

Sperry's balance sheet and they became assets of SLFC. SLFC retained the receivables on its balance sheet, and issued the asset-backed notes as supporting liabilities. Even though Sperry owned all the equity of SLFC, SLFC's balance sheet was not consolidated with Sperry's since GAAP then preferred the nonconsolidation of a financial subsidiary with a nonfinancial parent.[4]

For tax purposes, the lease-backed notes were structured so that they would be debt obligations of SLFC, rather than equity interests in the lease receivables. Such debt status was important so that the interest payments to the noteholders by SLFC would be tax-deductible, and thereby substantially offset the taxable income flowing to SLFC from the lease receivables. Chadbourne, Parke, Whiteside & Wolff rendered a tax opinion that the notes represented corporate debt of SLFC. The notes qualified for corporate debt tax treatment in part because of the presence of a significant layer of equity in SLFC. Sperry agreed to make an equity capital contribution of approximately $2 million to SLFC and to also contribute the title to the leased computer equipment to SLFC.[5] Since the lease-backed notes were corporate debt, not equity interests, for tax purposes, SLFC was able to largely offset its net income from the leases with tax-deductible interest payments to noteholders. The remaining taxable income to SLFC was consolidated for tax purposes into the consolidated federal income tax return of Sperry.

4. Payment Characteristics of the Notes. The 11 percent lease-backed notes were structured to pay monthly interest and principal. Interest was payable on the fifteenth day of each month on the basis of the amount of interest accrued in the previous month on the principal then outstanding. Principal was also payable on the fifteenth day of each month from the balance of the previous month's collections after the payment of interest and

---

[4] The relevant GAAP standard is set by ARB No. 51, Consolidated Financial Statements. However, FAS has adopted an amendment to ARB No. 51, that will reverse this nonconsolidation of financial subsidiaries with nonfinancial parents.

[5] As a result, SLFC would have a balance sheet debt to equity ratio of about 100 to 1, and a debt to equity ratio for tax purposes of about 10 to 1, assuming the residual value of the leased equipment to be about $20 million.

expenses, but in an amount no less than a minimum amortization amount which provided for the complete repayment of principal over approximately six years. SLFC retained a clean-up call right to redeem the balance of the notes once the outstanding principal balance fell below 10 percent.

As originally structured, the weighted average life of the notes was expected to be 2.07 years. However, early repayment of principal could occur due to several causes. Many of the leases provided purchase options under which the customers could purchase the leased equipment. Any exercise of such a purchase option would have the effect of a prepayment of the lease which could be passed through to the noteholders. Similarly, the lease contracts of a few customers permitted the exchange of equipment which could reduce monthly lease payments and thereby cause a partial prepayment. Also, the early termination of a lease contract, or the assignment of it to another customer, or a customer default could trigger Sperry's guaranty described next and result in prepayment.

Credit Enhancement. The 11 percent lease-backed notes were rated AAA by Standard & Poor's, a rating substantially in excess of Sperry Corporation's BBB+ general S&P credit rating.[6] This AAA rating resulted from substantial credit support both from Sperry Corporation and from a back-up, AAA-rated, third-party credit enhancer.

As noted earlier, the lease receivables came from lease contracts with 58 Sperry customers. The credit quality of these customers varied widely—43 percent of the note value of the lease receivables came from contracts with AAA customers, 8 percent with AA customers, 14 percent with A customers, 1 percent with BBB or lower-rated customers, and 34 percent from contracts with unrated customers. According to Standard & Poor's, the overall average customer rating in the receivables pool was "A." Also, the terms of the lease contracts varied widely. While most of the lease contracts were not cancellable by the customers, contracts with the federal government accounted for 37 percent of the value of the

---

[6] Sperry was rated A by Moody's; however, Moody's did not rate the lease-backed notes.

leases. Those federal contracts were terminable for the convenience of the government. Also, all of the federal leases and also the 12 percent of the leases with the Commonwealth of Pennsylvania were terminable if funds were not appropriated by the relevant governmental authority.

Investors in the lease-backed notes were exposed to these governmental risks, in addition to the credit risk that the commercial customers might go bankrupt or might simply default on their obligations to make lease payments. Also, of course, there was the risk that the leased equipment might somehow be damaged or destroyed. However, individual insurance contracts on the equipment covered the principal amount of the notes against such casualty losses. Finally, the lease payments under all the lease contracts may only have been due if Sperry (or a substitute) actually serviced the computer equipment. In sum, investors were exposed to a variety of risks that could result in the late payment or nonpayment of the lease receivables.

Accordingly, a substantial amount of credit support was necessary to obtain a AAA rating for the lease-backed notes. This credit support was provided first by Sperry Corporation's recourse obligation in the amount of 5 percent of the amount of the notes. Union Bank of Switzerland (UBS), a AAA-rated credit, provided a standby letter of credit supporting Sperry's 5 percent guarantee. This 5 percent credit support was available to meet any customer default in lease payments, including defaults resulting from nonappropriation or cancellation by the government customers.

In the event that credit losses exceeded the 5 percent coverage provided above, Union Bank of Switzerland provided a second letter of credit in the additional amount of 15 percent of the value of the notes. Because of the previously discussed bankruptcy concerns, Sperry Corporation could not have any obligation to reimburse UBS for payments made under this second letter of credit. UBS would only be able to recover any drawings upon it from SLFC. SLFC had about $2 million in equity capital and title to the leased equipment. In the event of a customer default and bankruptcy, SLFC would presumably be able to recover some funds to reimburse UBS, if necessary, by selling the equipment.

Thus a total 20 percent in credit enhancement supported the lease-backed notes. We estimate that the expected historic loss on the receivables was about 3.5 percent. Standard & Poor's determined that the 20 percent credit support from an AAA bank was sufficient in combination with the previously discussed structured protections to cause the notes to be AAA rated.

Placement and Trading. The First Boston Corporation was the lead manager for the issue which was underwritten by a ten member syndicate (see Figure 5.4). As lead manager, First Boston actually underwrote 53 percent of the $192,455,000 issue.

Servicing. Sperry Corporation remained the servicer of the lease contracts. As servicer, Sperry is responsible for taking all reasonable actions to collect all customer payments due on the lease receivables. In the event that a scheduled customer payment has

Underwriting syndicate

Underwriters	Principal amount
The First Boston Corporation	$102,455,000
Bear, Stearns & Co., Inc.	10,000,000
Dillon, Read & Co., Inc.	10,000,000
Goldman, Sachs & Co.	10,000,000
Kidder, Peabody & Co., Inc.	10,000,000
Merrill Lynch, Pierce, Fenner & Smith, Inc.	10,000,000
Morgan Stanley & Co., Inc.	10,000,000
Paine Webber, Inc.	10,000,000
Salomon Brothers, Inc.	10,000,000
Shearson Lehman/American Express, Inc.	10,000,000
Total	$192,455,000

Source: SEC Registration Statement.

Figure 5.4. Sperry Lease Finance Corporation, 11% Lease-Backed Notes, Series A.

not been received in a timely manner, Sperry as servicer will advance the payment and recover the advance from the Letters of Credit or other recoveries.

All customer payments under the lease contracts are made to a lockbox account in the name of SLFC. On a daily basis, Sperry as servicer transfers the lease payments from this account to a servicing account that is either federally insured or at a top-rated bank. Sperry receives any amounts in the servicing account that are not payments on the SLFC lease receivables.[7] Collections in the servicing account during the previous month are then paid into a collection account in the name of the Trustee. Monthly payments are then made to the noteholders on the fifteenth day of each month for the previous month's principal and interest. As servicer, Sperry is entitled each month to $1/12$ of its .325 percent annual servicing fee, together with a recovery of any monies previously advanced by Sperry as servicer.

Benefits

Sperry Corporation.   Through the Sperry Lease Finance Corporation, Series A issue, Sperry Corporation achieved its primary goal of eliminating the financing of the leases from its balance sheet. As a result, Sperry Corporation was able to eliminate interest rate risk, access the capital markets at the most economical AAA credit level, and eliminate substantial equity costs.

By engaging in the lease-backed notes securitization, we estimate that Sperry realized significant economic benefits compared to financing on Sperry's balance sheet. These benefits are graphically illustrated in the accompanying Figure 5.5 and represent our best estimate of the economics of the transaction. Since some financial details of the transaction are not publicly available, we have made reasonable approximations where necessary.

The first column in Figure 5.5 illustrates the cost to Sperry of the lease-backed notes. The 11 percent notes sold at 99.6 percent, which after an adjustment for payment timing produces an 11.24

---

[7] In some cases, customers will have made a single monthly payment part of which is attributable to the SLFC leases and part of which is for other equipment or services provided by Sperry.

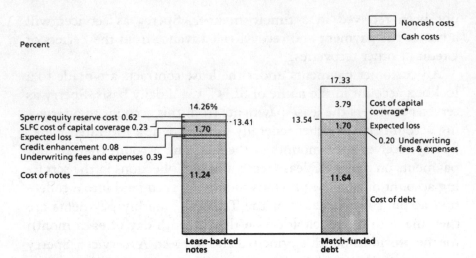

*Assumes IBM Credit's 7.8 leverage rather than Sperry's 1.91 leverage.

Source: McKinsey analysis.

Figure 5.5.   Sperry Lease Finance Corporation, 11% Lease-Backed Notes, Series A, comparative annualized pretax financing costs (March 7, 1985).

percent corporate bond equivalent yield to investors.[8] The next element of cost, 39bp, represents the underwriting and other direct costs of issuing the notes. The underwriting fees totaled $962,275 and the other issuance expenses totaled approximately $600,000.[9] The 39bp figure has been calculated by stating these expenses as a percentage of the note principal amount, and then annualizing over the 2.07 year expected average life of the issue. The credit enhancement fee has been estimated to be 37.5bp annually on the outstanding balances of the letters of credit, which approximately equals 8bp over the entire $192,455,000 issue.[10] Finally, we estimate Sperry's annualized expected loss on its recourse obligation to be about 1.7 percent, and we treat this expense as another cash cost

[8] This 11.24 percent CBE rate was calculated by First Boston.

[9] See Figure 5.4 for an itemization of the underwriters and Figure 5.6 for the particular issuance expenses.

[10] We believe this estimate to be quite conservative since the fee on the 15 percent back-up L/C may have been substantially less.

of the SLFC financing. Thus the annualized cash costs of the notes are approximately 13.41 percent—as shown by the shaded portion of the first bar in Figure 5.5.

However, we believe that the all-in financing costs of the notes require the consideration of two further noncash costs. The first such cost is the equity cost associated with Sperry's equity investment in SLFC. As we noted earlier, a Sperry investment of about $2 million in capital appears on SLFC's balance sheet. While it is possible that no cash actually made its way from Sperry to SLFC since SLFC's balance sheet also shows a $2 million demand note receivable from Sperry as an asset, we will nonetheless conservatively treat the $2 million as equity in SLFC. We estimate SLFC's pretax cost of equity to be 33.7 percent based upon a matched-maturity, risk-free rate of 10.7 percent, a market premium of 7.5 percent, a tax rate of 46 percent, and an estimated finance company beta of 1.0. SLFC's cost of capital coverage then becomes 23bp based upon that 33.7 percent pretax cost of equity, the 11.24 percent rate on the lease-backed notes, and SLFC's 100 to 1 ratio of assets to equity.

The second additional noncash cost is an equity cost incurred by Sperry. As previously mentioned, we estimate that Sperry's expected loss on its 5 percent recourse obligation over the life of the issue is about 3.5 percent. We have already factored in that 3.5 percent as a cash cost. However, we believe that Sperry may have elected to reserve a full 5 percent in equity capital against its recourse obligation, perhaps because of the uncertainty surrounding this expected loss. As a result, taking the most conservative view, Sperry had the further equity cost of holding an additional 1.5 percent equity capital against the SLFC financing. We estimate Sperry's pretax cost of equity to be 41.5 percent based upon a 10.7 percent risk-free rate, Sperry's 1.56 beta, a 7.5 percent market premium, and a 46 percent tax rate. The annual cost of holding this 1.5 percent in Sperry equity then amounts to 62bp. The resulting all-in financing cost of the lease-backed notes is 14.26 percent.

In contrast, we estimate the cash costs to Sperry of financing the $192,455,000 principal amount on Sperry's balance sheet to be

13.54 percent for the same period as shown by the second bar of Figure 5.5. This figure has been calculated as follows: We estimate that a 2-year straight debt financing would have cost Sperry, a BBB+/A credit (S&P, Moody's), 11.64 percent. We also conservatively estimate the associated issuance expenses to be 20bp. We then add the annualized expected loss on the computer leases of 1.7 percent. Thus the total cash cost of financing $192,455,000 would have been about 13.54 percent if it had been exclusively financed with debt.

However, Sperry actually financed a large proportion of its balance sheet with more expensive equity. According to its annual report, its book assets-to-equity ratio was 1.92/1. However, this leverage is a relatively low one, typical of a computer manufacturing company, rather than a computer finance company. We would be overallocating expensive equity if we were to use Sperry's overall leverage. Instead, we look to IBM Credit Corporation, whose ratio of assets to equity was about 7.8 to 1. Applying that leverage to Sperry's 41.5 percent cost of equity and 11.64 percent

Issuance expenses

Registration fee	$40,000
Attorneys' fees and expenses	75,000
Accountants' fees and expenses	70,000
Trustee's fees and expenses	96,700
Printing and engraving	213,000
Blue Sky expenses	26,500
Rating agency fees	60,000
Miscellaneous	18,800
Total	**$600,000**

Source: SEC Registration Statement.

Figure 5.6. Sperry Lease Finance Corporation, 11% Lease-Backed Notes, Series A.

cost of traditional debt, we get a cost of capital coverage of 3.79 percent. Therefore, the all-in financing cost of match-funded debt would be 17.33 percent.

In conclusion, as shown in Figure 5.6, we estimate that Sperry realized a small 13bp cash cost advantage and a large 3.07 percent all-in financing cost advantage as a result of the SLFC issue. Sperry also realized the further advantage of perfectly match-funding its computer lease receivables.

First Boston. First Boston and the nine-member underwriting syndicate earned up to $962,275 in fee income from the 50bp underwriting discount. As lead manager, First Boston actually underwrote 53 percent of the total issue. First Boston also earned the important competitive distinction of bringing to the U.S. public market the first issue of a AAA rated, asset-backed security, backed by nonmortgage assets.

Union Bank of Switzerland. As the third-party credit enhancer, Union Bank stands to earn an attractive fee over the life of the transaction.

Investors. Investors received AAA rated debt securities at an attractive 49bp spread to Treasuries. In fact, the Sperry lease-backed notes proved sufficiently attractive to both Sperry and the investor market that further issues of similar Sperry lease-backed notes followed in September 1985 and December 1986.

6

Commercial Mortgages

Commercial mortgages is an asset category that presents substantial credit securitization potential. Issuances of commercial mortgages are very large—$85 billion in 1986 alone—and the existing secondary whole loan market for income producing properties is quite limited. Moreover, the majority of commercial and multifamily mortgage loans were made by thrifts (31 percent) and commercial banks (29 percent). These lenders are likely to be interested in securitization of their commercial mortgage portfolios in order to cure asset-liability mismatch, to reduce capital costs, and to liquify existing portfolios while providing funding for new originations. Also, the owners of commercial properties are likely to see the securities market as an economically attractive alternative source of funds.

However, credit securitization is just beginning in commercial mortgages. In 1986, approximately $5 billion of the $85 billion commercial mortgage originations were securitized. As of November 1986, Standard & Poor's had rated approximately 20 commercial mortgage-securitized transactions. Most of these transactions have been sold in the Euromarkets or privately placed in the United States. However, in early 1987, the first U.S. public issue of a commercial mortgage-backed security came to market.

In this chapter, we will describe one securitized financing of a commercial mortgage by an active issuer —Olympia & York.

OLYMPIA & YORK
MAIDEN LANE FINANCE CORPORATION

One of the distinguishing features of this $200 million credit securitization is that it had to appeal to the ultimate borrower, as well as the financial intermediary. In the previous transactions, credit intermediaries like banks or finance companies have securitized loans in their portfolios so that the intermediaries could realize lower funding costs. Individual borrowers could not directly access the capital markets since the size of their credit card, auto loan, lease, or residential mortgage borrowing was far too small to directly access the capital markets.

However, as in this case, a commercial mortgage may be so large as to permit the borrower relatively direct access to the securities market for financing in order to obtain lower financing costs. This transaction came about because Olympia & York Maiden Lane Finance Corporation's existing mortgage loan with a Salomon Brothers subsidiary was expiring. While Salomon Brothers undoubtedly designed the securitized transaction and benefitted from it in several ways, the transaction could not have happened without Olympia & York seeing it as a relatively more attractive source of funds than alternative commercial mortgages from traditional lenders (see Term Sheet, Figure 6.1).

Structure

The structure of this transaction is summarized in Figures 6.2 and 6.3, and explained below.

Origination. Olympia & York Maiden Lane Company is a limited partnership whose exclusive business is the ownership and operation of a 44-story office building located at 59 Maiden Lane in New York City. The general partner of Olympia & York Maiden Lane Company is a corporate subsidiary of Olympia & York (U.S.).

The building at 59 Maiden Lane had an appraised market value of $280 million as of June 30, 1985, and was financed by a mortgage loan from Salomon Brothers Realty Corporation. Essentially, Olympia & York Maiden Lane Company entered into this

Issue:	10 3/8% Secured Notes
Parent/seller:	Olympia and York Maiden Lane Company
Offering date:	December 23, 1985
Rating (S&P):	AA
Principal amount:	$200,000,000
Collateral:	Mortgage note backed by mortgage on 59 Maiden Lane
Maturity (years):	10, callable after 8
Payment frequency:	Annually in arrears
Spread to Treasuries at offering:	141 bp
Credit enhancement (type/ provider):	$30,380,000 Insurance Policy/Aetna Casualty and Surety Company
Managing underwriter(s):	Salomon Brothers International/ Swiss Bank Corporation International Limited

Source: Offering Memorandum; Salomon Brothers.

Figure 6.1. Olympia & York Maiden Lane Finance Corporation.

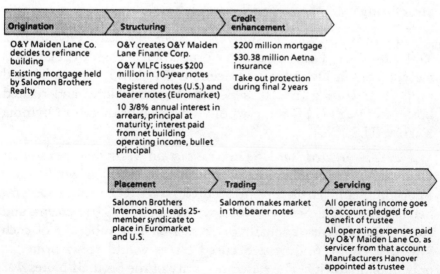

Source: Offering Memorandum.

Figure 6.2. Olympia & York Maiden Lane Finance Corporation, 10³/₈% Secured Notes.

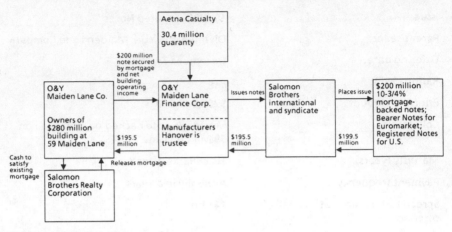

Source: Offering Memorandum.

Figure 6.3. Olympia & York Maiden Lane Finance Corporation, 10 3/8%
Secured Notes.

transaction in order to refinance that mortgage loan. Thus the net
proceeds from the offering of notes would be used to repay the
Salomon Brothers loan.

Structuring

1. Type/Creation of Special Purpose Vehicle. Olympia &
York Maiden Lane Finance Corporation (O&YMLFC) was
incorporated in Delaware on December 11, 1985, for the limited
purpose of issuing the 10 3/8 percent Secured Notes and related
business. O&YMLFC was a wholly-owned subsidiary of Olympia
& York (U.S.).

2. The Secured Notes. This transaction was structured so that
Olympia & York Maiden Lane Finance Corporation would issue
$200 million in 10 3/8 percent Secured Notes on or about Decem-
ber 17, 1985. The Secured Notes were priced at 99 3/4 percent, and
were to pay interest annually in arrears on December 31 of each
year (see Figure 6.4). The Secured Notes would repay principal
only upon maturity. The stated maturity of the Secured Notes was
10 years, but they were callable after 7 years.

The Secured Notes were primarily designed as a Euromarket
issue, although some of the notes were to be privately placed in the

Payment stream

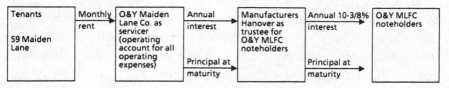

Source: Offering Memorandum.

Figure 6.4. Olympia & York Maiden Lane Finance Corporation, $10^{3}/_{8}\%$ Secured Notes.

United States. In order to appeal to the Euromarket, the Secured Notes were structured with the annual interest payment in arrears feature typical of Euromarket payment structures. The Secured Notes were initially represented by a "global note" which was deposited in London on behalf of Euro-Clear and CEDEL on or about December 23, 1985. Thereafter, bearer notes or registered notes would be issued to non-U.S. investors upon certification that the purchasers were not U.S. persons. Also, registered notes would be issued to sophisticated U.S. institutional investors upon certification that they purchased the notes in a private placement so that the Notes would be exempt from registration under the Securities Act of 1933.[1]

After the notes were issued, O&YMLFC would then lend the proceeds of the note offering to Olympia & York Maiden Lane Company, the owner of the property at 59 Maiden Lane. Olympia & York Maiden Lane Company would use such proceeds of the offering to repay the prior mortgage loan by Salomon Brothers Realty Corporation. That mortgage would then be amended and assigned to O&YMLFC and then to Manufacturers Hanover Trust Company as trustee for the noteholders.

In return for borrowing the receipts of the Secured Note offering, Olympia & York Maiden Lane Company would simultaneously provide the issuer, O&YMLFC, with a $200 million note that would be secured by the mortgage. This note would also be assigned to the trustee. As a result of this simultaneous transaction,

[1] See Chapter 1 for a discussion of the 1933 Act and its requirements.

the noteholders of the $200 million Secured Notes would be directly secured by a first mortgage on the $280 million building. While this mortgage would provide noteholders with assurance that they ultimately could recover their investment if necessary through a mortgage foreclosure and sale of the building, it would not provide noteholders with any assurance of the cash flow necessary for the timely payment of interest.

Accordingly, the trust indenture under which the Secured Notes were issued provided that all operating income from the building tenants would be paid into an operating account held by the trustee for the benefit of the noteholders. Olympia & York Maiden Lane Company will control that account and will be entitled to withdraw and pay current building operating expenses from that account. The money in the operating account will also be used to pay interest to noteholders.

3. *Timeliness of Principal Repayment.* As noted earlier, the noteholders only receive interest payments until the maturity of the notes. In order to secure an AA rating from Standard & Poor's, the issue had to be structured in a manner that would assure that sufficient cash would actually be available to repay the $200 million principal at maturity. As a result, O&YMLFC was required to provide cash, collateral, or credit support (liquid asset facility) by December 31, 1993, in an amount sufficient to cover full payment of principal at maturity, which is scheduled for December 31, 1995. O&YMLFC had the right to call the notes after December 31, 1992, by refinancing at that time instead of bearing the added cost of the liquid asset facility.

In the event that O&YMLFC failed to provide a liquid asset facility or otherwise satisfy Standard & Poor's of timely principal repayment, then there would be sufficient time (2 years) for the trustee to enforce the mortgage and, if necessary, sell the building to obtain the noteholders' principal in a timely manner.

4. *Protection against Bankruptcy Risk.* The O&YMLFC transaction was highly structured in order to assure that neither the issuer, O&YMLFC, nor the mortgagor, Olympia & York Maiden Lane Company, could become subject to a bankruptcy

proceeding. As noted earlier, the issuer of the Notes, O&YMLFC, was structured to be bankruptcy remote. Essentially, the issuer was prohibited from incurring debt other than the Notes and was limited in its business to functioning as a conduit that would hold the $200 million mortgage note that secured the repayment of principal. Also, O&YMLFC could not transfer the mortgage to any entity that did not also satisfy these criteria. More importantly, the owner of the property, Olympia & York Maiden Lane Company, was subject to the same restrictions, except that it could incur additional debt essentially if it would not adversely affect the rating on the Secured Notes.

Further, in order to protect the noteholders interest in the rental cash flows, those cash flows are deposited in an account held by the trustee for the benefit of the noteholders. Olympia & York Maiden Lane Company, the owner, may only withdraw monies from that account to pay building operating expenses or surplus not necessary for payments to noteholders under extremely conservative assumptions. Finally, the owner itself was restricted from transferring the property except to other Olympia & York related entities or to purchasers of AA or equivalent credit quality.

5. *Special Tax Features.* In structuring this transaction, it was important to assure non-U.S. investors that payments on the Notes would not be subject to withholding of U.S. federal income tax and that the identities of the noteholders would be confidential. Accordingly, O&YMLFC obtained an opinion from its counsel, Cleary, Gottlieb, Steen & Hamilton, that most non-U.S. investors would not be subject to such withholding and that non-U.S. owners of the bearer notes would not be required to disclose their identities in order to receive payments.

Credit Enhancement. The $10^{3}/_{8}$ percent Secured Notes were rated AA by Standard & Poor's due to their extremely strong capacity to pay interest and principal in a timely fashion. As a general matter, Standard & Poor's often requires at least 1.25 debt service coverage based upon a worst case scenario for a particular commercial property in order to obtain an AA rating.

The cash flows from 59 Maiden Lane were strong and reliable. Two tenants, the Home Insurance Company and the Federal Reserve Bank of New York, occupy 90 percent of the rentable space. Their leases do not expire until after the maturity date of the notes. The overall building occupancy rate was 99.94 percent and the building was a prime property located in the heart of the New York Financial District.

However, in order to obtain a AA rating, a $30,380,000 credit insurance policy had to be obtained from Aetna. Coverage under that policy was scheduled to decline annually to a minimum level of $5,696,000. The policy was particularly important to supplement the rental income in 1986 and 1987, after which there would be a significant increase in the payments required under the leases. As a result of the rental income and the third-party credit support, the Offering Memorandum projected the debt service coverage ratio would never be less than 1.33.

Also, of course, in order to secure an AA rating, Olympia & York Maiden Lane Company (owner) was required to maintain fire, liability, and other necessary insurance on the building. In the event of the building's destruction, the owner could then replace the building, prepay the mortgage note and the Secured Notes, or provide adequate substitute collateral.

Placing. Salomon Brothers International Limited was the lead manager for a 25-member underwriting syndicate (see Figure 6.5). Except for Salomon Brothers, the underwriters were restricted to placement outside of the United States to non-U.S. investors. Salomon Brothers could engage in private placements to U.S. institutional investors.

Trading. There has been a secondary market in the 10 3/8 percent notes. In fact, the notes seem to have been well accepted by investors since their spread to treasuries significantly declined between December 1986 and March 1987 to a level below the spread at issuance (see Figure 6.6).

Servicing. Olympia & York Maiden Lane Company (the owner) remained as servicer of the property. The owner will deposit the

Underwriting syndicate

Salomon Brothers International Limited
  Algemene Bank Nederland N.V.
  Banque Nationale de Paris
  CIBC Limited
  Credit Lyonnais
  Dai-Ichi Kangyo International Limited
  Deutsche Bank Capital Markets Limited
  McLeod Young Weir International Limited
  Samuel Montagu & Co. Limited
  Morgan Guaranty Ltd.
  Orion Royal Bank Limited
  Sumitomo Finance International
  Union Bank of Switzerland (Securities) Limited

Swiss Bank Corporation International Limited
  Banque Bruxelles Lambert S.A.
  Barclays Merchant Bank Limited
  Citicorp Investment Bank Limited
  Credit Suisse First Boston Limited
  Daiwa Europe Limited
  Generale Bank
  Merrill Lynch International & Co.
  Morgan Grenfell & Co. Limited
  Morgan Stanley International
  Sanwa International Limited
  Wood Gundy Inc.

Source: Offering Memorandum.

Figure 6.5. Olympia & York Maiden Lane Finance Corporation, 10³/₈% Secured Notes.

Date	Yield	Spread to treasuries
December 23, 1985 (issuance)	10.40%	141 bp
December 31, 1986	8.54	145 bp
March 31, 1987	8.43	100 bp

Source: Salomon Brothers.

Figure 6.6. Olympia & York Maiden Lane Finance Corporation, 10³/₈% Secured Notes (market price data).

lease payments in the trustee's operating account and withdraw operating expenses from that account. In the event that the balance in the operating account plus available credit support from Aetna is more than sufficient to cover the next due interest installment, the owner may draw excess net cash flow out of the operating account.

Benefits

Olympia & York Maiden Lane Company (Owner). Through the issue of the O&YMLFC 10³/₈ percent Secured Notes, the owner was able to refinance its mortgage at an attractive rate.

As shown in Figure 6.7, we have estimated the pre-tax financing costs of the 10³/₈ percent Secured Notes to the owner as 10.74

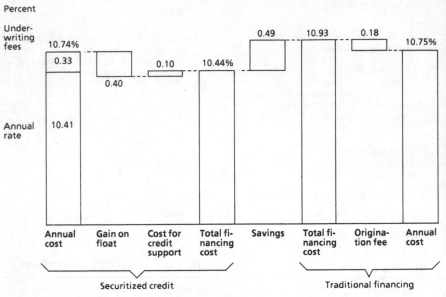

Source: Salomon Brothers; McKinsey analysis.

Figure 6.7.   Olympia & York Maiden Lane Finance Corporation, 10³/₈%
Secured Notes (comparative pretax financing costs).

percent. We make this estimate by taking the 10.37 percent
annual rate on the Notes and adjusting it up to 10.41 percent to
adjust for the 99³/₄ percent price to investors. We then add the $4
million gross underwriting spread annualized over the 10-year life
of the issue to produce an overall annual rate of 10.74 percent.[2]
Compared to typical commercial mortgages, this structure is unusual in that the owner only makes interest payments annually in
arrears, rather than monthly. Therefore, the owner benefits from
the use of monies that otherwise would have been paid out
monthly. The value of this float was 40bp assuming the owner
invested it at the then current short-term risk-free rate of 7.7
percent. Subtracting this 40bp from the 10.74 percent annual cost
of the notes yields 10.33 percent. We then add the estimated ⅝
percent cost of the Aetna credit support on the full $30,380,000

---

[2] We have adjusted this annualized expense upwards using a 10.62 percent discount rate
(10-year Treasury) in order to adjust for the time value of the money.

enhanced amount,[3] which amounts to 10bp on the entire issue. The resulting cost to Olympia & York Maiden Lane Company is 10.44 percent for the Secured Note financing.

In comparison, we estimate that the market rate for a comparable maturity, monthly pay, commercial mortgage was approximately 10.75 percent with a 1 percent origination fee. After allocating this 1 percent fee over the 10-year life of the loan and applying the same discount rate used above, the pre-tax financing cost of this traditional commercial mortgage was 10.93 percent.

Therefore, we estimate the all-in pre-tax savings from the Secured Notes to O&Y Maiden Lane Finance Corporation to be 49bp or $980,000 annually. Not only did Olympia & York Maiden Lane Company benefit from this estimated financing cost savings, but also Olympia & York opened up a potentially important new source of funds. Indeed, the significant decline in 1987 in the issue's spread to Treasuries may signify substantial investor acceptance that could cause similar issues to be even more economic in the future.

Salomon Brothers International Limited. The gross underwriting spread on this issue was 2 percent (1 3/8 percent selling concession plus 5/8 percent management commission) of the $200 million principal amount. As lead manager, Salomon Brothers International would receive a healthy portion of that $4 million fee with the balance flowing to other syndicate members. Through the O&YMLFC transaction, Salomon Brothers International succeeded in designing a way of realizing fee income from the refinancing of the 55 Maiden Lane building, without needing to extend another mortgage loan from its Salomon Brothers Realty Corporation affiliate and without losing O&Y's business to another lender.

Moreover, by structuring this first major offering of commercial mortgage backed securities, Salomon Brothers gained an important competitive distinction. Salomon Brothers developed skills, expertise, and a reputation for performance which would all be useful in securitizing this large asset class.

---

[3] This assumption is extremely conservative since the insured amount is scheduled to rapidly decrease each year.

7
Nonconforming Residential Mortgages

Residential mortgages is the asset class in which credit securitization has been most pervasive. For example, in 1986, about 70 percent of the $442 billion in new residential mortgage originations were securitized. The vast majority of these securitized residential mortgages were so-called "conforming" mortgages (see Figure 7.1). These mortgages were conforming in that they fell within the eligibility criteria of the three government-related credit enhancement programs—GNMA, FNMA, and FHLMC. The major factor in determining eligibility for these programs is the size of the mortgage—which presently cannot be greater than about $168,100.

In 1986, fully 92 percent of the conforming residential mortgages were securitized—largely through the government-related programs. The percentage of conforming residential mortgages securitized will vary from year to year, in part depending upon the mix of fixed rate and adjustable rate mortgages originated that year. Originators are especially likely to securitize their fixed rate mortgages, since these mortgages bear substantial interest rate risk. Borrowers are likely to change the rate at which they prepay such mortgages in response to changes in interest rates and other

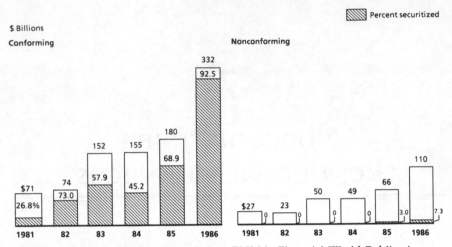

Source: Mortgage Banking Association; FNMA; Financial World Publications.

Figure 7.1.   Residential mortgage originations 1981–86.

factors (e.g., some borrowers are likely to refinance their fixed-rate mortgages after a substantial drop in interest rates). As a result, it is difficult or impossible for an originator to match fund fixed rate mortgages resulting in asset-liability mismatch risk. However, the ready availability of government-related securitization programs has permitted originators to freely offer fixed rate and variable rate conforming mortgages with the assurance that they will be able to sell the mortgages and thereby escape the risks associated with balance sheet funding.

While conforming mortgages have been thoroughly securitized with the assistance of the federal government, it is the remaining nonconforming mortgages (often referred to as "jumbo" mortgages) that present a quickly developing opportunity for securitization. While such nonconforming residential mortgages may of course be sold as whole loans, the structured credit securitization of such mortgages began in a small way a few years ago. The penetration of such securitization of these mortgages appears to be growing rapidly, albeit from a small base (see Figure 7.1).

Citibank, N.A. has actively securitized such nonconforming mortgages, and in this section we will analyze one of these Citibank issues.

CITIBANK, N.A., MORTGAGE PASS-THROUGH CERTIFICATES, SERIES 1986-Q

Citibank has been very actively engaged in a securitization program for nonconforming one- to four-family residential mortgages. In fact, in 1986 alone, Citibank originated at least 22 issues of residential mortgage pass-through certificates. The mortgages underlying these pass-through certificates typically were fixed-rate residential mortgages, many of which were jumbo mortgages. Citibank originated and serviced all of the mortgage loans pooled into its Series 1986-A through 1986-S pass-through certificates. Citibank also operated a conduit program under which it purchased, packaged, and serviced nonconforming mortgages originated by mortgage brokers, savings and loan associations, and banks.

The following transaction description describes the Citibank Series 1986-Q Pass-Through Certificates (see Figure 7.2).

Issue	9.00% Mortgage Pass-Through Certificates, Series 1986-Q
Parent/seller	Citibank, N.A.
Offering date	November 25, 1986
Rating (S&P)	AA
Principal amount	$110,000,000
Collateral	Residential mortgage loans
Payment frequency	Monthly
Limited recourse (amount/provider)	4-10%/Citicorp
Third-party credit enhancement (type/provider)	None
Managing underwriters	The First Boston Corporation ($\frac{1}{2}$ issue) Citibank ($\frac{1}{2}$ issue)

Source: Prospectus.

Figure 7.2. Citibank, N.A., 9% Mortgage Pass-Through Certificates, Series 1986-Q.

Structure

The structure of this issue is shown in Figures 7.3 and 7.4 and described next.

Origination. Citibank originated 15-year, fixed-rate mortgage loans in New York, New Jersey, and Connecticut. As of the November 1, 1986 cut-off date, the outstanding principal amount on the mortgage loans was approximately $110 million. The loans had a weighted average interest rate between 10.2 percent and 10.6 percent, and a weighted average maturity of 14.5 to 15 years.[1] The loans varied in size and type. No more than 10 percent of the mortgages had outstanding principal balances of more than $350,000, and no less than 60 percent had balances less than $150,000.[2] At least 65 percent of the loans were originated after July 1984. Also, at least 65 percent were secured by

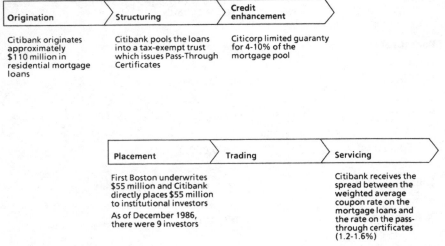

Source: Prospectus.

Figure 7.3. Citibank, N.A., 9% Mortgage Pass-Through Certificates, Series 1986-Q.

[1] The precise interest rate and maturity of the mortgage pool was slightly uncertain since the pool composition had not been finalized as of the date of the Prospectus.

[2] A substantial portion of these loans were nonconforming "jumbo" mortgage loans since the maximum ceiling on the size of a conforming loan at this time was about $133,250.

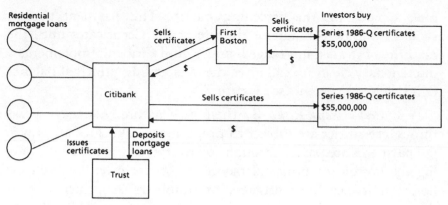

Source: Prospectus.

Figure 7.4. Citibank, N.A., 9% Mortgage Pass-Through Certificates, Series 1986-Q.

one-family dwellings, and no more than 30 percent by condominiums and row houses. No more than 20 percent of the mortgage loans had loan-to-value ratios of more than 80 percent, and all such loans had private mortgage insurance bringing the uninsured amount to no more than 75 percent of value.

Structuring

1. Type/Creation of Special Purpose Vehicle. Citibank created a trust by entering into a pooling and servicing agreement with a trustee, The United States Trust Company of New York. Citibank then conveyed the mortgage loans to the trust together with the mortgages and assignment forms. In return, the trust issued to Citibank approximately $110 million in Series 1986-Q Pass-Through Certificates, each of which represented a fractional undivided share of the mortgage pool.

2. Payment Structure of the Certificates. Since the Certificates were designed as pass-through instruments, investors would receive monthly payments of principal and interest. On the 25th day of each month, investors would be paid their proportional share of the principal payments made by borrowers in the preceding month. At the same time, investors would also be paid interest on outstanding principal at the 9 percent annual pass-through rate, accrued for the preceding month. This payment pattern should continue throughout the life of the Certificates until the maturity of the last mortgage loan, or until Citibank implements a discretionary clean-up call after the outstanding principal balance falls below 10 percent (see Figure 7.5).

3. *Prepayment Risk.* By their very nature, mortgage pass-through securities are subject to prepayment risk, since all principal payments are passed through to investors in the month following the borrower's principal payments. A borrower may sell his home, refinance his mortgage, or simply repay principal, and thereby prepay all or part of his existing mortgage loan; the investors will then receive their pro-rata shares of the resulting prepaid principal. Since prepayment rates tend to vary with interest rates and other economic conditions, the purchasers of mortgage-backed securities cannot be sure of the average life of the securities they purchase.

In the Prospectus to the 9 percent Pass-Through Certificates, investors were advised that HUD data indicated the average life of a pool of 15-year mortgages tended to be slightly under 7 years. However, the Prospectus advised potential investors that there was no way of reliably predicting the actual prepayment rate or average life of the mortgage loans in the Series 1986-Q mortgage pool. Of course, at any given time, market pricing for this or similar mortgage pools will incorporate the market's best estimate of the then anticipated prepayment rate.

4. *Accounting/Tax Structure of the Transaction.* An important element of the Citibank mortgage pass-through program is

Payment stream

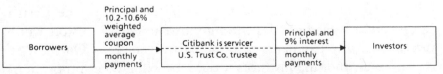

Source: Prospectus.

Figure 7.5. Citibank, N.A., 9% Mortgage Pass-Through Certificates, Series 1986-Q.

that it appears to be a true sale of the mortgage loans for RAP, as well as GAAP, purposes. As discussed in Chapter 1, banks usually cannot obtain asset sale treatment under RAP if there is any recourse back to the bank.[3] Nor can this no-recourse requirement be successfully evaded by structuring recourse back to a bank affiliate. In that event, the asset would still remain on the bank holding company's consolidated books for capital adequacy purposes. However, the banking regulators' no recourse policy does not apply to sales of participations in pools of residential mortgages, so long as the bank does not retain any significant risk of loss. While the question of what constitutes significant risk of loss is an open question, it is relatively clear that any such recourse must be less than 10 percent.

We believe that the Series 1986-Q Mortgage Pass-Through Certificates financing was structured to be a true sale under RAP. While there was no recourse back to Citibank for losses on the mortgage loans, there was some recourse to its holding company, Citicorp. However, pursuant to the Prospectus, the amount of such recourse to Citicorp was limited to between 4 and 10 percent. Therefore, we believe that Citibank and Citicorp were able to treat the sale of the mortgage loans as a true sale under RAP. As a result, neither Citibank nor Citicorp had to continue to hold capital against the mortgage loans. Of course, this transaction also satisfied the easier GAAP standard for a "true sale," as: (1) losses under the recourse obligation could be reasonably estimated; (2) Citibank could not call back the mortgage loans except for a minimal clean-up call when the outstanding principal fell below 10 percent of the initial balance; and, (3) the Certificate-holders could not put the loans back to Citibank or Citicorp except for the amounts covered by the recourse guarantee. The mortgage loans could therefore also be removed from Citibank's and Citicorp's balance sheets for GAAP financial reporting purposes.[4]

For federal income tax purposes, the transaction was structured as a sale by Citibank of the mortgages to a Special Purpose

---

[3] As a result, banks have been forced to use the spread account structure described in Chapter 1 in order to obtain RAP "true sale" treatment for nonmortgage assets.

[4] See Chapter 1 for a more detailed discussion of GAAP and RAP accounting.

Vehicle that qualified as a tax-transparent grantor trust. The transaction qualified as a grantor trust since principal and interest at the coupon rate were passed through to investors on a monthly basis and the trust was sufficiently passive to be a grantor trust.[5]

Since the structure qualified as a grantor trust, there would be no federal income taxation of the Trust. Instead, for tax purposes, the IRS would look through the Trust and simply view the transaction as one in which the investors were direct owners of pro-rata shares of the mortgage loans. Accordingly, the Certificate-holders would pay income tax at their individual tax rates on their pro-rata share of the taxable income from the mortgage pool. This income would flow through to the Certificate-holders without any taxation at the level of the Trust.

5. Protection against Insolvency of Citibank. As a bank, Citibank was exempt from the bankruptcy code and thus need not comply with all of the bankruptcy-remote structuring protections discussed in Chapter 1. Nonetheless, certain structuring steps were taken in order to protect Certificate-holders against the risk of a Citibank insolvency. Citibank assigned the mortgage loans to the Trustee (United States Trust Company of New York) and provided the Trustee with a schedule itemizing the individual loans. Also, Citibank delivered to the Trustee the mortgage notes, the original recorded mortgages, and mortgage assignments in recordable form. However, neither Citibank nor the Trustee was required to actually go to the trouble and expense of immediately recording the mortgage assignments. Absent such recording, other Citibank creditors might be able to exercise superior claims to the mortgage collateral in the event of Citibank's insolvency. In order to minimize that risk, the Trustee was required to demand that Citibank immediately record the assignments of the mortgage loans if Citibank's senior debt rating ever fell below an AA rating (S&P). Since the Certificates themselves were only AA rated as described below, the above structuring was deemed sufficient protection against insolvency risk.

[5] See Chapter 1 for a more detailed account of grantor trusts.

Credit Enhancement. The 9 percent Pass-Through Certificates were rated AA by Standard & Poor's due to their strong capacity to pay timely principal and interest. The basic source of this repayment capacity was the high quality of the Citibank-originated mortgages in the mortgage pool. Prospective borrowers were required to satisfy standardized eligibility criteria including filing financial statements, employment verification, a credit report, an appraisal of the property, and a satisfactory income coverage ratio. In addition, 80 percent of the loans in the mortgage pool had loan to value ratios at origination of 80 percent or less, and no loan had a loan to value ratio in excess of 90 percent. Those loans with loan to value ratios between 80 and 90 percent were required to obtain private mortgage insurance covering up to 25 percent of the principal of such loans.

Credit enhancement was provided by a Citicorp first loss Limited Guarantee in an amount that was not less than 4 percent and not more than 10 percent of the initial principal balance of the mortgage pool.[6] This Limited Guarantee was sufficient to raise the rating on the Certificates up to Citicorp's AA rating since the expected losses on the mortgage loans were extremely low. The loan loss experience on reasonably comparable loans originated by Citibank's New York Banking Unit was as follows:

	1983	1984	1985
Net annual loss ratio	.002%	0%	.001%

Thus the Limited Guarantee provided sufficient loss protection to fully raise the rating of the Certificates to the rating of the guarantor, Citicorp.

Placing and Trading. The distribution plan for the Series 1986-Q Certificates was that about $55 million of the Certificates would be placed by Citibank and/or its affiliate, Citicorp Securities Markets, Inc., with institutional investors at varying prices to be determined at the time of sale. The other $55 million in Certificates

---

[6] The precise amount of the Limited Guarantee was not disclosed in the Prospectus.

were to be underwritten by the First Boston Corporation. These Certificates would also be sold at prices to be determined at the time of sale. It is clear that the Series 1986-Q Certificates were placed with institutional investors since the SEC Form 10-K reported that as of December 31, 1986, all of the Certificates were held by only nine holders.

Servicing. Citibank remains the servicer for the mortgage loans, for which it receives the spread between the 9 percent interest rate on the Certificates and the 10.2 to 10.6 percent weighted average coupon rate on the underlying loans. As servicer, Citibank receives all payments from the borrowers, and then deposits into a certificate account all principal payments together with the portion of the payments necessary to pay interest at the pass-through rate. These deposits into the certificate account are made on the business day after the day the payment was received. Citibank, as servicer, then pays the accumulated principal and interest to Certificate-holders on or about the 25th day of each month. In the event of a delinquency by a borrower, Citibank may draw a voluntary advance from a subsidiary of Citicorp. In the event of a serious delinquency or default, Citibank may draw on the Citicorp Limited Guarantee. Under this Limited Guaranty, Citicorp will purchase any loans that are being foreclosed up to the amount of the guaranty. Citibank will pay Citicorp an annual fee of 10bp to 15bp of the outstanding mortgage pool principal for the Limited Guarantee. This payment will be made from Citibank's servicing compensation. As servicer, Citibank will give monthly notices to the trustee of the amounts distributed to the Certificate-holders, and Citibank will also provide each Certificate-holder with relevant information on a monthly basis.

Benefits

Citibank. Through the Series 1986-Q Pass-Through Certificates and the other issues in this series, Citibank has been able to originate a large volume of fixed-rate jumbo residential mortgages and fund them through credit securitization—thereby eliminating asset-liability mismatch risk. The elimination of this risk is particularly important for fixed-rate residential mortgage pools because of the variability of their expected average lives.

As noted earlier, prepayment rates on residential mortgages vary enormously. When interest rates substantially decline, prepayments tend to greatly increase as borrowers refinance their mortgages. When interest rates increase, the prepayment rate tends to decline since fewer borrowers refinance existing mortgages. As a result of this sensitivity of residential mortgage prepayment rates to these and other factors, it is extraordinarily difficult to match-fund fixed rate residential mortgage assets held on a bank's balance sheet.

This difficulty does not matter so much for conforming residential mortgages, which may be sold off the bank's balance sheet through securitization in one of the federally related programs. However, some banks have hesitated to offer jumbo fixed-rate residential mortgages since they could not be securitized through the federally related programs. Citibank solved this problem of the interest-rate risk inherent in fixed-rate jumbo mortgages by engaging in its own regular program of securitizing such mortgages. By this securitization program, Citibank was able to retain an attractive spread (1.2 to 1.6 percent in the Series 1986-Q) between the average yield on the mortgages, and the yield to the Certificate-holders. At the same time, Citibank eliminated these mortgage assets from its balance sheet and essentially transferred the prepayment risk inherent in the assets to investors who were better structured to take that risk.

Moreover, the securitization of the nonconforming mortgages through the Series 1986-Q Pass-Through Certificates produced another significant benefit for Citibank and Citicorp. As discussed in Chapter 1, the federal banking regulators require banks and their holding companies to maintain certain minimum ratios of primary capital to total assets. At the time of the Series 1986-Q issue, the minimum such ratio was 5.5 percent. However, as a practical matter, federally regulated banks and their holding companies maintained more than 5.5 percent capital to avoid too close regulatory supervision. As a result, many banks and their holding companies maintained a target primary capital ratio closer to 7 percent. Thus, Citicorp's primary capital ratio at year-end 1986 was about 6.82 percent.

As noted earlier, the securitization of the Citibank mortgages through the Series 1986-Q Pass-Through Certificates constituted a true sale for RAP purposes. As a result, Citibank and Citicorp were able to remove the mortgage assets from their balance sheets and to rededicate the expensive primary capital supporting these mortgage assets to other uses.

We cannot precisely estimate the all-in pretax financing cost advantage to Citicorp of financing the mortgages through a securitized sale, as opposed to matched-maturity balance sheet financing. One obstacle to preparing such an estimate is that we do not know the actual weighted average life of the mortgage pool, so we cannot satisfactorily identify the maturity and cost of matchfunded Citicorp debt. Another obstacle to preparing such an estimate is that we do not know the price or prices at which the Series 1986-Q Certificates were sold to investors. For these reasons, we have not prepared an exhibit showing the all-in financing cost advantage to Citicorp of the Series 1986-Q Certificates.

However, in order to offer a sense of such savings, we offer the following calculations together with their accompanying assumptions.[7] Assume that the Series 1986-Q Pass-Through Certificates were sold at a price that yielded 9 percent on a corporate bond equivalent basis. Also, assume a placement fee and issuance expenses of 8bp annually over a 7-year weighted average life. We add an expected annual net loss of 1bp as a result of Citicorp's recourse obligation.[8] The resulting all-in pretax financing cost of the Pass-Through Certificates would be 9.09 percent.

We then assume that Citicorp would attempt to match-fund this mortgage pool on its balance sheet with 7-year Citicorp notes yielding 7.80 percent. We estimate the annualized underwriting fees and other expenses of such notes to be 10bp and the expected loss to be 1bp. Finally, the pretax cost of capital coverage for such

---

[7] We will calculate these savings for Citicorp, as Citibank's parent holding company, since information is available to calculate a cost of equity for Citicorp and since the primary capital requirement applies equally at the Citibank and consolidated Citicorp levels.

[8] We do not include any credit enhancement fee, since the only credit enhancement was the internal Citicorp limited guarantee.

notes would be 1.86 percent assuming a 35 percent cost of equity[9] and a ratio of primary capital to assets of 6.82 percent. The all-in pretax cost of balance sheet funding of the mortgages would then be 9.77 percent—a cost 68bp in excess of the financing cost of the Pass-Through Certificates.[10]

While dependent on certain assumptions, the above calculations offer a sense of the significant all-in financing cost advantage to Citicorp of the Pass-Through Certificates. However, the more important point is linked to our inability to more precisely quantify this cost advantage. Neither we, nor presumably Citicorp, would be able to accurately estimate the weighted average life of the mortgage pool. Hence, match-funding of the mortgages at the time of their origination would be impossible as indicated by the following disclosure in the Series 1986-Q Prospectus: ". . . Citibank believes that no statistics of which it is aware provide a reliable basis for Certificate-holders to predict the amounts or the timing of receipt of prepayments on the mortgage loans." Therefore, a prime advantage of the Series 1986-Q securitization of jumbo residential mortgages was that it enabled Citicorp to offer this fixed rate product without taking the interest rate risk that could not easily be neutralized on its balance sheet due to the unpredictable life of the mortgage pool.

---

[9] This 35 percent pretax cost of equity is calculated from the capital asset pricing model using a 7-year risk-free rate of 7.09 percent, a Citicorp beta of 1.56, a market premium of 7.5 percent, and a tax rate of 46 percent.

[10] See the Appendix A for a more detailed description of this methodology for calculating comparative financing costs.

8

Receivables-Backed Commercial Paper Programs

The previous chapters have all been organized by individual asset classes. We have reviewed the credit securitization in asset classes ranging from auto loans to commercial mortgages, and we have analyzed individual transactions within each of these asset classes. Each of these transactions have been structured to match the cash flow from a fixed pool of a single type of assets with that of the holders of the asset-backed securities.

However, there is another asset-backed structure that has been widely used for pools of receivables that may include receivables of more than one asset class. This structure, the receivables-backed commercial paper program, generally does not directly link the cash flow from the assets to the payments to the commercial paper holders.

A receivables-backed commercial paper program typically works in the following manner. A special purpose corporation is established to issue the commercial paper. The special purpose corporation is structured to be bankruptcy remote, and the sole business of the corporation is to finance receivables. The special purpose corporation typically purchases the receivables from originators, but alternatively may lend money to them secured by "pledged" receivables. In either case, filings are made under the Uniform Commercial Code to perfect the special purpose corporation's ownership or security interest in the receivables. The special purpose corporation issues highly rated commercial paper to finance the receivables. Payments on the receivables are applied to repayment of the commercial paper. However, match funding the fixed-term commercial paper with the receivables is cumbersome and inefficient. As a result, maturing commercial paper is frequently funded with the proceeds from new issuances. A liquidity line of credit is generally provided by an irrevocable bank line of credit to support payment to the commercial paper holders in the unlikely event that the maturing commercial paper cannot be "rolled over" or if an originator's bankruptcy interferes with the receivables cash flow in a "pledge" transaction. The rating of a receivables-backed commercial paper program usually cannot be higher than that of the financial institution providing the irrevocable liquidity line of credit.

Credit support must also be supplied to cover credit losses on the receivables. Such credit support is generally provided by third-party credit enhancement, overcollateralization, and/or recourse to the originator. The amount of the necessary credit support is generally related to the credit history of the receivables.

As of March 1987, there were at least 9 active rated receivables-backed commercial paper programs with over $4 billion in issuance capacity. These programs were used to securitize a variety of assets such as credit card receivables, auto lease receivables, trade receivables, equipment lease receivables, and airline receivables. The receivables-backed commercial paper programs have proven to be very attractive to both originators of receivables and investors in the commercial paper. From the originator's perspective, such a program provides a continuing vehicle for the ongoing sale of financial assets through a structure that enables the originator to redeploy equity capital while sourcing funds through the highest quality commercial paper. From an investors' perspective, investors receive very liquid, high quality commercial paper supported by well-diversified cash flows.

Citicorp North America manages at least three such receivables-backed commercial paper programs (collectively referred to as

Corporate Asset Funding or CAF). These CAF programs are the market share leaders in receivables-backed commercial paper. In fact, by year-end 1987, the CAF programs had grown to about $6.6 billion in receivables-backed commercial paper. In this section, we will describe the largest of the CAF programs — Corporate Asset Funding Company, Inc. (CAFCO).

CORPORATE ASSET FUNDING COMPANY, INC.

With an approved commercial paper issuance capacity of $4.5 billion at year-end 1987, Corporate Asset Funding Company, Inc. (CAFCO), was the largest receivables-backed commercial paper program. The CAFCO program allows originators of trade receivables to sell their receivables to an issuer of the highest rated, A-1+/P-1 commercial paper. Originators can thereby remove the receivables from their balance sheets and redeploy expensive equity that would otherwise be necessary to support balance sheet financing of the receivables.

As will be discussed in this chapter, CAFCO differs from the previously discussed transactions in that CAFCO is an ongoing program rather than a one-time asset sale. The CAFCO structure gives originators the opportunity to continuously sell new receivables to CAFCO, subject to CAFCO's continuing willingness to purchase receivables from a given seller for an identified pool of obligors.

Structure

The structure of CAFCO is shown in Figure 8.1 and described next.

Origination. CAFCO supports its commercial paper with a group of receivables pools purchased from a number of different originators. For example, Figure 8.2 shows that these originators span a broad range of industries. The receivables generated by these originators are of different types. Some of the receivables pools have been generated by small retail sales to many thousands of customers who may each owe $200 to $500. Some of the

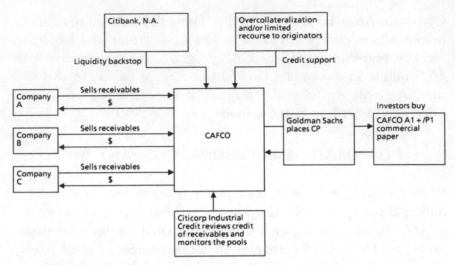

Figure 8.1. Corporate Asset Funding Co. (CAFCO) structure.

Representative industries

Pharmaceuticals	Film Production and Distribution
Chemicals	Consumer Products
Aerospace	Retailing
Telecommunications	Fast Foods
Insurance	Grocery
Paper	Automotive
Oil and Gas	Equipment Financing
Utilities	Surface Transportation
Finance Companies	Advertising
Oil Field Services	Mining
Food Services	Banking

Originator's credit ratings

S&P	Number	Size $ Millions	Percent
AAA	9	$1,210	16%
AA	6	1,674	22
A	13	1,587	21
BBB	17	2,175	29
Nonrated	10	895	12
	55	$7,541	100%

Figure 8.2. Combined corporate asset funding programs.

receivables pools are generated by larger sales ($1000 to $5000) to a smaller, but still broad base of 5000 or more customers. Finally, some pools are generated by very large sales to less than 100 customers. The receivables in CAFCO's pools are frequently of relatively short maturity—often with an average life of two months or less.

An originator typically enters into a purchase arrangement with CAFCO through an asset sales agreement. In accordance with that agreement, CAFCO purchases the receivables pool from the originator, and Citicorp North America serves as the manager for the receivables purchased by CAFCO (the "assets under management").

While CAFCO invests in receivables pools from a number of originators, CAFCO generally imposes several criteria upon all such originators to assure the credit quality of the receivables. For example, CAFCO looks for receivables pools whose credit-loss experience has been consistently low for a number of years. CAFCO requires originators to have sound credit and collection processes which generate sufficient data for regular portfolio monitoring. CAFCO also generally requires the originators of the receivables to be investment grade or, if not rated, of equivalent credit quality. (See Figure 8.2.)

Structuring

1. Type/Creation of Special Purpose Vehicle. CAFCO is a Delaware corporation primarily established for the limited purpose of issuing commercial paper and utilizing the commercial paper proceeds to purchase receivables from originators ("sale transactions").

2. The Revolving Period. As previously noted, the receivables in CAFCO's pools usually have very short maturities—often less than 2 months. However, the participants in the CAFCO program are interested in selling their receivables for much longer periods. Accordingly, to lengthen the funding period, the typical CAFCO pool is structured to be an "evergreen" facility with an ongoing revolving period, subject to continuing compliance with CAFCO credit standards, monthly reviews of portfolio performance, and annual onsite reviews of both portfolio and seller performance.

This revolving period works in the following manner. The agreement between CAFCO and the originator may provide for CAFCO to purchase a receivables pool up to a certain limit— $100 million, for example. Typically, the originator remains as the servicer (collection agent) for the receivables sold to CAFCO. The originator's customers, who owe the $100 million, send their payments to a bank lockbox account. The collection agent receives the lockbox payments and forwards the yield to CAFCO on its ownership interest in the pool. Payments which would pay down the $100 million in principal are typically reinvested in new receivables purchased from the originator. This automatic reinvestment may be terminated either by the originator or by CAFCO, in which event the $100 million pool would rapidly pay down. However, absent such a termination of reinvestment and subject to periodic credit review, CAFCO would continue to purchase a large receivables pool through this revolving feature.

3. Payment Structure of the Commercial Paper—Liquidity Support. It would be cumbersome and inefficient to precisely match-fund the receivables payments with maturing commercial paper. Instead, maturing commercial paper is normally funded with sales of new commercial paper. However, it is possible that market or other conditions might delay the placement of new commercial paper and thereby prevent the timely payment of maturing commercial paper. Such a possibility would be inconsistent with the high credit rating desirable for CAFCO's commercial paper. Accordingly, market liquidity is provided by the commercial paper dealer's ability to make a secondary market in CAFCO's commercial paper and to use its dealer inventory capability. Also, a liquidity backstop facility is provided for this and many other commercial paper programs by a commercial bank, in this case, Citibank, N.A.

4. Protection against Bankruptcy. Issuers of receivables-backed commercial paper, like CAFCO, are structured to be bankruptcy-remote entities. The issuer's business is limited to issuing commercial paper, using the commercial paper proceeds to purchase receivables and certain related activities. These limitations and others on the activities of special purpose vehicles like CAFCO are designed to ensure that the vehicle will not engage in any activities that could expose it to the business risk of a bankruptcy.

5. *Accounting/Tax Structure.* In a typical transaction, CAFCO will purchase a pool of receivables from an originator. As described next, the originator will provide some form of credit enhancement through overcollateralization or recourse to protect investors against credit losses. Pursuant to FAS Statement #77, the originator will be able to account for this transaction as a sale that removes the receivables from the originator's balance sheet, since the originator will be able to reasonably estimate its losses on its recourse or overcollateralization obligations. (See Chapter 1 for a more detailed explanation of GAAP accounting.)

From a tax perspective, the commercial paper issued by CAFCO appears to have been structured as debt. Depending upon the preferences of the parties and the structure of the particular transaction, this could be debt either of CAFCO or of the originator of the receivables. In either event, a tax deduction is available to the issuer of the debt for the interest payments to the commercial paper holders. For example, if the commercial paper was structured as debt of CAFCO, a tax deduction is available to CAFCO for the interest payments to offset income to CAFCO. Corporate debt tax treatment should be readily available to CAFCO since the payment frequency of the commercial paper clearly differs from that of the receivables and an adequate equity layer is present in CAFCO to further assure that the commercial paper payments will not be viewed as equity distributions. (See Chapter 1 for a more detailed discussion of taxation.)

Credit Enhancement. CAFCO received Standard & Poor's/Moody's highest A-1+/P-1 commercial paper credit rating. The CAFCO program has been designed to provide investors with several layers of credit protection. First, the CAFCO program requires that each receivables pool be creditworthy on a stand-alone basis, and that each originator provide credit enhancement for such pools (typically by overcollateralizing the pools). Such overcollateralization generally creates loss reserves several times the expected losses on the CAFCO pools. In order to establish the accuracy of the expected losses, originators are required to demonstrate their actual loss experience over a number of years. In addition, investors are provided substantial protection by the credit monitoring services of Citicorp North America, the manager of the CAFCO program. Citicorp North America constantly monitors the credit status of the originator and the receivables, and, in the event of a deterioration of credit status, CAFCO would refuse to purchase new receivables. As a result, the program would terminate relatively rapidly as the then-existing receivables were collected. Finally, further credit protection was built into the CAFCO program by its requirement that the participating originators all be investment grade companies, or, if unrated, of equivalent credit quality.

Placing. Goldman Sachs Money Markets Inc. is the dealer responsible for the placement of CAFCO's commercial paper.

Servicing. The originator of the receivables is usually appointed to act as the collection agent responsible for servicing. Payments on the receivables are generally made directly to a bank lockbox. The collection agent then collects such payments. At the end of each settlement period, the collection agent forwards the monies covering the daily yield on the commercial paper and the collection agent's fee to Citicorp North America (CNA), as the administrative agent for CAFCO. CNA then pays the yield to commercial paper holders and the collection agent's fee. Other monies collected by the collection agent may be paid to the originator of the assets as automatic reinvestment of principal. This automatic reinvestment may be terminated by either the originator or CAFCO.

Benefits

Receivables Originators. The numerous originators of receivables sold to CAFCO were able to gain significant economic benefits from their participation in the program. Most importantly, by selling their receivables to CAFCO, the originators are able to save substantial equity costs that would otherwise result from traditional balance sheet financing. While we lack the necessary data to particularly calculate this saving for originators participating in

CAFCO, we have prepared the following estimate for a hypothetical receivables-backed commercial paper program.

As shown in Figure 8.3, we estimate that a hypothetical receivables-backed commercial paper program would allow a particular hypothetical originator to save more than 3.0 percent pretax over the cost of match-funded traditional finance.

The first column of Figure 8.3 shows an all-in pretax cost of funds to the originator of between 6.87 and 7.40 as a result of a sale of receivables to a receivables-backed commercial paper program. This cost consists of: (1) a 6.50 percent yield to investors in the receivables-backed commercial paper; (2) a .075–.1 percent dealer's fee; (3) a .25–.75 percent program and back-stop facility fee; and (4) a .05 percent expected loss which the originator will incur because of overcollateralization or recourse.

This 6.87–7.40 percent pretax financing cost compares to an estimated 10.47–10.87 percent pretax all-in cost for traditional balance sheet financing by the originator. This 10.47–10.87 percent consists of a 6.50 percent cost of the originator's commercial paper (assuming that the originator has an A-1+/P-1 rating), a .1–.125 percent dealer's fee, a .125–.50 percent back-stop facility fee, and a .05 percent expected loss on the receivables. In addition,

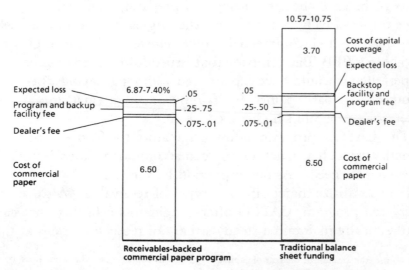

Figure 8.3. Hypothetical Receivables-Backed Commercial Paper Program, comparative vs. traditional originator financing.

there is a 3.70 percent cost of capital coverage, which represents the cost increment over the cost of debt necessary to reflect equity costs. In calculating the cost of capital coverage, we are adjusting the funding costs to allow for the fact that the originator funds its assets with both debt and equity. We therefore impute an equity cost to the financing in an amount that is proportional to the originator's overall ratio of debt and equity. (We assume the originator to be a captive finance subsidiary.)

Appendix A contains a detailed description of the methodology by which we calculated cost of capital coverage. For this example of a hypothetical originator, we have assumed a 25 percent pretax cost of equity, and a 5/1 leverage ratio of assets to equity. We then calculated the cost of capital coverage to be:*

$$\frac{25\% \text{ (Cost of equity)} - 6.50\% \text{ (Cost of debt)}}{5 \text{ (Leverage)}} = 3.70\%$$

In summary, we estimate that this originator could achieve an all-in pretax financing cost advantage of more than 3 percent by engaging in a receivables sale to a receivables-backed commercial paper program. This cost advantage essentially results from equity cost savings since the sale of the receivables eliminated the equity costs of balance sheet financing. In preparing this estimate, we have conservatively assumed that the originator could have itself issued A-1+/P-1 commercial paper. However, if the originator had been a BBB/Baa company that issued lower rated commercial paper, then it would have experienced additional savings, perhaps another 12.5 basis points, by gaining access to financing at the receivables program's higher credit rating.

The CAFCO program offers originators the above economic benefits through a structure that can accommodate a wide variety of originator needs. As noted previously, the CAFCO program is able to securitize many different types of receivables. Also, as an evergreen program, CAFCO offers originators a facility that can automatically maintain a steady stream of receivables sales at the

---

*Of course, the amount of the cost of capital coverage will depend upon the originators' cost of equity and leverage. It would be 1.85% for an originator with a 25% pretax cost of equity and a leverage of 10/1, and it would be 5.87% for an originator with a 30% pretax cost of equity and a 4/1 leverage.

level chosen by the originator. In short, CAFCO offers many types of originators a flexible structure that can economically serve a variety of financing requirements.

Citicorp North America. As the manager for the CAFCO program, Citicorp North America earns attractive fee income for its services in managing and credit-monitoring the CAFCO program.

Goldman Sachs & Company. The CAFCO program also ensures a substantial volume of fee business for Goldman Sachs Money Markets Inc., the dealer for the up to $4.5 billion in CAFCO commercial paper.

Investors. Investors, too, benefit from the CAFCO program, since it provides them with another source of the highest possible credit quality commercial paper (A-1+/P-1). In fact, more than 500 institutional investors regularly purchase the commercial paper issued by CAFCO and its two sister programs. And, as indicated in Figure 8.4, the investor community has over time recognized the

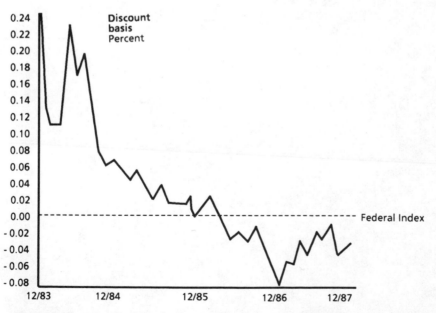

Figure 8.4. Typical Receivables-Backed Commercial Paper spread versus Federal Index

creditworthiness and liquidity of receivables-backed commercial paper to the extent that throughout the last two years it has typically sold at a yield competitive with the Federal Index for commercial paper issued by AA-rated industrial companies. The popularity of the CAF programs with investors may be seen from the performance of its commercial paper in times of financial turmoil. For example, during the market disturbances of October and December 1987, when financial companies saw their cost of funds rise appreciably, the CAF-managed asset-backed commercial paper programs experienced an actual decrease in funding costs.

Part 3

Perspective on Securitization

9

The Future of Credit
Securitization

In the previous chapters of this
book, we have demonstrated how credit securitization works and
illustrated its economics through a number of case examples. In
this concluding chapter, we will address three major questions
which the reader might raise. First, why hasn't credit securitization already displaced the bulk of traditional balance sheet lending? How might we expect credit securitization to evolve? Second,
how broad a reach do we eventually expect credit securitization to
have? Will it become a pervasive, generally employed technology
for intermediation, or will it remain a specialized technique for
financing only selected "niches" of financial assets? Third, how
great an impact will credit securitization eventually have on
bankers and other financial intermediaries?

HOW WILL THE CREDIT SECURITIZATION
TECHNOLOGY EVOLVE?

One might ask why credit securitization, given the significant
advantages which it offers, has not established itself more force-
fully already. Today, asset-backed financings (including the

broadly securitized residential mortgage market) still comprise only a small percentage of all outstandings. Does the relatively modest beginning of credit securitization foretell a limited impact or slow expansion in the future?

Securitization's slow start is, in fact, not at all surprising; most new technologies—even those which embody fundamental advantages over rival technologies and which eventually attain overwhelming dominance—begin modestly and tend to evolve, at least at first, gradually. Steam ships, for example, occupied a small, albeit growing niche against sailing ships throughout the better part of the nineteenth century. Similarly, major financial technological advances have commenced slowly before expanding in a nearly breakneck manner later on. Commercial paper, high yield (junk) bonds, and money market mutual funds have all exhibited slow starts followed by explosive growth. More specifically, new technologies, whether they represent physical advances in areas such as electronics, locomotion, and chemistry or in abstract areas such as finance tend to follow an S-curve in their development.[1]

THE S-CURVE OF TECHNOLOGICAL DEVELOPMENT

The curve is so named because it resembles an S whose ends have been pulled out (see Figure 9.1). It graphs the relationship between the effort which goes into developing a technology and the impact of this effort. At first, the benefits are modest, despite the heavy effort and time dedicated to refining and improving the promising new technology. We have labeled this period of a technology's advance as its inception. At some point, however, the process accelerates. The technology becomes rapidly accepted and enormous strides in its development are made with modest effort; this occurs throughout the growth phase. Eventually, the technological advance reaches its natural limits and progress once again comes very slowly, and only at the cost of great effort. This return to slow advances signals the onset of a technology's maturity

---

[1] We are indebted to our McKinsey colleague, Dick Foster, whose recent discussion of this phenomenon guided much of our thinking; see in particular his *Innovation: The Attacker's Advantage* (New York, 1986), pp. 31 ff.

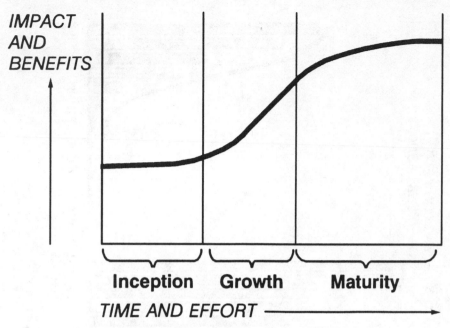

Figure 9.1.   The S-curve of technology and development.

phase. The market has mostly adapted to the technology and the period of rapid growth is now over.

Credit securitization is, as best as we can tell, still in its inception but is poised to enter its growth phase. Thus the modest growth of the past 3 years should soon be replaced by several years of explosive expansion. This would seem to follow not only from the S-curve phenomenon of new technologies in general, but more specifically from the similar pattern one can observe in a range of other financial technologies. The S-curve path can be readily recognized in the pattern of growth of commercial paper issued by industrial corporations; high yield or junk bonds; and money market mutual funds (see Figure 9.2).

The slow start of these, like most financial technologies, can be explained by the inertia which must be overcome in changing the behavior of borrowers and investors. We must also not underestimate the effort required to develop necessary infrastructures—markets, organizations, regulations, etc.—in support of these new forms of financing.

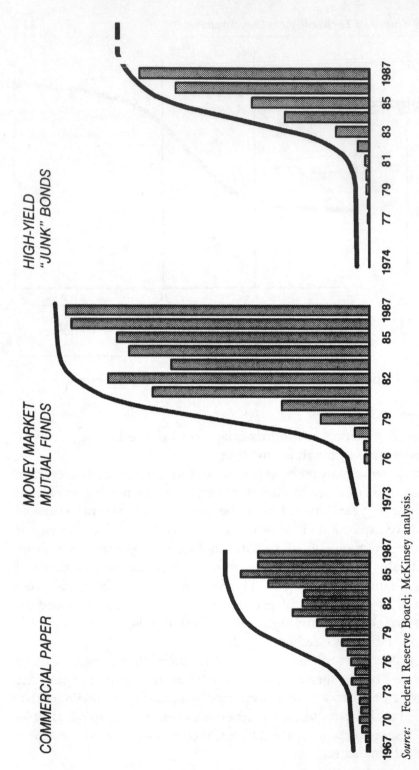

COMMERCIAL PAPER

MONEY MARKET
MUTUAL FUNDS

HIGH-YIELD
"JUNK" BONDS

Source: Federal Reserve Board; McKinsey analysis.

Figure 9.2. The S-curve of financial technologies ($ billions outstanding).

In the case of commercial paper, such developments took a long time. Until the late 1970s, only a small portion of highly rated industrial corporations replaced loans with commercial paper programs (at a savings of approximately 70 basis points[2] on their short-term borrowing costs). In fact, the early issuers viewed the commercial paper market as a supplemental source of liquidity to their bank borrowings rather than a lower cost substitute for such borrowings. It is not surprising, therefore, that the early surge of industrial commercial paper programs dates back to a period of credit tightening engineered by the Federal Reserve in 1966.

In discussions with early issuers of asset-backed securities, we have perceived an analogous motivation in the marketplace of credit securitization. Even in cases where the new technology is clearly seen as a lower-cost alternative to traditional funding, extra reasons such as interest rate exposures or capital constraints have typically been required to push "pioneer" issuers into using the technology. However, we expect that these extra motivations will, in the near future, no longer be necessary.

The industrial commercial paper entered its growth phase around 1978 and for the next 4 years it expanded at 40.7 percent annual rate. This acceleration did not occur in a vacuum. Commercial paper received a boost, as new techniques often do, from two sources; the emergence of a reinforcing technology, in this case money market mutual funds, and the effect of an external catalyst, in this case high interest rates. Let's look at each of these in a little more detail.

As Figure 9.2 illustrates, the rapid expansion of industrial commercial paper in the last decade coincided with an even sharper acceleration in the size of the nation's money market mutual funds. In fact, the coincidence was no coincidence at all; money market mutual funds have, for the past 10 years, been the single most important class of commercial paper investors, and commercial paper has constituted the single largest asset class in their investment portfolio. Money market fund managers invested heavily in commercial paper for its liquidity, yield and quality, while issuers

---

[2] This estimate is based on a comparison of commercial paper rates in 1970 with the full cost of bank borrowing by top grade companies at the time.

of the paper found ready funding in the ever-increasing assets that money market investors could provide. Both markets also benefited from the high interest rates of 1979 to 1984. Thus, growth of one market has tended to fuel the other—and both markets have been mutually reinforcing (see Figure 9.3).

The high interest rates of this growth period were instrumental in breaking the habits of borrowers and investors, as both saw their "costs" (an explicit cost for borrowers and an opportunity cost for investors/savers) rise in such an environment. Thus was highlighted the advantages of lower-cost commercial paper for borrowers and higher yield money market mutual funds for investors. When interest rates receded in 1983, high-grade borrowers did not switch back from commercial paper to bank loans, nor did investors shift away from money market mutual funds to traditional deposits. These customers had been sensitized to the greater efficiency of the newer financial intermediation alternatives. As long as these newer products offered better pricing for customers, they continued to maintain market share.

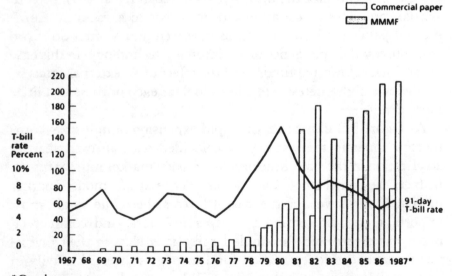

*October.

Source: Federal Reserve Board.

Figure 9.3.   Commercial paper and MMMFs vs. T-bill rate (outstanding balance 1967–87) ($ billions).

If history is to serve as a guide, we might expect the rate of credit securitization's growth to accelerate if: (1) a complementary or reinforcing technology is also developing, analogous to the mutual reinforcement of money market mutual funds and commercial paper 10 years ago; and/or (2) if it is driven by external catalysts, akin to 1979s run up in interest rates. In fact, both kinds of stimuli to growth can be observed in today's marketplace.

A technological development which should reinforce the spread of credit securitization exists in the increasingly automated (i.e., paperless) payments, collections and processing systems which handle trade and retail transactions. This increased level of automation greatly facilitates the collection and transformation of information—at the level of individual receivables—which is so often necessary for credit securitization. As for external catalysts, there are many possibilities on the horizon, anyone of which might trigger an acceleration in the growth rate of securitized financing. Four of these merit at least a brief mention: the development of the market for corporate control, recent changes in accounting conventions, more demanding capital adequacy guidelines for depositary institutions, and the increasing rate of acquisitions among financial service firms.

In the last 2 or 3 years, a lively market for corporate control has emerged. Corporations are learning that unless they work to raise the value of their stock, they are subject to the very real risk of a hostile takeover. As a result, many corporations are beginning to focus on increasing or maintaining their return on equity. Here credit securitization can play a valuable role; it allows corporations to maintain the level of business they desire, without tying up large amounts of expensive equity in financing the receivables generated by their basic operations. We expect more and more companies to be driven to increased usage of credit securitization as one of their fundamental tools to boost returns on equity against unwanted takeover attempts.

The strength of this catalyst to securitization will be further increased by a recent accounting change. New FAS rules will for the first time require nonfinancial business to consolidate the balance sheets of their finance subsidiaries. Thus nonfinancial businesses will no longer be able to remove receivables and other financial assets from the balance sheets by transferring them to unconsolidated finance subsidiaries. Here again, the power of securitized credit to remove balance sheet debt may make the technology an increasingly utilized tool in finance.

Capital adequacy guidelines which regulators set for depositary institutions, such as commercial banks and thrifts, will provide another important catalyst. Such guidelines have already provided an incentive for a number of asset-backed securities financings as institutions endeavor to free up their balance sheets in line with such regulations. However, stricter guidelines may even further increase the incentives for credit securitization in the future. In December 1987, regulators representing central banks in the United States, Britain, Japan, and nine other major industrial countries (The BIS) agreed to implement higher capital targets for lending institutions. Thus, the consequent pressure to free up capital through asset sales should only increase. Again, if recent trends hold, this regulatory catalyst will probably be reinforced by an increasing yield premium which the capital markets will demand from banks and bank holding companies for debt obligations.

Finally, credit securitization will probably also be stimulated by acquisitions activity among financial institutions, and the two trends must again be seen as interdependent. Securitization can expand the acquisitive capacity of a financial institution by freeing a portion of its capital for use in an acquisition; as the stakes for mergers and acquisitions in the industry rise, the value of the financing tool will only increase. At the same time, potential target firms will feel compelled to bolster their share price in this environment, at least in part by increasing the returns on their capital employed. Here once more, the securitization of their loan portfolio will provide an excellent means of doing so.

While we are confident that credit securitization will follow an S-curve in its development and that the technology now stands on the edge of a rapid growth phase, a great deal of uncertainty still remains. The actual pace of development is, for example, difficult to predict. In the other financial technologies we've mentioned, the steepness of the S-curve has varied. Industrial commercial paper outstandings grew at a compound annual rate of 22.1 percent between 1967 and 1977 before entering a rapid growth phase which spanned 1978 to 1981; the compound annual rate of growth was 40.7 percent. Money market mutual funds, while following a similar S shape in their development, grew much faster. This technology's low growth inception phase lasted 5 years, from 1972 to 1977, a period in which fund balances grew very slowly. However, once money market funds entered their high growth phase, and were stimulated by the then rapid growth of industrial commercial paper (1978 to 1981), these funds expanded at a staggering 144.7 percent compounded, per year. It remains to be seen whether credit securitization will follow a relatively sedate growth path, as exhibited by industrial commercial paper, or a blistering path more akin to that traced by money market mutual funds. In all events, we foresee an S-curve for credit securitization. At this time, however, we cannot tell how "lazy" the shape of the "S" will be.

HOW PERVASIVE WILL ASSET-BACKED SECURITIZATION BECOME?

Three fundamental technologies exist today for debt financing: balance sheet lending, "traditional" securities financing, and credit securitized or asset-backed securitized financing. Since the first two technologies are quite mature, and the third is still in its early development phase, we should expect "market share" to shift from balance sheet lending and traditional securities funding towards securitized credit financings. The question is how large will this shift be?

Today, balance sheet lending, considered in all of its forms across the entire economy, represents approximately $3.9 trillion in outstandings, a number which is fairly close to the $4.9 trillion in traditional debt securities outstanding. Asset-backed outstandings account for a mere $770 billion, which shrinks to less than $100 billion when mortgages guaranteed by federal government agencies are removed from the total. Five or ten years from now, we would expect this picture to change dramatically, with asset-backed securities accounting for a total level of outstandings which would be roughly comparable to traditional loans and traditional securities. In other words, we do not expect credit securitization to fully replace either traditional loans or securities, but we do expect that it will become at least as important as these older technologies. Where is this growth in asset-backed financing going to come from? Let us answer this question by looking first at retail financing and then at commercial financing.

As we described in the earlier chapters, certain types of financial assets (individual loans) are amenable to the pooling and structuring processes which credit securitization currently employs. Such individual loans are typically quite homogenous, often secured by real assets and are generated and monitored along predominantly formulaic credit criteria. These loans lend themselves to actuarial analyses when grouped in large portfolios and, therefore, facilitate the more efficient risk management and risk absorption techniques which were described in the first chapter of this book.

Most retail lending fits into this category of "readily securitizable" financial assets. Formula-driven credit scoring and credit monitoring techniques are widely used for such loans, and most retail lending programs therefore result in homogenous loan portfolios. Credit securitization has already been used as a lower cost, more efficient financing alternative in residential mortgages, revolving debt generated from credit cards, secured consumer installment loans (e.g., automobile financing), and unsecured consumer installment loans. These asset classes make up the vast majority of retail borrowings.

Even if the other classes of retail loans such as private banking demand loans, and trading account margin loans prove to be inappropriate for credit securitization, the bulk of retail lending is already "grist for the securitization mill." Furthermore, our economic analysis of securitization's relative benefits leads us to believe that almost all of these eligible assets would be more efficiently funded by asset-backed financing than they would be if they remained on their originators' books. In our opinion, it is, therefore, only a matter of time before credit securitization becomes the dominant technology for retail lending. And the length of time required will probably be determined more by the motivation and behavior of the financial service firms who originate retail loans than any other factor.

Commercial financing presents a more complex case. Some commercial lending is already done in a way which makes the original loans amenable to credit securitization. Accounts receivable financing, equipment leasing, equipment finance, and some commercial mortgage lending tend to exhibit the same properties of homogeneity and actuarially predictable behavior as retail financial assets. In fact, asset-backed securities have already been structured and issued from these asset classes. This book reviews a commercial mortgage issue done by Olympia & York, an equipment lease receivables backed issue originated by Sperry Corporation and the credit securitization of accounts receivable by a receivables-backed commercial paper program. Asset-based commercial lending, in short, can generate financial assets which are economically securitizable using the technology's existing techniques. Credit securitization, moreover, provides a more efficient, lower cost alternative means of funding such loans to traditional balance sheet lending. Thus we would also expect securitized financing to become the dominant technology for asset-based commercial lending.

Unlike retail lending, however, the potential volume of commercial lending eligible for credit securitization is relatively small. Asset-based lending is a less prominent loan origination and monitoring technique than is general obligation corporate lending; and it is the latter that represents the overwhelming majority of commercial debt financing, in the form of traditional securities such as bonds, notes, and commercial paper. General obligation commercial lending is much harder to securitize using the techniques currently available to the market.

This may change in the future, as the credit securitization technology evolves and its infrastructural support system grows. At the present time, however, general obligation corporate credits present two obstacles to the technology. First, these credits are nonhomogeneous, so that understanding the risk of a portfolio generally requires understanding the "story" behind each of the individual credits which comprise it. This requirement reduces the effectiveness of the portfolio risk measurement and risk management tools which credit securitization employs. Second, the Investment Company Act of 1940 makes the issuing of public securities backed by general purpose obligations an arduous and, in some cases, impossible task, as we described in Chapter 2. Such obligations, unlike those backed by real estate, accounts receivables, or those generated by retail lending, often do not possess an automatic exemption from the legislation.

Several efforts are underway to address the first of these obstacles; standardized loan pricing and credit grading techniques are, for example, being developed and tested. Similarly, though no major initiatives are now at hand, the second obstacle might be removed through legislative repeal. Notwithstanding, the private placement market has and will continue to be available as a source of investors, regardless of the restrictions on public issuance imposed by the Act. Thus, the possibility that credit securitization will become a cost-effective means for funding general obligation corporate credits cannot be discounted. Even if this were not the case, we believe that credit securitization will become a major and perhaps the dominant technology for commercial debt financing through the expansion of asset-based lending.

Our analysis of asset structures of most American companies suggests that a majority of their general obligation borrowings can be replaced by asset-backed obligations or outright asset sales. Account receivables owned by the U.S. commercial and industrial sector exceed $700 billion, which in itself surpasses the total commercial and industrial loan outstandings which represent (roughly $600 billion in borrowings). However, the distribution of ownership of these receivables among companies is unlikely to permit the replacement of anywhere near the total balance of C&I loans. On the other hand, if other eligible corporate assets, such as certain types of real estate, equipment and commodity inventories are used to supplement receivables financing, then a major portion of general obligation loans could probably be refinanced using credit securitization.

Such refinancing would only take place if corporate borrowers are given an incentive for their efforts, e.g., lower pricing. And lower pricing will, in turn, require greater intermediation efficiency. As we have illustrated throughout this book, credit securitization can provide reduced funding costs vis-à-vis balance sheet lending and, in many cases, vis-à-vis traditional securities financing. If asset-based lending remains a prerequisite for credit securitization, the higher operating costs involved in this form of loan origination and servicing would counterbalance the savings available from securitized funding. The new technology's cost advantage would thus be reduced and at times even eliminated. Since these operating costs are substantial, they will probably hold back the rate at which credit securitization is employed in commercial lending.

Even this operating cost disadvantage is likely to be only a temporary barrier which will be removed as the payments and collections process in this country shifts from a paper-based to a fully electronic approach. Once invoicing, payment, and settlement is done electronically (and several European economies are already well along in this transformation), the extra information which asset-based lending requires will already have been collected. The payments and collections systems will provide it effectively and cheaply.

HOW WILL CREDIT SECURITIZATION CHANGE THE FINANCIAL SERVICES INDUSTRY?

Throughout this book we have made the argument that the customers of the financial services industry (i.e., saver/investors and borrowers) will benefit from credit securitization. In these closing pages we will consider how the new technology will affect the financial service firms who link the savers and borrowers together. Senior management of these firms are increasingly asking themselves how credit securitization will affect their profitability, change the structure of the industry in which they compete, and whether it will place new demands on their firms' core institutional skills. In the next few pages we consider these three issues.

Potential Profit Impact

Three developments which we mentioned earlier in this chapter—the growth of the industrial commercial paper market, the development of the junk bond market, and development of money market mutual funds—have already had an enormous impact on this country's commercial banking system. We estimate that roughly $15 billion in annual pretax profit contribution has been diverted from the industry, in the form of lost loan volumes, reduced loan spreads, lost deposit balances, and higher cost deposits. This loss in contribution for the banks has not led directly to a like-sized decline in bottom line profits since commercial banks have restructured their costs over this period and expanded their activities in high margin areas such as retail banking. Nevertheless, the impact of "traditional" securitization (that is, commercial paper, junk bonds, etc.) on the banking industry's profitability has been great. What will be the impact of *credit* securitization?

Credit securitization should reduce the *gross* revenues from financial intermediation (i.e., the entire process of deposit taking and lending) for the industry as a whole. The very aim of the technology is, after all, the reduction of the intermediation spread so as to leave borrowers and investor/savers better off. Fortunately, credit securitization also provides financial service firms with the tools needed to reduce their costs as gross revenues drop. For many individual firms, and perhaps for the industry as a whole, these costs will decline further than gross revenues, thus leading to higher profitability.

We must, however, reemphasize our definition of costs, lest the challenge facing financial institutions be misunderstood. Throughout this book, we have treated capital, including equity capital, as a cost. This treatment of capital costs is widely accepted among capital markets investors, corporate finance professionals, and financial theorists. Capital is not, however, treated as a cost in a conventional accounting sense, and this tendency to think of capital as a free or, at least, an inexpensive resource is often reflected in the attitudes of managers throughout the financial services industry. The realization of costs savings made possible by credit securitization will require the redistribution of capital throughout the financial services industry and probably require the overall reduction of capital employed at the industry level. This development should change the attitude of management with regard to capital and other costs. And, as these attitudes change, they will accelerate the restructuring of the industry. It is a change long overdue.

In any event, credit securitization will also bring savings which extend beyond a reduction in capital costs. Credit losses across the industry should fall, once the technology is adopted, since securitization supplements the credit analysis of the originator with multiple downstream reviews from credit enhancers, rating agencies and conduits. Over time this will lead to better credit decisions at the point of origination, as those lenders who can satisfy these skeptical downstream participants displace their lower skilled competitors. In general, fewer bad loans will be made.

Credit securitization will probably lead to reduced operating costs as well. The decline should be a result of the industry-wide disaggregation that the technology will foster; today credit securitization is already replacing vertically integrated firms who handle all steps of financial intermediation, from deposit taking through lending, with firms which focus on a narrower set of roles such as origination, loan servicing, credit enhancement and securities placement. Since the economies of scale vary enormously from role to role, industrial disaggregation will permit individual firms to configure their operations according to their best skills and franchises, thereby reducing unit operating costs. This development is already well underway in the residential mortgage sector of the business. Individual originators, servicers, conduits, dealers and investors are increasingly replacing the multiple intermediation tasks that were traditionally performed by single institutions, from loan origination to deposit capture.

CHANGE IN INDUSTRY STRUCTURE

In addition to reduced costs (seen in many other similarly restructured industries), the disaggregation fostered by credit securitization should bring about two other advantages to financial services firms, and thus further change the structure of this industry. First, it should reduce the degree of head to head competition which many financial institutions now engage in. Today, too many firms look alike. They are vertically integrated suppliers of the same "full" product line. Credit securitization and its disaggregation will permit a far wider degree of differentiation from firm to firm.

As we have already mentioned, the differentiation will admit greater opportunities for focus among players within the industry. Some financial firms will focus on pure origination across a very broad product line within a certain geographic area, while others will opt to become national servicers or conduits of individual products. The number of reasonable combinations (of roles, products, and customer markets) which players can select from is immense. As new combinations evolve, the greater differentiation among firms will permit more fruitful competition—based on distinctively different service levels or fundamentally lower costs— than the head to head competition which now characterizes financial services. The industry, thus, could look very different in a few years, stripped of the unsustainable pricing and eroded credit standards that is characteristic of much of today's marketplace.

Second, industry disaggregation and competitive differentiation should help small institutions, such as community banks, survive the industry's worsening profit squeeze. These smaller banks and thrifts are often very efficient originators of credits and gatherers of savings. A credit securitizing industry structure would permit less formidable players to focus on their high "value-added" customer contact roles and subcontract the servicing, interest rate risk management, wholesale funding and other activities in which they are ill-equipped to compete. With credit securitization they would, moreover, be able to supplement their existing asset, liability and service product lines with "private label products," such as mutual funds sponsored by other firms.

IMPACT ON CORE SKILLS

We define core skills as those "institutional capabilities" which reside at the operating level of firms, that is on the "front line" or "in the trenches." Credit underwriting, operations management, and marketing/sales are examples of core skills which are particularly important for financial institutions. These core skills will become even *more* important as a result of credit securitization. As we have seen, the new technology will make credit underwriting skills more transparent as skeptical downstream purchasers, guarantors and rating agencies review the quality of what originators generate for securitized transactions. Credit underwriting skills will also become a major differentiator of competitive costs, as explained in Chapter 1, since credit securitization will lead to capital costs that rise in direct proportion to expected credit losses.

In coming years, as the financial world securitizes, core skills in marketing and sales will similarly become a greater determinant of success; in the new era, competitive rivalry will no longer be checked by capital size and growth. Core skills in operations will also grow in importance, as banks, thrifts and finance companies find themselves competing with focused competitors who possess improved configurations and operate at volumes determined by scale economies.

Contrary to appearances, these traditional financial skills in credit, marketing and operations will not be swamped or made obsolete by newer skills in structuring and securities sales. Instead, with securitized credit, the traditional skills will become even more valuable as industry competition becomes more explicit— and more demanding. Thus, top managers will have to ensure that their own institutions continue to build these skills, deeply and distinctively.

That task may be even more demanding than top management's other major challenge—charting a strategic course in terms of products, markets, geography, and, now, roles. As the global arena of financial services continues to intensify, developing the right strategic vision will not be easy. But the difficulty of the job will be compounded by the ever increasing need for every player to mobilize individuals down through the levels of organization, and equip them to compete in the rapidly changing game. Winners will be those institutions who rise to these multiple challenges, and thereby most effectively leverage the many opportunities provided by the new technology.

Appendix A
Methodology for Financing Cost Calculations

In our view, a central advantage of securitized credit is that it is a significantly lower-cost financing technology than traditional financing intermediated through bank or finance company balance sheets. Therefore, it is important that we are quite clear about the methodology by which we have analyzed financing costs. In this appendix, we will:

- Explain the methodology we selected to calculate the economics of the transactions analyzed in Part 2.

- Explain why we chose this methodology over other technical calculation alternatives.[1]

[1] Ron Wippern, currently an independent consultant and formerly professor at Yale School of Management, and Tim Koller of McKinsey & Company were extremely helpful in discussing and developing the concepts treated in this appendix. Ron repeatedly created time to push forward our thinking about some of the more difficult concepts embedded in the above methodology. Tim made extremely valuable contributions to the corporate finance theory underlying our approach to credit securitization, and he was also kind enough to review this appendix.

METHODOLOGY FOR CALCULATING
THE COMPARATIVE COSTS OF CREDIT
SECURITIZATION VS. TRADITIONAL FINANCE

We have generally attempted to compare the all-in pretax financing costs to the originator of financing through a particular securitized credit transaction with match funding in a traditional manner. We have tried to include estimates of the transaction costs associated with both alternative forms of finance. The resulting comparative costs show our best estimate of the all-in pretax cost advantage to the originator of engaging in the securitized credit transaction.

Let us now look at an example of one of these calculations in order to understand the details of this calculation. Consider the Asset Backed Securities Corporation transaction calculations that were presented in Chapter 3 (see Figure A.1).

The second column of Figure A.1 shows the cost of match-funded traditional GMAC debt. We calculated that cost in the following manner. First, we estimated that GMAC medium-term notes at a matched 2-year maturity would have yielded about 7.01 percent, and that the associated underwriting fees and other issuance expenses would have amounted to another 20bp on an annual basis. We then adopted a 50bp loan loss allowance to reflect a maximum estimated amount that GMAC would reserve and actually lose each year on the car loans that were being financed. While this loan loss allowance may not technically be a financing cost, it is important that it be included in the calculation to balance the expected loss to GMAC on its recourse obligation in the comparable securitized financing.

While the above calculations may be somewhat difficult in practice, since some estimated costs (especially that for match-funded debt)[2] may be difficult to obtain, these calculations do not present any theoretical difficulty. Unfortunately, the same cannot be said for the remaining cost item, the cost of capital coverage.

---

[2] Theoretically, it might pay GMAC to traditionally match-fund the auto receivables with a blend of commercial paper and medium-term notes of various maturities that, blended together, had about the same maturity as the 2-year notes. Such a blend might lower GMAC's cost of funds by a few basis points. However, given the uncertainties in our estimate of the cost of such notes, any such attempted further refinement would not be meaningful.

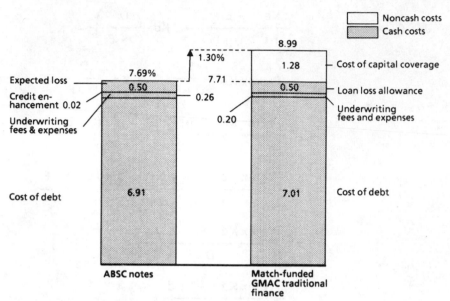

Source: GMAC Annual Report, McKinsey analysis.

Figure A.1. Asset-Backed Securities Corporation, Asset-Backed Obligations, Series 1 comparative annualized pretax financing costs (October 14, 1986) (percent).

The cost of capital coverage represents the incremental additional cost of equity over the cost of 100 percent debt financing. In other words, we define cost of capital coverage to be the weighted average cost of capital (WACC) minus the cost of debt. In our calculations, we have calculated this cost of capital coverage on a pretax basis by the following formula:

$$\frac{\text{Pretax Ke} - \text{Kd}}{\dfrac{\text{Assets}}{\text{Equity}}} = \text{Cost of capital coverage}$$

In this formula, Pretax Ke means the pretax cost of equity, Kd is the cost of debt, Assets is the total value of debt plus equity, and Equity is the value of the equity. This formula is simply a shorthand way of calculating WACC − Kd, as shown in Figure A.2.[3]

---

[3] We believe that George Feiger of McKinsey & Company deserves credit for this formula, although he is, of course, not responsible for our application of it.

$$
\text{WACC} - \text{Kd} \quad = \left(\frac{\text{Ke}}{1\text{-}t} \, \frac{\text{E}}{\text{D} + \text{E}} \; + \; \text{Kd} \, \frac{\text{D}}{\text{D} + \text{E}} \right) - \text{Kd}
$$

$$
= \text{Pretax Ke} \, \frac{\text{E}}{\text{D} + \text{E}} \; + \; \text{Kd} \, \frac{\text{D}}{\text{D} + \text{E}} - \text{Kd}
$$

$$
= \frac{\text{Pretax Ke} \;\; \text{E} \; + \; \text{Kd D} \; - \; \text{Kd (D} + \text{E)}}{\text{D} + \text{E}}
$$

$$
= \frac{\text{Pretax Ke} \;\; \text{E} \; + \; \text{Kd D} \;\; - \;\; \text{Kd D} - \text{Kd E}}{\text{D} + \text{E}}
$$

$$
= \frac{\text{Pretax Ke} \;\; \text{E} \;\; - \;\; \text{Kd E}}{\text{D} + \text{E}}
$$

$$
= \frac{\text{Pretax Ke} \;\; - \;\; \text{Kd}}{\dfrac{\text{D} + \text{E}}{\text{E}}}
$$

$$
= \frac{\text{Pretax Ke} \;\; - \;\; \text{Kd}}{\dfrac{\text{Assets}}{\text{Equity}}}
$$

Figure A.2. Derivation of cost of pretax capital coverage formula.

One difficulty in applying this formula is that the leverage ratio Assets/Equity should be applied at market values. To do this, we would need the market value of GMAC's equity and of its debt. However, GMAC is a wholly owned subsidiary of GM. Thus, no market value is available for GMAC's equity. Accordingly, we decided to use the book value of GMAC's equity on the theory that this book value was a reasonably good proxy, since GMAC's assets were relatively short-term financial assets. We also decided to use the book value of GMAC's debt as a reasonable proxy for the market value of that relatively short-term debt. Thus we were able to develop an Assets/Equity ratio for GMAC.

Of course, the use of this ratio shows one of our fundamental assumptions. We have assumed that GMAC and the other originators were not over-capitalized—that they were not holding excess equity in their capital structure. Therefore, we have assumed that in the event that GMAC or another originator were to fund the assets by traditional balance sheet finance, the originator would hold its proportion of debt and equity constant before and after the financing. We believe this to be a very reasonable assumption, since GMAC and the other originators are large financial institutions very active in the capital markets. These companies are not likely to be over-capitalized. In fact, these companies may occasionally be under-capitalized, in which event our Asset/Equity ratio would understate the amount of equity required to support traditional balance sheet finance.

After resolving the above question of how to calculate leverage, the only remaining difficulty in calculating the cost of capital coverage was to calculate GMAC's cost of equity. To calculate that cost, we used the capital asset pricing model (CAPM) in the simple form of: $Ke = Rf + \beta(M)$. Of course, CAPM presents some difficulties in application. We ultimately decided to use a market premium of 7.5 percent, together with a risk-free rate matched to the average life of the assets we were funding.[4] The remaining difficulty was to determine a proper beta (β), since no market prices exist for GMAC's equity. We considered adopting the 1.1 levered beta of Household International, the only independent public finance company for which a beta was available, but instead decided to simply use a beta of 1.0 as one generally appropriate for banks and finance companies. Therefore, we were able to estimate GMAC's cost of equity using CAPM to be:

$$Ke = Rf + \beta(M)$$
$$= 6.1 + 1.0(7.5)$$
$$= 13.6\%$$

Finally, we divided that 13.6 percent by 1 minus the marginal tax rate of 46 percent to get:

---

[4] One example of these difficulties is the question of which market premium to use. We decided to use a 7.5 percent premium calculated by Ron Wippern, however we recognize that others may prefer to use a premium closer to 6 percent.

$$\text{Pretax Ke} = \frac{13.6\%}{1 - .46} = 25.2\%$$

We could then proceed to calculate the cost of capital coverage:

$$\text{Cost of capital coverage} = \frac{\text{Pretax Ke} - \text{Kd}}{\dfrac{\text{Assets}}{\text{Equity}}}$$

$$= \frac{25.2\% - 7.01\%}{\dfrac{90.8}{6.4}}$$

$$= 1.28\%$$

And it is this 1.28 percent that is the cost of capital coverage used in Figure A.1. Please note that this calculation is generally sensitive to several factors: the marginal tax rate (the higher the tax rate, the higher the cost of capital coverage), the beta (the higher the beta, the higher the cost of capital coverage), the market premium (the higher the premium selected, the higher the cost of capital coverage), and the leverage (the greater the leverage ratio of assets to equity, the less the cost of capital coverage).

Using the above methodology, we were able to calculate an all-in pretax cost to GMAC of 8.99 percent for traditional financing (Figure A.1). The 8.99 percent consisted of a "cash cost" of 7.71 percent together with a "noncash cost" of 1.28 percent, which represented the imputed cost of equity in excess of the cost of debt.

We compare this 8.99 percent with the all-in financing cost of the ABSC Notes. The first element of this cost is the 6.91 percent (CBE) cost of the ABSC Notes. This 6.91 percent was a little bit more difficult to estimate than in other transactions since ABSC issued three tranches of Notes, each with different coupons and maturities. The 6.91 percent figure represents an average of the corporate bond equivalent yields[5] of each tranche,

---

[5] Corporate bond equivalent means that the yield has been adjusted to the effective yield of a typical corporate bond that pays every 6 months, even though the ABSC Notes actually pay quarterly. We make this adjustment in order to fairly compare the ABSC Notes to GMAC traditional finance for which a 6-month payment pattern has been assumed in the cost of the debt.

weighted by the relative size and weighted average life[6] of each tranche.

The second element of cost is the 26bp annualized cost for underwriting fees and expenses. This figure includes two component parts: $15,942,500 in underwriting fees payable at the time of issuance of the Asset-Backed Notes, and another $1,450,000 in other issuance expenses. These fees and expenses are incurred at the start-up of the transaction, and therefore theoretically ought to be stepped up by an appropriate discount rate in order to be properly annualized. While we have so annualized these costs for certain transactions including this ABSC Series I transaction,[7] we have not done so in other transactions when the difference in cost is minimal.

The third cost element of the ABSC Notes was the credit enhancement fee paid to Credit Suisse. We estimate that fee to have been 3/8 percent annually on the 6 percent of the principal that was guaranteed. We then spread the fee over the full 100 percent of the issue's principal to get a 2bp annual cost.[8]

The fourth and final cost element of the ABSC Notes was the 50bp annual maximum expected loss. We include this cost since we are attempting to calculate the all-in cost to GMAC of the ABSC financing. The expected loss is a cost because GMAC has made a 5 percent first loss limited guarantee on the vehicle receivables. Therefore, GMAC will absorb the actual credit losses on these receivables over the life of the issue. In fact, GAAP accounting specifically requires GMAC to recognize this cost associated

---

[6] The weighted average life of an asset-backed security is the average amount of time required for principal to be repaid to investors. We use that weighted average life period for the purpose of comparing asset-backed securities which regularly pay principal and interest with straight corporate debt, which only repays principal at maturity. Technically, this comparison might more precisely be made between the durations of the two securities. However, weighted average life is the standard used for these comparisons by the securities industry, and, as a result, it is relatively easily available. Accordingly, we have decided to work with the weighted average life, which is reasonably accurate given the relative imprecision of the other elements in these calculations.

[7] For example, we did perform this discounting for the Olympia & York transaction which had a much longer maturity (10 years) and had significantly differing upfront fees.

[8] The amount of the Letter of Credit tends to decline in proportion to the reduction of the amount of principal outstanding. Therefore, it is usually appropriate to measure this cost to the WAL of the issue.

with the recourse obligation by reserving the expected loss at the time the ABSC Notes were issued. We believe that the expected loss on the vehicle loans was slightly less than 50bp annually, but we decided to use a 50bp annual loss figure since we believe that is approximately the amount that GMAC reserved for the expected loss.

The all-in financing cost of the ABSC Notes then amounts to 7.69 percent, which is 130bp less than the 8.99 percent all-in cost of traditional GMAC finance.

Our Financing Cost Calculation Methodology vs. Alternatives

It is important to be aware of a fundamental technical assumption in our methodology for calculating the cost to GMAC of the ABSC issue.[9] We assume that the total cost to GMAC of its 5 percent recourse contingent obligation is no more than the 1 percent expected loss on the vehicle loans over the life of the issue. We make this assumption because we know that GAAP only requires GMAC to reserve for the 1 percent expected loss, and we also know from GMAC's Annual Report that in fact the company does approximately make such a 1 percent reserve.

However, while GMAC itself may properly only recognize a 1 percent cost associated with its recourse obligation, it is possible that the investor market could effectively impose a greater cost. At least one possibility springs readily to mind. Investors might effectively require GMAC to reserve a full 5 percent in equity against GMAC's 5 percent recourse obligation—even though the reasonably expected loss was only 1 percent. Investors could

---

[9] We also make one fundamental theoretical assumption to which we would draw your attention. That assumption is that the financing cost savings realized by GMAC as a result of the ABSC issue are not disturbed by consequent increases or decreases in GMAC's cost of equity or cost of traditional debt. It is possible that by effectively increasing GMAC's financial leverage, securitization could increase GMAC's cost of equity and cost of traditional debt. It is also possible that by creating an asset portfolio that generates greater net cash flow and fewer balance sheet risks, securitization could decrease GMAC's cost of equity and cost of traditional debt. We have not attempted to quantify any such cost increase or cost of traditional debt. An analysis of the corporate finance theory underlying our decision to assume no change in GMAC's cost of equity or traditional debt would be beyond the scope of this book.

effectively impose this higher 5 percent requirement by subtracting that amount of equity as dedicated to the ABSC issue, before calculating the amount of equity available to support GMAC's general credit debt obligations.

In order to examine this possibility, we interviewed rating agencies and institutional investors shortly after the ABSC issue. While this recourse issue had been considered, it was our understanding that as of that date the market had by and large decided not to impose any additional equity cost upon issuers of asset-backed securities for recourse in excess of expected losses. In fact, some market participants indicated that they were considering whether to award equity bonuses to issuers of asset-backed securities. Such a bonus might be appropriate since the asset-backed issuers were matched asset-liability financings which necessarily eliminated interest rate mismatch risk that might otherwise be present in the originator balance sheets. Therefore, we concluded that the most accurate way of portraying the cost of the ABSC and other issues was to simply show the cost of the expected loss to the originator from their recourse obligations. This treatment was consistent with GAAP accounting and, equally importantly, consistent with the then current view of the overall investor market.

However, it is possible that at some time in the development of credit securitization the investor market may fully impute equity to support outstanding recourse obligations. It is possible that the relative insignificance of the potential recourse exposure in light of the originators large balance sheets may have obscured any such equity costs in the developmental stage of credit securitization. It is critically important to note that while such an action by the investor market would reduce the all-in financing cost advantage of securitization, we do not believe that the fundamental economics would change. In the case of ABSC, such treatment would nevertheless result in an equity cost savings for GMAC since the 5% recourse level for the ABSC issue still would require significantly less equity than the 7% equity that GMAC held against assets on its balance sheet. More importantly, though, a market decision to require equity to fully support recourse obligations could result in the reconfiguration of credit enhancement structures to eliminate unnecessarily high levels of recourse.

For example, consider the credit enhancement structure of the ABSC issue. In that issue, there was 5 percent recourse back to the originator, GMAC. That 5 percent recourse level was far in excess of the less than 1 percent expected loss on the vehicle loans over the life of the issue. This excess recourse has been structured into some asset-backed issues, like ABSC, in part because it was free since the investor market was not requiring equity to support such excess recourse. As a result, the "extra" recourse was a costless way of lowering the fee for third-party enhancement. For example, in the ABSC transaction, the 5 percent recourse to GMAC was backed up by a 6 percent Letter of Credit from Credit Suisse. We estimate the price of that Letter of Credit to have been only 3/8 percent annually, a price that may have not been obtainable with a lower level of recourse.

Suppose that the ABSC transaction had been more traditionally structured and that recourse to GMAC had been limited to no more than 2 percent. As a result, let us also suppose that the price of the Credit Suisse Letter of Credit rose to an unprecedentedly high annual rate of 1 percent of the amount enhanced. In that event, the comparative annualized pretax financing costs of ABSC versus traditional GMAC finance would be as shown in Figure A.3. The first column of Figure A.3 shows the cost of the restructured ABSC financing. The 6.91 percent cost of the ABSC notes, the 26bp underwriting fees and expenses, and the 50bp expected loss, all remain unchanged from our original ABSC cost calculations.[10] The new credit enhancement fee of 1 percent on the 6 percent amount enhanced, when spread over the full $4 billion issue, amounts to a 6bp cost of credit enhancement. Finally, we must add one new cost that did not appear in our original calculation. That cost is the cost of capital coverage for the 2 percent recourse, which we are supposing must be supported by equity.

The most conservative way of viewing this equity cost would be to treat it exactly as we did the 7 percent equity used in traditional GMAC finance. Calculated in that manner, the cost of capital

---

[10] The calculations of the cost of the ABSC transaction as originally structured appear in Figure 3.5.

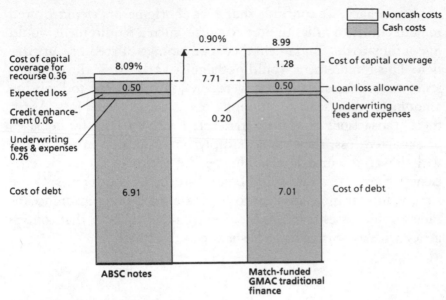

Source: McKinsey analysis.

Figure A.3. Asset-Backed Securities Corporation, Hypothetical Alternative Structure for Asset-Backed Obligations, Series 1, comparative annualized pretax financing costs (percent).

coverage arising from allocating 2 percent equity as a result of the 2 percent recourse obligation would be:

$$\frac{25\%(\text{Pretax cost of equity}) - 6.91\%(\text{Cost of debt})}{\dfrac{100}{2} \ (\text{Assets/Equity})} = 0.36\%$$

In that event, the all-in financing cost of the ABSC Notes would be 8.09 percent which would still be a significant 90bp cheaper than traditional GMAC finance (Figure A.3).[11]

---

[11] The above 36bp cost of capital coverage attributable to 2 percent equity may theoretically be slightly too conservative, since our cost calculations have already included a portion of that recourse cost. We have done so by counting the 50bp annual expected loss from the recourse obligation. Accordingly, the cost of capital coverage only for an average of 1.5 percent equity has been unaccounted for over the approximately 2-year average life of the issue. The cost of capital coverage for this 1.5 percent would be 27bp. At that level, the all-in financing cost of the ABSC notes would be 8.00 percent—99bp cheaper than traditional GMAC finance.

In summary, we conclude that even if originators were required to hold equity to fully support recourse, such a requirement would not eliminate the fundamental cost advantage of credit securitization. This requirement would not significantly affect the economics of those transactions that were already structured to limit the amount of recourse to an amount close to the expected loss. As for those transactions previously structured with recourse far in excess of expected loss, they would simply be structured in the future with lower recourse levels. Hence, the ultimate economic efficiency of securitization would be undisturbed in both cases. Quite simply, it is far more efficient to purchase third-party insurance for catastrophic losses than it is for the originator to cover that contingency with expensive balance sheet equity capital.

Appendix B
List of Securitized Credit Transactions

The first part of this Appendix lists the public issues of non-mortgage asset backed securities in chronological order from the first such issue in 1985 through year end 1987. The second part of this Appendix lists the 1985 to 1987 public issues of mortgage backed securities that were securitized without the assistance of government-related credit enhancement programs.

These listings are included so that the reader may gain a sense of the scope and development of securitization.

TABLE B.1. PUBLIC ISSUES OF NONMORTGAGE ASSET-BACKED SECURITIES 1985–87

Originator	Issue Date	Issuer	Amount ($ millions)	Asset Class	Offer Yield (percent)	Coupon (percent)	Moody's/ Standard & Poor's Rating at Offering	Expected Average Life (years)	Lead Manager
Sperry Corporation	03/07/85	Sperry Lease Finance Corp., Series A	$ 192.46	Leases - data processing equip.	11.24	11.00	NR/AAA	2.1	First Boston
Valley National Bank	05/15/85	Valley National Financial Corp.	100.50	Auto and truck	9.75	9.50	Aa1/NR	1.9	First Boston
Marine Midland Bank	05/15/85	MM 1985-1 CARS Trust	60.17	Auto and truck	9.72	9.63	NR/AAA	1.6	Salomon Brothers
Home Federal S&L	08/01/85	Home Fed. 1985-1 CARS Trust	103.21	Auto and truck	9.74	9.75	NR/AAA	2.0	Salomon Brothers
Sperry Corporation	09/12/85	Sperry Lease Finance Corp., Series B	145.81	Leases - data processing equip.	9.93	9.45	NR/AAA	2.4	First Boston
General Motors Acceptance Corp.	12/12/85	GMAC 1985-A Grantor Trust	524.68	Auto and truck	8.71	8.45	Aa1/AA+	1.9	First Boston
Western Financial Savings Bank	12/13/85	Western Financial FASTBACs 1985-A Grantor Trust	110.00	Auto and truck	8.76	8.38	Aa1/NR	1.7	Drexel Burnham Lambert
General Motors Acceptance Corp.	01/23/86	GMAC 1986-A Grantor Trust	423.55	Auto and truck	8.81	8.55	Aa1/AA+	1.9	First Boston
General Motors Acceptance Corp.	04/16/86	GMAC 1986-B Grantor Trust	1,049.49	Auto and truck	7.34	7.10	Aa1/AA+	2.0	First Boston
Empire of America Federal Savings Bank	06/19/86	Empire of America FSB 1986-A Grantor Trust	190.22	Auto and truck	7.98	7.7	Aaa/NR	1.5	First Boston
General Motors Acceptance Corp.	06/20/86	GMAC 1986-C Grantor Trust	755.07	Auto and truck	8.04	7.8	Aa1/AA+	2.1	First Boston
Chrysler Financial Corp.	07/23/86	CARCO Series 1986-1	250.00	Auto and truck	7.42	7.5	NR/AAA	1.4	Salomon Brothers
Nissan Motors Acceptance Corp.	07/24/86	NMAC 1986-B1 Grantor Trust	112.73	Auto and truck	7.55	7.25	Aaa/AAA	1.3	First Boston
		NMAC 1986-B2 Grantor Trust	69.70	Auto and truck	7.55	6.7	Aaa/AAA	1.9	First Boston
		NMAC 1986-B3 Grantor Trust	5.01	Auto and truck	7.50	5.7	Aaa/AAA	1.5	First Boston
General Motors Acceptance Corp.	08/19/86	GMAC 1986-D Grantor Trust	354.75	Auto and truck	7.08	6.5	Aa1/AA+	1.5	First Boston
		GMAC 1986-E Grantor Trust	725.07	Auto and truck	7.29	6.9	Aa1/AA+	2.1	First Boston

Issuer	Date	Issue	Amount	Type			Rating		Underwriter
General Motors Acceptance Corp.	10/14/86	Asset-Backed Securities Corp. Class 1-A Class 1-B Class 1-C	$2,095.00 585.00 1,320.00	Auto and truck	6.30 6.96 7.27	6.25 6.9 6.95	Aaa/AAA	1.1 2.2 3.1	First Boston
Western Financial Savings Bank	11/13/86	Western Financial FASTBACs 1986-A Grantor Trust	191.93	Auto and truck	6.84	6.625	NR/AAA	1.4	Drexel Burnham Lambert
Banco Central Corp.	11/17/86	Banco Central 1986-A Grantor Trust	66.61	Auto and truck	6.25	6.15	NR/AA+	1.4	First Boston
General Motors Acceptance Corp.	11/18/86	GMAC 1986-F Grantor Trust	326.96	Auto and truck	7.00	6.85	Aa1/AA+	1.9	First Boston
General Motors Acceptance Corp.	12/02/86	Asset-Backed Securities Corp. Class 2-A Class 2-B Class 2-C	95.00 25.05 60.16	Auto and truck	6.30 6.77 6.97	6.25 6.65 6.85	Aaa/AAA	1.1 2.2 3.1	First Boston
Goldome FSB	12/05/86	Goldome 1986-A	205.71	Leases - data processing and telecommunication	6.80	6.6	NR/AAA	1.4	First Boston
Bank of America National Trust & Savings Assn.	12/12/86	California CARS Grantor Trust 1986-A	514.22	Auto and truck	6.75	6.8	Aaa/AAA	1.5	Salomon Brothers
Unisys Corp.	12/17/86	Sperry Lease Finance Corp. Series C	174.45	Leases - data processing	7.14	7.05	NR/AAA	1.6	First Boston
General Motors Acceptance Corp.	12/17/86	GMAC 1986-G Grantor Trust	444.86	Auto and truck	7.03	6.85	Aa/AA	1.9	First Boston

TABLE B.1. (Continued)

Originator	Issue Date	Issuer	Amount ($ millions)	Asset Class	Offer Yield (percent)	Coupon (percent)	Moody's/Standard & Poor's Rating at Offering	Expected Average Life (years)	Lead Manager
RepublicBank Delaware	01/16/87	Credit Card Backed Notes Series A	199.50	Credit card	7.24	7.15	NR/AAA	3.2	Goldman Sachs
Bank of America	02/24/87	California Credit Card Trust 1987-A	400.00	Credit card	6.95	6.90	Aaa/AAA	1.8	First Boston
Western Financial Savings, Santa Ana, CA	03/19/87	Western Financial Auto Loans 2, Inc.	125.00	Auto and truck	6.86	6.75	Aaa/AAA	1.4	Drexel Burnham Lambert
General Motors Acceptance Corp.	03/24/87	GMAC 1987-A Grantor Trust	163.60	Auto and truck	N/A	7.00	Aa1/AA	1.9	First Boston
General Motors Acceptance Corp.	04/22/87	GMAC 1987-B Grantor Trust	162.50	Auto and truck	N/A	N/A	Aa1/AA	1.9	Salomon Brothers
RepublicBank Dallas	05/25/87	Auto Loan Pass-Through Certificates, Series A	230.00	Auto and truck	8.46	8.50	Aaa/AAA	1.2	Goldman Sachs
General Motors Acceptance Corp.	05/29/87	GMAC 1987-C Grantor Trust	166.10	Auto and truck	N/A	N/A	Aa1/AA	1.9	First Boston
General Electric Credit Corp.	06/03/87	GECC 1987-1 Grantor Trust	146.90	Auto and truck	N/A	8.50	Aaa/NR	2.0	Kidder Peabody
Marine Midland Automotive Financial Corp.	06/04/87	Marine Midland 1987-1 CARS Trust	600.10	Auto and truck	8.41	8.45	Aaa/AAA	1.5	Salomon Brothers
Chrysler Financial Corp.	06/11/87	CFC-1 Grantor Trust	515.90	Auto and truck	8.49	8.30	Aaa/AAA	1.9	First Boston
Bank of America	06/22/87	California Credit Card Trust 1987-B	300.00	Credit card	8.21	8.20	Aaa/NR	1.8	Salomon Brothers
General Motors Acceptance Corp.	06/22/87	GMAC 1987-D Grantor Trust	323.30	Auto and truck	N/A	8.15	Aa1/AA	1.9	Salomon Brothers

Issuer	Date	Security	Amount	Collateral			Rating		Underwriter
Imperial Savings Assn.	06/23/87	Imperial CARDS Trust 1987-1	100.00	Credit card	8.30	8.25	Aaa/AAA	2.5	Salomon Brothers
Mack Financial Corp.	06/30/87	Truck Receivables Underlying Certificates, Series 1		Auto and truck			Aaa/AAA		Shearson Lehman Brothers
		Class 1-A	103.70		7.22	7.15		0.5	
		Class 1-B	111.50		8.13	8.05		1.9	
General Electric Credit Corp.	07/02/87	Asset-Backed Securities Corp.		Auto and truck			Aaa/NR		First Boston
		Class A	$ 15.30		7.53	7.40		1.0	
		Class B	10.40		8.52	7.45		3.3	
Security Pacific Credit Corp.	07/16/87	Security Pacific Credit Corp. 1987-A Grantor Trust	103.00	Auto and truck	7.92	7.70	Aaa/NR	1.6	First Boston
General Motors Acceptance Corp.	07/28/87	Asset-Backed Securities Corp., Series 4		Auto and truck			Aaa/AAA		First Boston
		Class A	971.20		7.47	7.40		1.1	
		Class B	439.60		8.38	8.30		3.1	
Western Financial Savings, Santa Ana, CA	07/29/87	Western Financial Auto Loans 2, Inc.	110.00	Auto and truck	8.00	7.80	Aaa/AAA	1.5	Drexel Burnham Lambert
First National Bank of Boston	08/24/87	Salomon Brothers Receivables, Inc.	102.00	Auto and truck	8.30	8.25	Aaa/NR	1.7	Salomon Brothers
Mattel, Inc.	09/17/87	Mattel Funding Corp.	62.5	Trade receivables-backed preferred stock	5.4 initially		Aaa/AAA	Unlimited	First Boston
Union Carbide Corp.	09/23/87	Union Carbide Finance Corp.	249.00	Trade receivables-backed preferred stock		Class A - 5.55, Class B - 5.60, Class C - 5.65	Aaa/AAA	Unlimited	First Boston
Great American First Savings Bank, San Diego	09/23/87	Great American Credit Card Trust-A	110.00	Credit card	9.22	9.05	Aaa/AAA	2.5	Goldman Sachs
Imperial Savings Association, San Diego	09/24/87	Imperial Savings Assoc.	100.00	Corporate junk bonds	9.48	9.38	Aaa/AAA	-	Drexel Burnham Lambert
First Chicago Corp.	09/29/87	First Chicago CARDS	800.00	Credit card	9.23	9.15	Aaa/AAA	1.9	Salomon Brothers

TABLE B.1. (Continued)

Originator	Issue Date	Issuer	Amount ($ millions)	Asset Class	Offer Yield (percent)	Coupon (percent)	Moody's/ Standard & Poor's Rating at Offering	Expected Average Life (years)	Lead Manager
Green Tree Acceptance Corp.	09/30/87	Merrill Lynch Mortgage Investors, Inc. Trust 1987-1	71.50	Manufactured homes loans	10.63	10.20	NR/AA	5.0	Merrill Lynch
American Airlines	10/02/87	American Airlines 1987-A Grantor Trusts		Leases - notes financing aircraft leveraged leases			A1/A+		Morgan Stanley
		Class 1	3.45		8.96	8.96		0.2	
		Class 2	6.52		9.13	9.13		1.2	
		Class 3	9.93		9.42	9.42		2.2	
		Class 4	7.88		9.65	9.65		3.2	
		Class 5	1.71		9.97	9.97		4.2	
		Class 6	19.95		10.52	10.52		8.0	
		Class 7	43.19		11.11	11.11		13.8	
Volkswagen of America	10/08/87	Volkswagen Lease Finance Corp.	150.00	Auto leases	9.95	9.75	NR/AAA	4.0	Dillon, Read
UST Corp., Boston	10/09/87	UST FASTBACs 1987-A	109.10	Auto and truck	9.39	9.20	Aaa/AAA	1.6	Drexel Burnham Lambert
General Motors Acceptance Corp.	10/13/87	Asset-Backed Securities Corp., Series 5	142.70	Auto and truck	9.53	9.40	Aaa/AAA	1.6	First Boston
Empire of America Federal Savings Bank Buffalo	10/23/87	Empire of America 1987-A Grantor Trust	265.00	Auto and truck	9.05	8.85	Aaa/NR	1.6	First Boston
Marine Midland Bank NA	11/05/87	Salomon Brother Receivables, Inc.		Auto and truck			Aaa/AAA		Salomon Brothers
		Class 1Y	176.80		N/A	8.15		N/A	
		Class 1A	265.80		N/A	8.50		N/A	

Issuer	Date		Amount	Type			Rating		Underwriter
Chrysler Finanical Corp.	11/12/87	CFC-2 Grantor Trust	1,000.00	Auto and truck	8.79	8.55	Aaa/AAA	1.9	First Boston
Household Finance Corp.	11/12/87	Household Bank fsb		Unsecured consumer loans			Aa3/AAA		
		Class A	151.70		7.60	7.45		0.5	Goldman Sachs
		Class B	280.40		8.65	8.25		1.0	
BMW Credit Corp.	11/18/87	Asset-Backed Securities Corp. Series 6		Auto and truck			NR/AAA		First Boston
		Class 6-A	36.04		7.69	7.55	Aaa/NR	0.5	
		Class 6-B	88.50		8.78	8.65		2.0	
UST Corp., Boston	11/20/87	UST FASTBACs 1987-B Grantor Trust	100.00	Auto and truck	8.71	8.55	Aaa/AAA	1.6	Drexel Burnham Lambert
Maryland National Bank	12/09/87	MBNA Credit Card Trust 1987-A	500.00	Credit cards	9.21	9.05	Aaa/AAA	3.5	First Boston
Green Tree Acceptance Corp.	12/17/87	ML Mortgage Investors, Inc.	112.00	Manufactured housing loans	10.1		NR/AA	5.5	Merrill Lynch

Source: *Asset Sales Report*, The First Boston Company, Goldman, Sachs & Co.

TABLE B.2. PUBLICLY OFFERED PRIVATE MORTGAGE BACKED SECURITIES ISSUES 1985–87

Issue Date (month/year)	Amount ($ millions)	Yield (percent)	Issuer
03/85	$ 38.50	11.9	Sears Mortgage Securities Corp.
04/85	160.00	12.5	Citibank
05/85	100.00	12.3	Citibank
	82.72	11.5	Manufacturers Hanover Mtg.
	50.00	11.5	Citibank
06/85	29.58	Varies	Sears Mortgage Securities Corp.
	31.92	11.3	Sears Mortgage Securities Corp.
	100.00	12.0	Citibank
07/85	100.00	11.0	Citibank
	39.30	10.5	Sears Mortgage Securities Corp.
08/85	100.00	10.0	Citibank
09/85	100.00	12.0	Citibank
10/85	100.00	11.0	Citibank
	22.00	Varies	Sears Mortgage Securities Corp.
	100.00	8.0	Citibank
	48.02	11.3	Sears Mortgage Securities Corp.
11/85	150.00	11.0	Citibank
	99.53	10.5	Sears Mortgage Securities Corp.
	75.80	10.5	Sears Mortgage Securities Corp.
12/85	157.00	10.5	Salomon Brothers Mtg. Securities IV
	167.00	10.5	Salomon Brothers Mtg. Securities IV
	75.00	10.5	Citibank
	30.00	Varies	Sears Mortgage Securities Corp.
1985 Total = $1,956.37			
01/86	75.00	10.5	Citibank (New York Bank)
02/86	168.54	–	Sears Mortgage Securities Corp.
	52.17	10.0	Salomon Brothers Mtg. Securities IV
	75.12	10.0	Salomon Brothers Mtg. Securities IV
	100.00	10.5	Citibank
	50.00	10.0	Citicorp Homeowners, Inc.

Issue Date (month/year)	Amount ($ millions)	Yield (percent)	Issuer
	40.00	10.5	Citibank
03/86	50.00	7.5	Citibank
04/86	100.00	10.0	Citibank (New York Bank)
	100.00	10.0	Citibank (New York Bank)
	75.00	9.5	Citicorp Homeowners, Inc.
05/86	75.00	10.0	Citibank (New York Bank)
	60.00	9.5	Citicorp Homeowners, Inc.
06/86	100.00	10.0	Citibank (New York Bank)
	131.57	9.5	Salomon Brothers Mtg. Securities IV
	120.14	10.3	Salomon Brothers Mtg. Securities IV
	24.92	8.4	Salomon Brothers Mtg. Securities IV
	100.10	10.0	Travelers Mortgage Services
	50.05	10.0	Travelers Mortgage Services
07/86	403.37	10.0	Home Savings of America (sen/sub)
	67.00	10.0	Travelers Mortgage Services
	55.00	9.5	Travelers Mortgage Services
	121.08	9.5	Salomon Brothers Mtg. Securities IV
	29.09	9.0	Salomon Brothers Mtg. Securities IV
	43.41	9.0	Salomon Brothers Mtg. Securities IV
	64.62	9.8	Salomon Brothers Mtg. Securities IV
	62.73	9.5	Salomon Brothers Mtg. Securities IV
	75.00	9.5	Citibank (New York Bank)
	75.00	10.0	Citibank (New York Bank)
	120.00	10.0	Citibank (New York Bank)
	50.00	9.0	Citicorp Homeowners, Inc.
	45.00	9.5	Citicorp Homeowners, Inc.
08/86	75.00	9.5	Citibank

Issue Date (month/year)	Amount ($ millions)	Yield (percent)	Issuer
	53.50	8.5	Citicorp Homeowners, Inc.
	100.00	9.5	Citibank
	52.17	9.0	Sears Mortgage Securities Corp.
	125.90	9.5	Sears Mortgage Securities Corp.
	54.00	9.0	Sears Mortgage Securities Corp.
	116.00	8.0	Travelers Mortgage Services
	46.04	9.2	Salomon Brothers Mtg. Securities IV
	51.19	8.0	Salomon Brothers Mtg. Securities IV
	109.04	9.5	Salomon Brothers Mtg. Securities IV
09/86	80.00	9.0	Citibank (Conduit series: Citimae)
	75.00	9.0	Citibank (New York Bank)
	60.00	9.5	Citicorp Homeowners, Inc.
	140.00	9.0	Citicorp Homeowners, Inc.
	125.00	9.5	Citibank (New York Bank)
	88.00	9.0	Sears Mortgage Securities Corp.
	104.73	9.0	Salomon Brothers Mtg. Securities IV
	50.25	8.0	Salomon Brothers Mtg. Securities IV
	150.60	9.5	Salomon Brothers Mtg. Securities IV
10/86	85.76	9.0	Sears Mortgage Securities Corp.
	190.00	9.5	Salomon Brothers Mtg. Securities IV
	55.00	9.0	Salomon Brothers Mtg. Securities IV
	60.00	10.0	Citibank (Conduit series: Citimae)
	75.00	9.0	Citicorp Homeowners, Inc.
	75.00	9.5	Citicorp Homeowners, Inc.
	50.00	9.0	Citibank (New York Bank)
	125.00	9.5	Citibank (New York Bank)

Issue Date (month/year)	Amount ($ millions)	Yield (percent)	Issuer
11/86	119.80	8.0	Travelers Mortgage Services
	150.00	9.5	Citibank (New York Bank)
	40.00	9.0	Citibank (Conduit series: Citimae)
	160.00	9.5	Mechanics and Farmers SB (sen/sub)
	110.00	9.0	Citibank (New York Bank)
	100.20	9.5	Salomon Brothers Mtg. Securities IV
	65.00	10.0	Citibank (Conduit series: Citimae)
12/86	75.30	7.5	Travelers Mortgage Services
	59.50	8.0	Travelers Mortgage Services
	89.44	8.8	California Federal Savings
	238.97	6.0 & 3.98	Salomon Brothers Mtg. Securities IV
	125.00	9.0	Citibank (New York Bank)
	125.00	9.0	Citibank (New York Bank)
	100.00	8.5	Citibank (New York Bank)
	70.00	9.5	Citibank (Conduit series: Citimae)
	72.00	8.5	Citicorp Homeowners, Inc.
	59.49	9.0	Sears Mortgage Securities Corp.
	101.87	9.5	Salomon Brothers Mtg. Securities IV
1986 Total = $6,992.66			
01/87	123.00	9.00	Citicorp Homeowners, Inc.
	125.00	8.50	Citibank (New York Bank)
	110.00	8.50	Citicorp Homeowners, Inc.
	100.00	9.00	Citibank (New York Bank)
	100.00	8.50	Citibank (New York Bank)
	194.00	8.50	Security Pacific National Bank
	116.00	8.00	Security Pacific National Bank
	101.68	8.45	Imperial Savings Association

Issue Date (month/year)	Amount ($ millions)	Yield (percent)	Issuer
	100.00	6.50–2.50	Kidder, Peabody Acceptance Corp. 1
	75.80	7.50	Travelers Mortgage Services
	59.50	8.00	Travelers Mortgage Services
02/87	96.43	8.50	Salomon Brothers Mtg. Securities 87-1
	99.53	6.50	Salomon Brothers Mtg. Securities 87-3
	106.88	7.00	Salomon Brothers Mtg. Securities 87-4
	138.08	8.00	Salomon Brothers Mtg. Securities 87-2
	122.70	7.50	Travelers Mortgage Services
	125.00	9.00	Citibank (New York Bank)
	200.00	9.50	Kidder, Peabody Acceptance Corp.
	80.00	9.00	Citimae (Conduit series)
	60.00	9.50	Citimae (Conduit series)
	341.77	8.80	Imperial Savings Association
	445.00	9.50	First Boston Mtg. Securities Corp.
	125.59	7.50	Travelers Mortgage Services
	53.00	7.50	Republic Federal S&LA Series 1
03/87	102.00	6.50	Dean Witter Mortgage Capital Corp.
	125.00	8.50	Citibank (New York Bank)
	200.00	IO/PO	Salomon Brothers Mtg. Securities (REMIC)
	200.00	IO/PO	Salomon Brothers Mtg. Securities (REMIC)
	100.00	8.50	Citicorp Homeowners, Inc.
	100.00	8.50	Citibank (New York Bank)
	76.00	8.50	Mechanics and Farmers Savings Bank
	275.00	9.00	First Boston Mtg. Securities Corp.

Issue Date (month/year)	Amount ($ millions)	Yield (percent)	Issuer
	270.00	8.50	Security Pacific National Bank
	35.00	8.50	Security Pacific National Bank
	75.16	6.50	Travelers Mortgage Services
	77.70	6.50	Sears Mortgage Securities Corp.
	84.50	7.00	Citicorp Homeowners, Inc.
	117.95	8.50	Salomon Brothers Mtg. Securities S1
	84.70	8.28	Residential Funding Mortgage Sec. 87-5
	100.00	8.50	Citicorp Homeowners, Inc.
	126.90	11.00	First Boston Mtg. Securities Corp.
04/87	88.00	9.00	Citicorp Homeowners, Inc.
	110.00	10.82	First Boston Mtg. Securities Corp.
	125.00	9.00	Citicorp Mtg. Securities, Inc.
	75.00	8.50	Citicorp Mtg. Securities, Inc.
	120.69	8.50	Residential Funding Mortgage Sec. S2
	150.00	8.50	Citicorp Homeowners, Inc.
05/87	75.00	8.50	Citicorp Mtg. Securities, Inc.
	100.00	9.00	Citicorp Mtg. Securities, Inc.
	48.48	7.75	Citicorp Homeowners, Inc.
	125.00	8.50	Citicorp Mtg. Securities, Inc.
	59.00	8.50	Citicorp Homeowners, Inc.
	100.00	9.00	Citicorp Mtg. Securities, Inc.
	114.00	8.87	Residential Funding Mtg. Sec.
	110.00	9.13	Residential Funding Mortgage Sec. S4
	126.77	8.50	Residential Funding Mortgage Sec. 87-6
	92.00	9.16	Sears Mortgage Securities Corp.
06/87	50.00	9.00	Citicorp Mtg. Securities, Inc.
	73.00	8.50	Citicorp Mtg. Securities, Inc.
	147.00	ARMs	Imperial Savings Association
	75.00	9.00	Citicorp Mtg. Securities, Inc.

Issue Date (month/year)	Amount ($ millions)	Yield (percent)	Issuer
	75.00	9.00	Citicorp Mtg. Securities, Inc.
	104.76	9.00	Travelers Mortgage Services
	59.00	10.00	Citicorp Mtg. Securities, Inc.
	30.90	9.44	Residential Funding Mortgage Sec. 87-7
7/87	72.00	9.50	Citicorp Mtg. Securities, Inc.
	188.19	9.80	Imperial Savings Association 1987-4
	72.60	Varies	First Boston Mortgage Securities 1987-1
	170.00	8.75	Kidder, Peabody Acceptance Corp. 1
	75.00	9.50	Citicorp Mtg. Securities, Inc.
	204.00	Varies	Great Western Savings
	72.06	8.75	Residential Funding Mortgage Sec. S5
	73.81	10.00	Residential Funding Mortgage Sec. S6
08/87	47.00	9.50	Citicorp Mtg. Securities, Inc.
	150.12	Varies	Residential Funding Mortgage Sec. 87-8A
	95.19	9.00	Residential Funding Mortgage Sec. 7
	67.57	10.25	Residential Funding Mortgage Sec. 8
	25.08	Varies	Residential Funding Mortgage Sec. 87-8B
09/87	65.00	9.50	Citicorp Mtg. Securities, Inc.
	88.00	Varies	Merrill Lynch Mortgage Investors, Inc.
	49.56	9.63	Sears Mortgage Securities Corp.
	100.00	12.50	Salomon Brothers Mtg. Securities (REMIC)
	120.00	8.75	Kidder, Peabody Acceptance Corp.

Issue Date (month/year)	Amount ($ millions)	Yield (percent)	Issuer
	81.00	10.00	Travelers Mortgage Services
	61.83	10.50	Residential Funding Mortgage Sec. S9
	50.00	9.50	Citicorp Mtg. Securities, Inc.
	71.47	10.20	Merrill Lynch Mortgage Investors, Inc.
10/87	100.00	Varies	Home Owners Federal S&L
	75.00	7.25	ComFed Savings Bank (Lowell, MA)
11/87	113.00	8.70	California Federal S&L
	57.00	9.00	Travelers Mortgage Services
	73.30	8.14	Salomon Brothers Mtg. Securities
	182.76	9.16	Salomon Brothers Mtg. Securities
12/87	42.02	7.01	Republic Fed. S&LA Series 2
	50.71	7.66	Republic Fed. S&LA Series 3
	40.00	10.00	Citicorp Mtg. Securities, Inc.
	52.00	9.00	Countrywide Funding Corp.
	100.00	7.50	Home Owners FS&LA
	43.90	Varies	Residential Funding Mortgage Sec.
	194.49	7.49	Columbia Savings & Loan Association
	50.00	Varies	Countrywide Funding Corp.
	80.51	Varies	Salomon Brothers Mtg. Securities
	60.00	7.50	ComFed Savings Bank (Lowell, MA)
	37.40	10.50	Security Pacific National Bank
	52.80	Varies	Residential Funding Mortgage Sec. 9
	112.30	10.10	Merrill Lynch Mortgage Investors
1987 Total = $11,100.02			

Source: Financial World Publications, *Inside Mortgage Capital Markets.*

Index

259

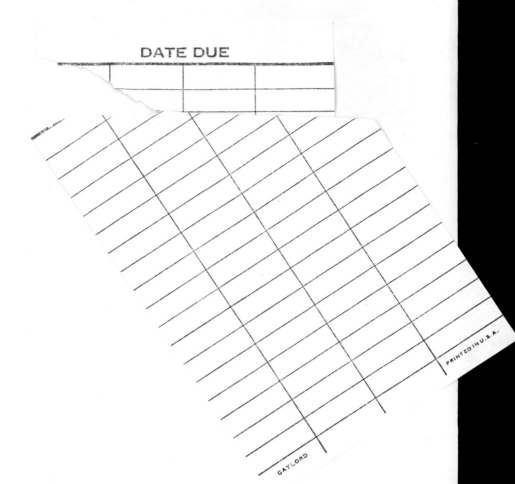

DATE DUE

GAYLORD

PRINTED IN U.S.A.